LIFE ON ICE

LONNIE DUPRE

KEEN EDITIONS

This is a work of nonfiction. The events and experiences detailed herein are all true and have been faithfully rendered as I have remembered them, to the best of my ability.

Photo credits: Roger Pietron, John Peterson, Lonnie Dupre, Bering Bridge Expedition, Larry Roepke, Kelly Dupre, John Hoelscher, Greenland Expedition, Tim Knight, Tine Lisby Jensen, Tom Surprenant, One World Expedition, Stuart Smith.

ISBN: 978-0-9846603-1-5

Book design by Adria Chilcote

Cover design by Ann K. Ryan and Adria Chilcote

Published by Keen Editions and printed in the USA.

Dedicated to Kelly and Jacob Dupre, the two people in my life who have sacrificed the most for my unusual calling.

I am forever grateful.

LIFE ON ICE

25 YEARS OF ARCTIC EXPLORATION

"I bless the whole journey, forgetting hardship
and chance misfortune by the way."

—Knud Rasmussen,
Danish Arctic explorer

PROLOGUE

Is this it? Is this how it's going to end? Buried alive in a snow cave just 3,000 feet short of the Denali summit? Everything has gone well so far except for this—70-mile-an-hour winds and below-zero temperatures that make it suicide to step outside my 3-foot by 6-foot ice shelter. I want to be the first to make a successful solo summit in January of Denali, the highest peak in North America. My training and equipment are serving me well. There's not a major flaw in my plan. What I couldn't foresee was an earthquake and weather that won't break long enough for me to make the last climb—to the peak, at 20,320 feet above sea level. All I need is 13 hours of clear weather to make it to the top and back, but I'm not sure I'll get it.

Simply trying such a feat sounds crazy to a lot of people, but then most people think that a lifelong love affair with the Arctic is crazy. And perhaps they're a little bit right. Most people's idea of paradise is sun, heat and a tropical island. Not me. I love the winter cold of a northern snowscape.

* * *

I first encountered the dangers of cold and ice when I was six years old. I was spearfishing with my dad on a lake near our Minnesota farm. It was a bitter cold December day with a stiff breeze. As the sun set, we picked the frozen fish out of the snow and threw them like cord wood onto the snowmobile sled. Already chilled through as we headed for home, Dad took a short cut across a cattail swamp.

Suddenly our snow machine broke through thin ice. There I was, floating among ice chunks, temporarily held up by the air trapped in

1

my snowsuit. The cold water rushed into my boots, around my legs, up to my waist, then up to my chest and neck. The shock of the cold water on my warm skin was immediate. I was terrified, but as suddenly as I went into the frigid water, a strong hand grabbed the seat of my snowsuit and pushed me onto the breaking ice.

I slid to a halt on shifting plates of ice, my wet chopper mittens sticking to the ice. Too scared to look behind me, I steeled my eyes straight ahead, recalling a story I'd been told about a trapper lost in this swamp. He was found after several weeks when someone walking across the ice stepped on a soft patch. It was the top of the trapper's head sticking through the ice.

When I finally looked around, Dad was trying to keep the snow machine from completely sinking. He stood to the side of the machine in 5 feet of ice water and goosed the throttle to keep the skis up on the breaking ice edge. He knew what awaited us if our Ski-Doo sank, leaving us soaking wet, cold and far from home. I could hear the machine coming closer and the muffled exhaust rising through the boggy water. The ice began to break around me and water covered my shoulders. Again, pushed up and out by the seat, I slid ahead on smooth ice.

We finally made it to ice thick enough to support us, and Dad put me on the machine between him and the handle bars in hopes I would get at least a little heat from the engine. We sped for home. My dad kept reminding me to wiggle my toes and fingers no matter how difficult it was or how much it hurt.

He carried me into the house like a frozen fish, my clothing too stiff to bend. Mom thawed my frozen snowsuit with warm water and tugged me out of it while Dad held the cuffs. As my suit and I thawed, baby bullheads wriggled out of my pockets. Wrapped in blankets on the sofa, I shivered violently. My teeth chattered so hard my jaw ached. Tears ran down my face as my feet started to thaw.

Until that moment I loved everything about our long winters: building caves in snowbanks, sledding down steep hills, whipping behind our yellow Ski-Doo on a plastic saucer, and standing on thick ice waiting to spear the next fish. Now, for the first time, I hated the cold. I slept for 24 hours straight.

Two days later, I was back on the same lake, following mink tracks through the cattails with my brother, Todd. Now an authority on bad ice, I motioned to him not to go near the thin spots. Just moments after my caution, I heard a commotion. I ran in the direction of the spring where we speared pike to find my brother's muddy arm sticking out of a hole in the ice. As he tried to grasp the edge, I sprawled out and stretched my own arm out to reach my brother's. I pulled him from the water as he coughed out brown, wet bog bottom. Remembering what Dad had said to me, I told him he needed to keep wiggling his toes and fingers. We ran all the way home.

Being dunked in frigid water had two very different outcomes for my brother and me. Todd still lives in Minnesota but his winter travels always take him south. Not me. I remain fixed on the north, heading to the Arctic every chance I get, no matter the season. It is where I feel my place in the world.

DRAWN TO THE NORTH, 1961–1990

"All true wisdom is only to be found far from the dwellings of men, in the great solitudes; and it can only be obtained through suffering."

—Inuit Shaman

CHAPTER 1

LEARNING ABOUT THE NORTH

My whole life feels like an extended training period for Arctic exploration. I was born on April 17, 1961, and grew up on a farm in rural Minnesota. We depended on what we grew or raised, and on what my father brought home from hunting and fishing. Our mainstays were venison and sweet corn. From as early as I can remember, I was taught to fish and hunt. I never recall a time when I wasn't curious about nature and wildlife. Why doesn't the water freeze inside a muskrat house? How do animals stay warm in winter? What made those tracks? I was especially interested in the north. How far does "up north" go? Who lives there? How do they handle the cold? Do people there still subsist on hunting, fishing and gathering?

I was not a natural student if you define that as a classroom book-learner. But that doesn't mean that I wasn't a reader. I spent hours in the library reading Foxfire books about surviving in the wild, building a log cabin, smoking fish and tanning skins. By the end of middle school, I was a self-proclaimed expert on North American animals. I read all the material I could get my hands on about the Inuit and the Arctic, and waited for the day when I could experience first-hand the vast lands of the Inuit, caribou, polar bear and musk oxen. I came by this yearning to explore remote regions naturally. One of my mother's ancestors is the 15th-century Breton explorer Jacques Cartier, who claimed the territory we now know as Canada for the French.

I didn't know how I could make a living from my passion, but it didn't dampen my fascination. When I was 13, I started to learn carpentry. It began with a shovel, then graduated to a saw and other tools. I learned from my dad, just as he had learned from his dad. Carpentry was the way my dad supplemented our small farm income. Through high school, I spent nearly every weekend and some school nights in primitive camps near our house with my good friend Jay. Our hero was a movie character, Jeremiah Johnson. We lived under a tarpaulin lean-to, ate squirrel on a stick by the fire and ran hound dogs until all hours of the night. We ate venison, duck, beaver and grouse. In one two-week period, another friend and I trapped 80 beavers and sold the skins at the century-old Winnipeg Fur Exchange.

By the time I was 22 years old, I was ready to venture out of Minnesota. With naive hopes of striking it rich fishing commercially and working on the Trans Alaska Pipeline, my cousin Dan and I headed for Alaska in a three-quarter-ton Chevy pickup. The rundown vintage camper we hauled was so loaded with canned goods and supplies it swayed back and forth as we drove along I-94. It was the summer of 1983. From Anchorage, we flew north of the Aleutian Islands and pitched our canvas tent on the sand dunes of Ugashik Bay. We'd picked a place with weather so bad the sun shines an average of only one day a month. A hard wind blew the dunes' fine sand through the tent walls and coated everything inside—dishes, bedding, toothbrushes, us.

Sick of sand in our teeth and the sound of flapping canvas, we moved a few miles down the beach to a small log hut built of horizontal planks and driftwood. Carved in a log above my bunk was the name Eli Kal, a notorious mad man from the village of Pilot Point. Kal, the stories went, lived like a stray dog under old boats and bits of canvas, and stole whatever he could get his hands on. He hadn't been seen in years, but the locals say his spirit enters people staying in the area and turns them into crazed murderers. Just that spring a village man went nuts and shot seven people unlucky enough to pass by him. They all died.

One day, I opened the door of our isolated hut to a short, stocky, slightly unkempt man wearing a wool sea captain's hat. I offered my hand. "Can I help you?"

With a half-hearted shake, he said, "We planned on using this hut to fish out of."

"Sorry," I answered. "The hut wasn't being used, and since it doesn't belong to anybody, we moved in. You have another place to stay?"

"We want to stay here," he shot back.

"Sorry," I said again. "We're staying for a couple weeks. You can have it after that."

Grudgingly, he stormed off. That night we heard gunshots down the beach. It was common for fishermen to set off shots at night to scare bears away from their camps, so we gave it no thought.

When I went outside the next morning to take a leak, I noticed large brown bear tracks in the sand next to our shack. Looking over my shoulder, I saw a plane on the beach. Handcuffed to the struts was yesterday's visitor. In front of the plane an arm stuck out of the sand. Two law enforcement officers were digging out the attached body. The man in custody, whiskeyed-up, had gotten into a fight with his fishing partner over their earnings. He emptied his pistol into his partner's chest, buried the body in the sand and continued fishing in front of our hut as if nothing had happened. A third partner returning from a walk sensed something was wrong and hoofed it to the village to inform the authorities.

This was my first real experience of the human "wild" factor and the scarcity that the wilderness could hold. We didn't strike it rich—from either oil, gold, fish or game. In fact, we barely got by. My kid's play was over. Yet even these precarious months didn't dampen my spirit. I was all the more eager to travel even farther into the Arctic. With fishing season at an end, we headed back to Anchorage, where practicality meant a return to carpentry. My next Arctic experience would have to wait.

CHAPTER 2

VENTURING NORTH

By the fall of 1985, I was pining for another adventure. While sitting in my 15-foot travel trailer near downtown Anchorage, John Petersen, a Minnesota lumberjack, and I sketched out an expedition into Alaska's bush. We wanted to spend the winter living off the land. We opened up a map of Alaska on the combination table and bed, closed our eyes and put our fingers down on the map. Halfway between wherever our fingers landed was to be our destination. Our fingers both came down on the Brooks Range region, and between them was Deadman's Lake in Kanuti Flats. You'd think the name alone would have put us off, but we were young and had more dreams than wisdom.

We pooled our money, $1,500 total, and loaded John's El Camino with food, wool clothes, traps, rifles, 30 penny nails, a chain saw, a wood stove, Visqueen plastic and four rolls of Copenhagen. We traveled north 500 miles and camped next to the Yukon River on the haul road to Prudhoe Bay. We rolled out our bags on Visqeen next to the car. It was October 25 and -20°F.

Our next segment was by air. Our pilot, Ron, landed on a small gravel strip next to the road. We stuffed the Cessna 208 well beyond its capacity. It took the whole runway plus a couple of feet to get off the ground. I raised my head to look out. Bowed upwards under the strain, the wings just cleared the treetops.

The lake was about 50 miles southwest of Bettles. My Foxfire book knowledge and carpentry skills along with John's excellent logging skills paid off at first. In five days we had built an 11-foot by 11-foot cabin out of 25 stunted Arctic birch we'd dragged across the lake. Because we lacked good trees to make full walls, we dug the floor out from the inside to give John headroom. He is much taller than I am, which isn't saying much. At five-feet-six, I'm slightly taller than a thermos bottle. We used the dirt to insulate the roof and the sides. When we finished, our cabin looked like a cross between a beaver house and a dirt pile with a 3-foot-square door and a stovepipe sticking out the top. The only flaw in our design was that as we heated the cabin, the permafrost floor melted into a mud pit. We fixed the problem with crude floorboards cut with a chain saw, but the musty tundra smell never left our cabin.

Naively optimistic about our plan to live off the land, we had left Anchorage with only enough money to get us here by car and plane. We also left with only enough food for half the time we expected to be gone, hoping to supplement our diet with what we could hunt or trap—lynx, martin, wolverine and beaver. Selling our furs at the end of our stint was to pay for the flight out and for gas for the drive back to Anchorage. We hoped to have some money left to show for our months of work.

On December 12, it was -43°F. We had been gone for 53 days without so much as seeing a plane overhead. We snowshoed nearly every day on trap lines, 13 miles round trip, but we caught few animals and bagged only one grouse. Our Bisquick mix, Krustease pancakes, sugar, butter and canned Spam had run out. We were down to eating fruit cocktail and Celebrity canned bacon for breakfast. The bacon was so salty that we had to rinse each piece in hot water before cooking it.

Dinner was a continuous pot of thin stew made from the scrawny rabbits we snared around the cabin, plus canned vegetables. It hardly offered us the calories we needed to cope with the cold. Finally we broke down and ate a fox—my one and only. Cooked fox smells like urine. John said it tasted like chicken. For me, not even close. We lacked fat in our diet because all the animals we caught were about as skinny as we were now. Blue veins ran like a road map across my belly. John's suspenders, once taut and bowed by his thick frame, hung straight down to a slack waistband.

During the coldest days, we stayed put to conserve energy. We often ran the trap lines separately to cover more ground and grab some time alone, a relief from living on top of each other. Our solo travels also added new topics to our depleted conversations. The obvious dangers of traveling alone in extreme cold weighed on our minds. We were far away from any possible help. Losing fingers and toes to frostbite, or, worse, breaking through thin ice and freezing to death miles from the cabin were real dangers.

One day John did break through the ice; luckily, I was with him. I'd crossed some marginal ice, and John, 50 pounds heavier, followed in my tracks. He broke through and was up to his chest in frigid water, 3 miles from the cabin. I pulled him out and we raced for the cabin, pushing hard to keep John's temperature up. By the time we arrived, his wool clothing was frozen stiff, straight as a board except for slight angles at the elbows and knees. We both worried about his feet as he painfully thawed them next to the stove. But after a few hours, he said his toes were beginning to feel like their old selves. After that, we had a rule: no travel below -38°F.

At that latitude, daylight on December 21 is only an hour long. As I watched the low orange glow of the sun "rising" in the crisp air, I concluded it would be a good day to stay put and whittle a birch spoon. We'd left Anchorage two months earlier, and we were discouraged that our pilot hadn't flown in to check on us as he'd promised.

For Christmas dinner, we fixed lynx loins wrapped in Celebrity canned bacon and ate John's bush cookies, made from ingredients I didn't want to know, since, to my knowledge, we had no makings for cookies. After dinner we had a contest, racing to open cans of fruit cocktail with an Army-issue P38 can opener. Loser had dish detail. John won. He'd been practicing.

The day it hit -58°F was so still we could hear a spruce grouse eat a cone across the lake. Ice an inch thick formed around the edges of the door and from floor to ceiling in the cabin's corners. We had planned to stay in the camp until the end of February but decided to pack it in on January 4. I was getting worried because we'd lost too much weight and weren't having much luck with our hunting. We also knew it was quite possible our pilot might not come for us at all. We buttoned up the cabin and took only the bare essentials—matches, two cans of Sterno, a can of bacon and two cans of fruit cocktail—for a forced march in thigh-deep snow to Allakaket, which we estimated was 32 miles away. From this Athabaskan village we would contact our pilot for a pick up. We'd each logged about 450 miles of snowshoeing during our stay and thought we were up for the task.

The Sterno produced no heat in the bitter cold, the salty bacon made us even thirstier and the fruit cocktail froze solid as a brick. We alternated breaking trail every half-mile as we followed a several-week-old snowmobile trail made by Athabaskan trappers. It was buried so deeply under snow, we had to follow it by feel. Our lives depended on not losing the faint trail through the taiga. Even with large snowshoes, we sank to our knees on the trail and floundered in snow up to our waists when we ran off the trail.

After 10 hours of brutal trail breaking, we stopped to rest. For dinner, we ate our can of bacon raw. We had no reserves left in our bodies to heat our sleeping bags, so we kicked our feet and shook in our bags all night. We hugged the cans of frozen fruit cocktail in hopes they would thaw by breakfast.

Five hours later, after downing spoonfuls of slushy fruit cocktail, we moved away from our camp. The sun wasn't up yet. We started out exhausted, and grew weaker and weaker with each trail-breaking

12

turn. Our legs and feet ached, and our backs and shoulders hung like lead. "My body is giving my head a good fight," John said. Although it wasn't very cold out, 6°F or so, John was out of energy and unable to stay warm. I helped him untie his wool coat from around his waist and put it on. I began thinking we should have stayed at the hut and waited for our pilot.

It seemed there was no end to the walking. Extremely dehydrated, we dipped our mitts into the snow to melt it in our dry mouths. We didn't realize that the energy it took to melt the snow was leaving us even more dehydrated. Our minds tempted us with the thought of sleep, if only for a few minutes, but we knew that giving in to the impulse would mean certain death.

"This endurance test, survival walk, whatever you want to call it, is the hardest thing I've ever done," coughed John. I couldn't have agreed with him more. We were now walking a fine line between getting to Allakaket and meeting our creator.

After nearly three more hours, we came down a steep bank to a wide, hard-packed snowmobile trail. Off came the snowshoes. After all those miles high-stepping through powder, it seemed deceivingly effortless to walk on the hard trail. By now it was pitch dark. We were disoriented. Was the village a mile away, or 10 miles? And which way was it? If we guessed wrong, we would probably die within hours. We headed left.

A half-hour later, John spotted the light of a small cabin through thin trees. We went up to the door, knocked and heard a voice say, "Come in." When John walked in, the young Athabaskan woman in the cabin looked horrified. Behind the door was a mirror, and for the first time in months John saw himself. He looked like a dying wild man, with dark sunken eyes and a frosted bush beard.

"Is there a place we can stay?" John said in as calm a voice as he could muster.

13

"Principal of the school," she said, pointing to the far end of the village.

Allakaket is nestled on the south bank of the Koyukuk River, a vein of life offering fish, game and transportation in summer. On both sides of the trail, log cabins belched birch smoke straight up through the cold Arctic air. Kids sporting Pine Marten hats looked us over as we walked by, strange-looking, woolly white men. One of the kids was a chewer. "Nasty habit," I said, and bought half a tin of Copenhagen from him for $20. I'd run out a week earlier.

John Stone, the principal, gave us a key to the school cafeteria. We could sleep there and eat what we found in the cupboards. The first thing I found was a pound bag of shredded coconut. I devoured the whole bag while John worked on a large can of Cheese Whiz.

On January 7, after three days waiting for a plane—any plane—to show up, we knew we were wearing out our welcome. A few of the young men were angered that we'd been trapping on what they believed was their land. They let us know with an ass chewing that was essentially this: The white man already has enough land. Finally a plane arrived. It belonged to a company running weekly commercial flights to Bettles. The pilot agreed to take us if we signed an I.O.U. for our fare. As we climbed aboard, a young village official shouted, "Don't come back, and tell your pilot Ron not to be so generous with our lands."

When we arrived in Bettles we looked up Ron, who said, nonchalantly, that he'd planned on flying to our camp in a couple days. We didn't believe him. The next morning, Ron flew me back to our cabin to retrieve our furs and supplies. All through the flight I was nervous about what we might find. As we circled the cabin from about 500 feet, disappointment hit me hard. Our belongings were scattered all around the cabin, and snow machine tracks obliterated our snowshoe trail.

"Looks like they ransacked the place. Sorry," Ron muttered.

"It doesn't look good," I said. "Put her down on the lake, and I'll see if there's anything worth collecting."

I ran to the open door of the cabin and went to the shelf that once held my camera and diary. It was bare. I sat back on my old bunk. I did not want to believe the thieves had taken them. I glanced at the scattered clothes and cookware on the frozen floor. I thought about the beloved .22 lever-action rifle John's dad gave him as a young man. To my amazement, our furs were still in a bundle, hanging undamaged from the ceiling. Rifles, packs, sleeping bags, clothes, chain saw—nearly everything else was gone. Only the furs remained.

We loaded the plane with the furs, the gear that was left, jugs of Coleman fuel and kerosene, and a bag of crumpled, frozen clothes I picked up around the cabin. When we landed back in Bettles, John approached the plane. He sensed something was wrong. "They took most everything, John, but left the furs," I said.

"Why not the furs?" John asked. "That's all we really took from them. A few animals off a chunk of land! Alaska, the promised land, the land of rugged beauty, pure air and water, and the same scummy people you can find in any rotten city. It makes me sick."

I couldn't find words to tell John about his stolen rifle. He read it in my face and walked away in tears. Ron flew us back to the Prudhoe Bay haul road, and we dug the El Camino out of the snow. The gauge showed that we would be slightly short of fuel to reach Fairbanks where we were to sell our furs, so we poured a five-gallon mixture of kerosene and Coleman fuel into the tank. It worked. We drove straight through and pulled into Fairbanks close to midnight. We got $606 for our furs. After settling up for our flights, lodging, gas and the repair of three very expensive flat tires, we each had $20 left when we arrived in Anchorage on January 10. We had been gone 82 days. The final blow to our failed adventure was the $100 fine from Alaska Fish and Game for building a cabin on state property without permission.

My first venture into the far north was far short of successful by any measure except one: I learned how *not* to live in the icy wilderness. It was a lesson that served me well as I began planning more serious Arctic ventures.

CHAPTER 3

OWNING MY FIRST SLED DOGS

By 1986, Alaska's economy had collapsed, and you couldn't buy a job. I was newly married, and my wife, Bonnie, was pregnant, so we packed up my carpentry tools and drove back to Minnesota. During long hours working construction over the next two years, my mind was always on the north. I knew that if I wanted to see more of the Arctic, I would need a dog team, the workhorses of that land and the most efficient transporters of men and supplies.

Locating a team of Inuit dogs for sale was luck of timing. Respected hunter Jacobie Avingyak from Igloolik in Canada's high Arctic was getting too frail to handle a dog team. I contacted Paul Schurke of Ely, Minnesota, and asked if he wanted to buy a share of the team. Schurke had made a North Pole expedition by dog team with Will Steger in 1986 and wanted to start an adventure business with dog teams. He agreed to share the cost of the dogs, and we bought them sight unseen.

I first saw my new dogs through the bars of plastic airline kennels when they arrived in the belly of an Arctic cargo plane in Ottawa, Canada. Black, brown, beige and white, they looked as wild as wolves and stank like wet horse blankets. They were big dogs, but a feast-and-famine lifestyle under cold, hard-working conditions had left them skinny and mangy. The females weighed about 60 pounds, the males about 80. These were not the fast runners like the lanky Alaskan huskies trained to compete in the 1,100-mile Iditarod Trail Sled Dog Race. They were the Sherman tanks of the mushing world: big, strong, heavily furred, easy to care for, and accustomed to pulling packed sleds through Arctic storms. They were the perfect dogs for an expedition.

Explorer Geoffrey Hattersley-Smith, who worked with both dogs and machines along the edge of the Arctic Ocean, said that his dogs could always move faster over rough patches of ice than any snowmobile. They always started in low temperatures, he added, and they didn't break down.

I put on a pair of gloves and wrapped a thick towel around my arm for protection. In my most comforting voice, I talked to them as I reached in to pet them between growls. Tucking my fingers behind their sealskin collars, I eventually pulled the reluctant, clawing dogs, one by one from their kennels. They calmed down immediately.

It was a hot July day, and I faced a 1,000-mile drive back to Minnesota. I loaded the dogs in the truck, each of them in its own straw-lined box. To keep air moving over my panting Arctic payload, I stopped only for gas and water.

Although I was still living in the Twin Cities, I worked for Paul Schurke that fall of 1988, helping him launch Wintergreen Adventure, which took clients dog sledding in Minnesota's Boundary Waters Canoe Area Wilderness. I felt a real kinship with the Inuit dogs. Barely domesticated enough to handle, they were scrappers, ready to fight among themselves, but loyal to their driver. Each had a distinct personality. Some couldn't get enough affection. Others were grumpy and responded to petting as if it were torture.

I was convinced that learning to work with dog teams was an essential element of successful Arctic travel. My dream of exploring the Arctic was advancing. It felt like my destiny. My home situation was another matter. By now, Bonnie and I could see that we were different in too many ways to have a future together. We had married young. It was apparent to me that the worlds we wanted to inhabit were too far apart to reconcile. She would never be at peace in my "wild," and I would never be happy in a more traditional, urban life.

What we did agree on after our two-year marriage was that we both deeply loved our young son, Jacob.

CHAPTER 4

SPREADING GLASNOST ON THE BERING BRIDGE

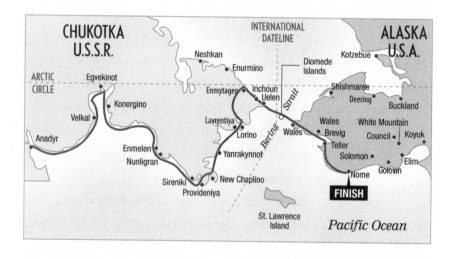

In March of 1989, Paul Schurke and I joined 10 others on a joint Soviet-American Arctic expedition to promote peace between the two countries in the spirit of Mikhail Gorbachev's new policy of openness. Because of the Cold War, families in the Bering Bridge region had been separated for more than 40 years by the "Ice Curtain." It was Paul's idea to have an expedition to encourage the two governments to allow indigenous people to travel back and forth freely.

Six Americans and six Soviets were to traverse, by dog sled and ski, a thousand miles "on the wings of Glasnost." We would visit indigenous villages between Anadyr, Russia, and Nome, Alaska. Three members of each team were indigenous people from the Bering Straits region and represented Yupik, Inupiat Inuit and Chukchi reindeer herders.

Alaska Airlines provided a Boeing 737 to carry the American team, along with our dogs and gear, to Anadyr, Siberia. It was the first time the Soviet Union had allowed a U.S. plane to fly into this militarized air space. Rows of obsolete jet fighters, which had been used to patrol the U.S.-Soviet border, were parked along the runways as we landed. I hoped that the era of hostility between the two countries was itself becoming obsolete and that our trek would contribute, at least a little, to the reconciliation of American and Soviet citizens.

At the start of our journey in Anadyr, we ran our dogs down the main street. I could spot nothing but fur-hatted people in all directions. We were the first Americans many had ever seen. Before our departure, we went through a series of medical tests sponsored by a medical university in Moscow. Many of the tests included blood samples. Between drags on his cigarette, the doctor fished around in a bowl of alcohol for a needle. Putting his lips on the back of it, he blew out any remaining alcohol and fastened the needle to the syringe. It was as dull as a 16 penny nail and looked nearly as big. The doctor held the back of my arm to gain leverage. Wincing in pain, I thought longingly of the new-age needles and syringes in our expedition medical kit.

With wires hanging from our bodies and clothespins on our noses, we breathed into plastic bags as we peddled bikes until, desperate for oxygen, we tore the clothespins off. For our last test, we submerged our bare hands in a tub of ice water for 20 minutes and then held them under an infrared screen to see how long it took to restore circulation. The thawing was excruciating, but I was pleased to have the second best return-of-circulation time in the team.

We left Anadyr in early March 1989 and traveled across a region locked in cold and desolation. With treeless valleys and mountains on one side, and the shifting ice of the Bering Sea on the other, we skied and sledded, carrying our personal gear in backpacks. Heavier group equipment, food and fuel went on the sleds.

For breakfast and dinner each day, we ate a bland mixture of buckwheat, dried meat and milk. Knowing it would do me good, I forced it down. For lunch, we had salted side pork, dry Russian rye bread, dried fruit and halva (a sweet confection of honey and sesame butter) or chocolate. It was much tastier than breakfast.

We saw our first village in a valley at the bottom of a long, steep drop. Nicolai "Cola" Attinya, one of our Russian teammates, and I moved closer to the edge with our teams to survey our options. It appeared far too steep for a dog team. I scanned the area to our right looking for a more gradual decline. I found none. Nicolai shrugged his shoulders and commanded his dogs to go forward over the lip of the steep incline.

At that moment, Paul skied up from behind. "My God, what is he doing?"

We both watched Nicolai expertly brake his sled with a large, steel-pointed wooden pole jammed into the snow between the runners. Then he disappeared in a cloud of snow. A minute late we spied him and his team as they slid to a stop at the bottom. In the distance, a tiny arm waved from below to indicate all was well.

Encouraged by Nicolai's successful run, Paul removed his skis and lashed them to the sled. We moved dogs and sled to the edge where Paul pulled out the dog's nightly stake-out chains and wrapped them around the sled runners for added drag. The dogs, eager to run down nearly any kind of grade, gave a tug. Paul and I, on each side of the sled, dug our heels in and grabbed the upstanders. We exchanged a look—maybe we should rethink this—but it was too late.

The dogs pulled us over the lip, hell-bent down the valley wall. As we strained to provide drag, the snow built up in front of our legs. We picked up speed. The sled was riding right on the heels of the dogs. Three quarters of the way down the slope, we hit a whale's back—a ridge in the snow—and we all went airborne. "Yahoo," I yelled. I glanced at Paul, his expression something between exhilaration and fear. I imagine mine was a mirror image.

The sled landed on its side with both of us dragging behind, desperately holding the upstanders. The dog-driver's rule—never let go of the sled—was stuck in our heads. When we slid to a halt on the valley floor, snow was crammed into my cuffs and collar, and inside my glasses. My snow-packed ears muffled the cheers. I tried to stand. Paul, laughing from the excitement, gave me a good slap on the back, popping loose some of the snow in my ear.

The second village we visited, Velkal, was a village rarely seen by outsiders. It was a military radar installation, a rustic version of the Distant Early Warning (DEW) Line sites in the Arctic region of Alaska, Canada, Greenland and Iceland. It reminded us of how fragile Gorbachev's policy of glasnost was. "No cameras allowed" was just one sign of this reality. We raised American and Soviet flags, and were greeted by some 2,000 people, waiting in subzero temperatures with banners of peace and friendship. Out came the vodka, along with talk of repression and hope for the future.

When we entered New Chaplino, another teammate, Darlene Apungaluk from the village of Gambell on Alaska's St. Lawrence Island, felt right at home. With hugs and tears, she met long-lost relatives, including old aunts who had cultural tattoos from their foreheads to the bottom of their chins. The tattoos were made with needle and fine thread rubbed in soot or gunpowder, and then drawn

21

through the skin. I felt as if had stepped back hundreds of years.

New Chaplino's modest houses were made of vanilla-colored plaster over cement. Their steep-pitched roofs were covered with rusty tin. The women were dressed in long, blue-beaded coats. When tattooed older women banged out a traditional dance on drums of walrus gut stretched over wooden hoops, Darlene recognized the steps and joined in. The mayor, a red-haired woman sporting a complete set of bright gold teeth, toasted us and welcomed us into the community. Villagers presented us with gifts of caribou parkas, mittens, hats and seal-skinned kamiks (boots). When the ceremonies were over, we sat down to a feast of jellied reindeer patties, Russian rye topped with salted salmon eggs, pea and onion salad, and reindeer tongue, all punctuated by toasts with vodka and salmon-berry juice.

The next evening, when Paul made a scheduled radio call to Nome, we learned that the Exxon Valdez had spilled 11 million US gallons of crude oil in Prince William Sound. I was devastated. I considered Alaska my second home.

When we reached our next stop at the town of Enmelen after nearly a month without a good wash, we stripped down and ran barefoot in the snow to the banya, a wood-fired sauna and bath hut. Hot steam soothed our chilled and aching bodies. Two large Russian men, one at my head and one at my feet, gave me a combination massage and scrub, rotating me while I lay on a bench. Another thrashed me from head to toe with Siberian silver birch boughs. When I could no longer stand the heat, I staggered to the adjacent room and jumped into an oval, 6-foot-deep pool of ice water. The concrete pool had large openings on both ends to allow the town's stream to flow through. Our reward for surviving this awaited us in the next room: white sheets to wrap in, then tea and salmon-berry jam.

During the festivities, I was given a cap made from the head skin of a three-day-old reindeer for my three-year-old son Jacob. A hat with reindeer ears like the one I received is intended for the child of a reindeer herder. A hat without ears is for the child of a fisherman.

We were not back on the trail for long when a fierce storm forced us to set up camp. We were all cold and tired after a 25-mile day, and the wind was fierce. The dogs burrowed deep into the snow and curled up tight with their feet tucked next to their warm bellies and their tails wrapped around them to prevent heat loss.

We built block walls of snow to protect our tents and then rebuilt the collapsed walls every couple of hours. The wind, gusting to 75 miles an hour, ripped gaping holes in our tent, requiring middle-of-the-night repairs. Outside, we could barely stand upright. During one repair effort, the wind tore the mitten shell from my right hand. I chased it for a few yards before giving up. I dug an old wool sock out of my pack and slipped it over my frozen fingers. The strong, frigid wind penetrated my wind pants and froze my penis. I ran around camp with both hands in my pants, which, of course, greatly amused my teammates.

The next day, looking through my ice-covered face mask as my sled runners glided across virgin snow, and seeing only ice and rock and snow, I felt humbled by this vast mystical land. I thought of what we were doing—12 adventurers trekking across a dangerous, inhospitable landscape in the cause of peace and brotherhood. This journey was larger than either of our two nations. It was an example for people everywhere.

At a mountain trail near Enmelen, Nicolai's lead dog, bored by the bleak, white landscape, chased a low-flying snow bunting over a cliff, taking Nicolai and the other dogs with him. They tumbled down the escarpment with the sled rolling over driver and dogs. We stood, stunned, as Zoya, our team doctor, screamed Nicolai's name over the cliff edge. Ten minutes later, we were relieved and amazed to see Nicolai skillfully driving his team up a near-vertical section of hillside to our left, screaming obscenities in Chukchi to his dogs. His face was bloodied from a broken nose. He looked possessed as he thrashed his lead dog with a ski pole.

The next villages, Sereniki and Yanrakynnot, subsist on the 40,000 walruses that live on the nearby Arakamchechen Island. These two villages still build traditional walrus-skinned boats. The umiaks, about 25-feet long, have a frame of spruce lashed together and covered with walrus skins. We negotiated the purchase of a umiak that would be shipped ahead for our Bering Strait crossing.

On the trail, Paul and I sometimes slept in dog sleds to get some relief from the crowded tents. One morning, I was awakened by something wet, cold and furry pushing against my face. At first it didn't register. Then I thought, "Bear!" Rolling on my side, I clawed desperately at the sleeping bag drawstring pulled tight against my face. I gave a scream in a lame attempt to scare the intruder away. Sweating and panicking, I burst upright to find a curious reindeer with a nice rack of horns chewing grass a few feet away.

Our teammate Zoya was excited when we entered her village. The villagers threw a party for us, and we feasted on seal liver, beluga whale and reindeer between Inuit games and traditional dances. We joined in games of finger pull, kneel jump and high kick, in which you jump, feet together, and kick at a fur ball suspended from a pole. I won the kicking prize—a 10-pound loaf of Russian rye.

A week later we arrived in Uelen, the easternmost point in the old Soviet Union—6,200 miles from Moscow and only 52 miles from Alaska's mainland. This is where Mongolian nomads migrated over a land bridge to North America, and eventually traveled across vast stretches of the Arctic to Greenland. Uelen is named for two large black granite rocks that stick out of a hilltop in the otherwise flat area. During winter these rocks are free of snow when all else is covered in white. Snow seems to melt the second it hits them, and because they can be seen for 50 miles the black markers serve as a navigational reference for the Chukchi and Inuit.

Knud Rasmussen, a Danish Arctic explorer who was born in Greenland, drove a dog team from Greenland, across Canada, Alaska and the Bering Strait, to Uelen in the early 1920s. He led the 1921–1924 Fifth Thule Expedition, a three-and-a-half-year dog-sled trip to test the premise that the peoples of the north were linked by a common lifestyle and culture. When we arrived in the village, I discovered that his thesis still held 65 years later. Uelen was the end of the line for Rasmussen's expedition and near the end of Russia for us. This place, at the narrows of the Bering Strait, is known as a birthplace for storms. While we were there, conditions were normal: blinding snow and 70-mile-an-hour winds gusting to 80. It was impossible to stand upright. At one point, it took me a full 40 minutes of stumbling and crawling to reach the dogs to feed them—just 200 yards away from the small school where we were staying.

A ship came once a year to deliver supplies to Uelen, forcing the villagers to rely on themselves. They carefully nurtured cold-weather vegetables in little greenhouses. Onions, radishes, cucumbers and potatoes were the staples, along with the occasional tulip, which was an amazing site in the middle of all the ice and snow. On April 17, 1989, my 28th birthday, our new friends, the schoolteacher Ludmilla and her husband, presented me with the only tulip in town. I cherished this gift, a perfect symbol of the heart of this place.

While in Uelen, a 17-year-old Russian girl begged me to hide her in my sled when we left. She was desperate to leave the Soviet Union and come to the United States. I told her it was impossible. Before I left, she wrote me a poem in broken English, which said in part [as written]: "In lunar light dark I recollect you face cheerful and together with this mysterious look on dark sky, I remember you eyes bright and brilliant...." To this day I regret not helping her achieve freedom.

From Uelen we made our most daring excursion, to Soviet-owned Big Diomede Island in the middle of the Bering Strait, 2.5 miles from Alaska's Little Diomede and 22 miles from the Alaska mainland. The extreme dangers of crossing the notorious strait meant that while half the team would cross in a 25-foot umiak, the other half would bring the dogs in a Soviet military helicopter. I wondered which was safer: an overloaded walrus-hide tub or a cobbled-together Russian military helicopter that had seen action in Afghanistan and resembled a school bus with a prop wired to the roof?

As I watched the ice moving in the 2-mile-an-hour current of the strait, I realized it didn't make much difference. Either way, if we ended up in the water, we would be dead long before we could be rescued. The dogs couldn't be transported by boat, so that made my decision easier. I went by helicopter with the nervous canines. Looking out at the ice and open water about 300 feet below made me nervous, so I occupied myself trying to spot the occasional seal lying on the ice.

Big Diomede, 5 miles in diameter, has a steep, mountainous shoreline locked in isolation and drifting sea ice. The area is constantly stormy, and the sun almost never shines. On the seaward edge of a wind-swept plateau 300 feet above the sea, a dozen weather-beaten, concrete structures stand, home to young Soviet soldiers who serve as border guards and are assigned to the island for two years without leave. That would be my definition of hell. Their faces seemed to say they felt the same.

To help relieve their boredom, we enlisted them in a game of soccer. The game came to an abrupt end when our only soccer ball got booted over the 300-foot cliff into the sea. While the team regrouped and visited with our new hosts, Nicolai and I took our dogs to survey a safe route around the steep island and onto the thin ice toward Little Diomede. Once we had a route, we hauled supplies out to the international dateline, an invisible border on the sea ice between the two islands, one Russian, one American. From there we could clearly see Alaska's flat-topped Little Diomede. Being one of the few Americans to see our country from this vantage point gave me pause.

On April 23, we packed our sleds and buckled on skis for the crossing to Little Diomede and the United States. There we met Jason Davis from KSTP TV in St. Paul, who was co-producing a National Geographic documentary on our expedition. An Alaskan telecommunications company was also on hand for a live broadcast of our crossing. Some 125 Inuit live on Little Diomede. They subsist on whale, walrus, seal, ducks and bird eggs. Darlene Apungaluk and I were treated to herring eggs and dried salmon dipped in seal oil, which ran down our forearms and off our elbows.

From Little Diomede, we continued to Wales, on the Alaska mainland, where we were greeted with a celebration of traditional dancing, potluck meals and lots of stories. We mushed out of Wales on April 28 and followed the coast south. The sea on our right was a buckled mass of ice too rough for travel. Eventually we made it to Nome, the old Gold Rush community that is now the finish line of the Iditarod Trail Dog Sled Race. It was growing warmer by the day, and the dogs and I twice broke through the thin ice on a shallow stream on our way into town. Although we were cold and wet, I didn't care. I was ecstatic. We'd made it to our finish line and the end of the expedition.

I was pleased with what we had accomplished on our trip. After decades of separation, we helped bring peoples and families from both countries closer together. A few months later, in mid-September, officials from Washington and Moscow ratified the free-travel agreement that Alaska Gov. Steve Cowper and his Soviet counterpart, Vyacheslav I. Kobets, signed when our teams crossed the U.S.-Soviet border between Big Diomede and Little Diomede.

Natives of the Bering region in both countries could now traverse the strait without visas. The natural crossroads of continents no longer served as a roadblock that separated families of the Yupik and Inupiat people.

This was a significant step in my journey to be an Arctic explorer. I learned, from both my teammates and the Inuits I met, the importance of companionship in a harsh environment. I learned to value simple tools and materials. My immersion into this native culture left me feeling at home with the Arctic people. I also came away with a much greater appreciation for my American freedoms and blessings. The old gulags and Soviet military posts, the teenager who wanted to escape in my sled, the Soviet citizens doing without the most basic medical and dental services, they all made me feel extremely grateful for what we have.

As I flew out of Alaska on May 11, 1989, I looked down on the magnificent Denali (Mount McKinley) and its vast valleys. I thought of the Japanese mountaineer and polar explorer Naomi Uemura, who perished during a winter solo ascent of the mountain. His body still rests on the mountain. I felt for the first time that I had joined the list of adventurers who are fueled by a dream to explore. I could also see that even those who perish in their quests remain flickers of hope in our planet's grand landscape.

LEARNING TO MAKE A DIFFERENCE, 1991–1996

"I've started to feel the layers of civilization peeling away; it takes weeks to find your animal self. I wake up, grunt at the sun, perform the day's chores, sniff the north wind, and automatically pick out the best route and the safest campsites....I've found the rhythm. I think I can do this."

—Børge Ousland,
Norwegian polar explorer

CHAPTER 5

CROSSING THE NORTHWEST PASSAGE, WEST TO EAST

After the Bering Bridge Expedition, I came home to a new reality. Bonnie and I were finalizing our divorce. It was a sad time, but we both knew it was a necessary choice. I also came home to find a letter of congratulations from Kelly Bowden, a woman I'd met during a winter camping excursion in the Boundary Waters. She was raised in the Twin Cities, but she was keen to live an outdoors life. She had just finished biking 3,000 miles across the United States. We started dating soon after I returned from the expedition.

I wasn't home long before I had a serious case of Arctic Fever. I read the stories of Sir John Franklin's ill-fated Northwest Passage exploration in 1845, and Roald Amundsen's successful expedition in 1906. I yearned for more first-hand knowledge of this unique environment. I wanted to immerse myself in the cultures of the people who live there. In short, I wanted to explore the vast lands from Alaska to Greenland.

Nearly 70 years ago, explorer Knud Rasmussen wrote that he was glad Arctic exploration by dog sled was not yet a thing of the past. He was the first explorer to travel the Northwest Passage by dog sled. I thought his words were still true, so I planned a 3,000-mile dog-sled expedition from Prudhoe Bay, Alaska, to Churchill, Manitoba. It took two and a half years to put this trip together, and it became a critical experience in my development as a polar explorer. My plan, built on a skimpy $75,000 budget, was to start in late 1991 and finish in late spring 1992. It would be the first west-to-east winter crossing of the famed Northwest Passage.

I wanted to learn everything possible about Inuit culture and compare our findings to Rasmussen's experiences in 1923–24. Much of the trip would follow Rasmussen's course but in reverse. What had taken him three years, we planned to do in six months. I knew it was a bold undertaking, with -40°F temperatures, constant winds and two months of polar night. What I didn't know was that I would be tested as never before.

Three men joined me in this expedition: Jon Nierenburg, Tom Viren and Malcolm Vance. Dark-bearded Jon Nierenburg is a mix of East Coast upbringing and Alaskan bush experience. Jon worked as a naturalist and park ranger in Alaska's Denali National Park and had several dog-sled expeditions under his belt, including a first ascent by dog sled of Mount Sanford in the Wrangell Mountains. He had also traveled through the Arctic National Wildlife Refuge and made a lengthy trip through Alaska's interior.

Tom Viren is tall, stocky and mild-mannered. His biology degree is backed by a great deal of outdoors experience. He is an emergency medical technician, a National Outdoor Leadership School instructor and a staff member of many outdoor adventure businesses in Minnesota and Alaska. I'd worked with Tom in northern Minnesota when we led winter wilderness treks together.

Malcolm Vance is a commercial fisherman who lives in a modest log cabin in McCarthy, Alaska, with his partner, Mary Naukpuk. McCarthy is a bygone mining town of rusted iron nestled at the foot of the Wrangell-St. Elias Mountains. Malcolm had twice completed the Iditarod Trail Sled Dog Race between Anchorage and Nome. Known as "fly-by-the-seat-of-your-pants Vance," he grew up near Lake Tahoe and ran a bungee-jumping business with his twin brother, Mark. They also owned a salmon fishing permit for Bristol Bay.

The Northwest Passage trip was by far the largest I'd organized. Along with the North and South Poles, the Northwest Passage was one of the few mystical territories left for explorers. I wanted to learn first-hand more about Knud Rasmussen's journey, the Inuit people and the historical search for a shorter shipping route in the north.

I also wanted to see the mess created by the DEW Line stations along the Arctic coast. The DEW Line is a relic of the Cold War, built between 1953 and 1961, at a cost of $347 million. From Alaska to Greenland, 31 remote sites were spaced over 3,600 miles to protect North America from Russian aircraft. Some were still active, but others had been abandoned. Few people realize the extent of the environmental wounds these radar stations had inflicted on their previously pristine environment. Fuel, PCBs and dioxins all seeped into the tundra and then into the water. Inevitably, they find their way into the food chain, moving from fish to seals to bears and humans, with humans receiving the largest dose.

We planned to pass through a number of Inuit communities, and we shipped supplies ahead to depots spaced a hundred miles apart in villages and at DEW Line stations that were still staffed. I had just been married eight months, so even though Kelly knew she'd married an explorer, our parting and separation was difficult. It's not easy being married to someone who lives on the edge the way polar explorers do. Our spouses and partners ride the emotional roller coaster along with us. I was conscious of what I was asking of Kelly: living alone for months at a time and going to bed at night not knowing whether I was safe or in peril. Luckily, by now we were settled on a small farm in Buffalo, Minnesota, and Kelly had started a job in special education at the local middle school. I hoped our first long separation wouldn't be too hard on her.

Along the bumpy road from Fairbanks to Prudhoe Bay, in three trucks packed with sleds, food, gear and 36 canines, Jon, Tom, Malcolm and I stayed close together. Fearing our old, cobbled-together trucks would break down, we didn't dare lose sight of each other. Along the way, we broke a water pump, thermostat, alternator and windshield. A flat tire hardly registered. A sign marked the last tree along the road. It was the last tree we would see for six months. Then came a sign marking the Arctic Circle. We were ready to leave behind all the stresses of preparation, but we were jittery about starting the expedition, a wise sentiment, I thought.

Giant tongues of fire licked the sky at Prudhoe Bay, burning off natural gas from the British Petroleum Company (BP) oil rigs. The fires and the rigs seemed out of place on the otherwise serene landscape. Company officials welcomed us with plenty of food and comfortable lodgings. Home to about 8,000 workers, the base had all the trimmings—swimming pools, gyms, racquetball courts, saunas and solariums. Not a bad place to be stranded during the four-day blizzard that raged outside, though after three days Malcolm described it as "a plush prison."

Company officials gave us clearance to depart from BP's main oil platform, Endicott, which would save us some miles crossing uncertain terrain to the coast. Endicott is an enormous man-made island of gravel with a drill rig in the center. Imagine pouring gravel into a space the size of a football field a mile deep.

We mushed out of Prudhoe Bay at mid-afternoon on October 23, 1991, under a soupy sky. A crowd of workers waved us off. The temperature was 28°F. Because of the trip's 3,000-mile length, we had to set off from Prudhoe Bay uncomfortably early in autumn to make sure we reached Churchill before the spring thaw. This meant our first days of travel would take us over the season's thinnest ice. We had no idea how dangerous that would prove to be. For the first time, all of our team—four men, 36 dogs, equipment, gear, food and stove gas—was assembled in one place: the edge of the Arctic Ocean.

My Inuit dogs, though young and unruly, were born for Arctic travel. Their constitution allowed them to sleep in the harshest weather and travel on subsistence rations. They were also as ornery as a pride of lions, constantly fighting with each other. We traveled on the tundra with each sled carrying about 750 pounds of gear because the sea ice wasn't yet thick enough to hold us. At this latitude, with the sun low in the sky, the elongated shadows made it look as if I were driving a team of horses and a huge covered wagon. It was a lasting Arctic impression.

When we came to our first DEW Line station at Bullen Point, it resembled a junkyard in an apocalyptic movie. Thousands of empty, rusting 55-gallon oil drums were strewn about, washed up on the snowy beach for a mile in most directions. Some still contained small amounts of fuel leaking onto the tundra. It was an enormous insult to the environment. It's shocking how many governments treat the fragile Arctic with such brutal disregard. Just a short distance to the east lay the Arctic National Wildlife Refuge (ANWR), which some people want to open for oil drilling. Environmentalists strongly oppose drilling, and I am wary of anything that tampers with the Arctic's fragile ecosystem.

We crossed our first set of polar bear tracks at Camden Bay, about 22 miles west of Kaktovik. The next day, traveling in a bad ground blizzard that restricted our visibility, a bear passed within 200 yards of Jon and Tom. Apparently more interested in hunting seals than investigating dog teams and men, the bear ran down a ridge strewn with oil drums. We could tell it was not a young bear by its yellow coat, stained from greasy seal fat.

We camped at Camden Bay, another abandoned DEW Line station and another complete mess smack in the middle of ANWR. More than a thousand abandoned oil and fuel drums dotted the tundra. The next morning's incredible sunrise over the Brooks Range to the south served only to highlight the dump left by the U.S. military and its contractors.

When we arrived in the whaling village of Kaktovik, we took an informal poll of some of the 200 residents. We wanted to know how they felt about oil drilling in ANWR. I was startled to find that 70 percent of the Inuit we asked favored drilling. It would bring jobs and revenue to their community, they said. It was mostly the elders who opposed drilling. I tried to imagine Prudhoe Bay-style oil exploration, with natural gas flares and gravel pads, intruding into this wild home of musk oxen, caribou and polar bears. The picture disturbed me.

Musk oxen were reintroduced here in the 1960s after centuries of absence. There are more each year, crowding out the caribou, which are better to eat. The Inuit here hunt huge bowhead whales from small open boats. They are allowed two strikes a year. In other words, if they harpoon one and lose it, tough luck. It takes the whole village 36 hours to butcher a whale.

In early November, we made camp 7 miles west of the line across the tundra and taiga that separates Alaska and Canada. Fog obscured all but the peaks of the Brooks Range, and everything felt damp. Old sod buildings appeared to be remnants of a trading post from the end of the 19th century. Six graves stood a few yards away. I made out one name on a wooden headboard: ANNIE (spelled with backward Ns), December 21, 1919. I wondered if the darkest day of the year had done her in. More likely, it was the Spanish influenza.

In the 1920s, when Knud Rasmussen traveled through the area, he wrote of finding "fine, smooth ice just inside the barrier" formed by sandy reefs, "very different from the tumbling pressure ridges beyond." The dogs, he noted, "move at a steady trot, and we ourselves were growing accustomed to trotting alongside." Like Rasmussen and his team before us, we ran alongside our sleds.

November 4 was a brutally windy day, with gusts blowing to 60 miles an hour. Progress was slow, both because of the wind and because the newly formed sea ice was sticky under our sled runners. This was the first time salty sea ice affected the expedition. It was a harbinger of difficulties to come. As we moved along on the new ice, Tom found it easier to jog than to ski. It was 0°F, but the ice was covered by a thin layer of wind-blown snow over a layer of slush the consistency of sticky dough. On skis, we had no glide at all, and the sleds moved as though riding on sand.

Depending on conditions, we typically mushed 15 to 25 miles a day. All the while, we were losing sunlight to the Arctic winter. The sunrise now was close to 11:30 am, with sunset about 4:15 pm. Temperatures dipped further below 0°F. Malcolm observed that dressing each day was like getting ready to do battle against Mother Nature. We took turns cooking. Each morning, breakfast was hot cereal, raisins, granola bars, and sometimes a few M&Ms as a treat. We ate lunch on the go.

On November 8, our drinking water tasted of salt, and the sticky ice slowed us again. We were frustrated. The smooth surface looked so inviting for travel, but we couldn't find any snow that wasn't salty. The constant wind had distributed the brine over the coastal landscape. Heading into this world unknown to us, Tom expressed nervousness about entering this unavoidable tunnel. I was nervous, too, but I'd prepared myself for just such uncertainty. When I make a professional commitment—to myself or to someone else—I hold myself to a high standard. This keeps me going at moments when fears and surprises could easily undermine my confidence.

We reached Shingle Point, another DEW Line station, in mid-November after a 13-hour run of 30 miles. We'd seen the station's lights from miles away—how many miles we hadn't known—but we were drawn to them, so we'd pressed on well into the night. It was our longest haul. The station manager, Ron Hilton, gave us a pleasant welcome, and offered coffee and leftover barbecue spare ribs. The DEW Line guys needed to be fed pretty well to keep them there. I shaved my thick beard off for the first time in five years. I was sick of de-icing it.

Whenever we stopped, the first task was dog care. I was mushing 11 dogs, though most of the time I skied or ran beside the sled. Whenever possible, we found a sheltered place to stake the dogs, and we checked for sore feet, harness rubs and other minor infirmities. The dogs never ceased to amaze us. They pulled their hearts out all day, and at night curled up and slept easily in temperatures that would freeze me solid. In the morning, they hopped up and did it again, and in good spirits. It's hard to imagine more inspiring traveling companions than our Inuit dogs.

Once the dogs were seen to, we got the tents up and began cooking dinner, a two-hour process that began with melting ice. While we prepared dinner, we talked over the day, studied maps and planned the next day. Then we ate our pasta or rice meals fortified with butter and drank hot beverages, usually tea, cocoa, coffee or a fruit drink. After a month on the trail, we seemed to be eating well enough. No one seemed terribly skinny or worn down. Even at -22°F, it didn't seem that cold. We were getting acclimated. Each morning it took us nearly four hours in pitch dark to break camp and get on the trail. We got up at 6:30 and were on our way by 11:15.

Jon noted that the nature of our travel changed about two-thirds of the way between Kaktovik and Tuktoyaktuk (Inuit for "it looks like a caribou"), "Tuk" to us. Where once we crossed tundra, lake and swamp, we now traveled almost exclusively on the frozen Beaufort Sea. The route was taking us due east to the MacKenzie River Delta, a maze of swamp and river. About 48 miles from Tuk, in the middle of the MacKenzie River Delta, the clear, smooth 16-inch-thick ice looked at times like open water.

When we got to Tuk, we met an elder named Emmanuel Felex, Sr. In the 1920s, he'd shaken hands with Knud Rasmussen. Emmanuel, 11 years old, had been one of the town's few inhabitants. Rasmussen, dressed like an Eskimo, had been traveling with an Inuit woman, "his girlfriend," Emmanuel remembered some of the village women whispering. "No, she's just traveling with me," Rasmussen had answered, amazing the Inuit that a white man knew their language.

During our two-day stay, villagers gave us loaves of bread and bannock, and asked that we stay awhile, but the polar night was creeping up and we had to keep moving. We planned to take a well-deserved rest in Paulatuk, our next stop.

By November 21, it was getting dark enough to see the moon peek weakly around ribbons of cloud alongside the low-lying sun during the day. We knew this was to be our last sight of the sun for weeks. The polar night had begun. With little or no snow on land, we were again traveling on newly formed ice. From Tuk to Paulatuk, a 320-mile stretch, it was slow going again. The surface was still salt sticky; it looked great but gave no glide.

As Thanksgiving approached, we had our coldest day yet. At -30°F, it was a head-down, teeth-clenching, tough-it-out day. No matter how much I ran alongside the sled, I couldn't get warm. At the end of the day, Tom helped guide my team to the lee side of a palisade. Once out of the wind, he figured we had it made. He took off his skis, strapped them to his pack and started up a slope to get a better view of the route ahead. Halfway up, he stumbled over a not-long-dead ptarmigan. We all understood that death was common in this harsh environment, but Tom's encounter with the ptarmigan served to remind us that we were easy prey. The Arctic kills anything, even animals adapted to it.

No matter how long the day, our Inuit dogs still had enough spare energy to fight. Their scrappiness is part of what makes them so strong. The human team didn't get along much better. Jon often questioned my leadership. Our squabbles—mostly about our rate of travel and my unruly dogs—left a bad taste in everyone's mouth. It was my first real lesson in group dynamics. I came to learn how important personality is when choosing a team. Ability isn't everything.

I also began to see my shortcomings as a team leader. One of my strongest skills is being able to improvise when it comes to equipment and the elements. However, when it came to solving problems relating to people, I had a ways to go. I became frustrated and crabby when the plan wasn't going as scheduled. I tried my best to curtail my frustration, and I kept reminding myself how hard we were pushing ourselves, how much we were accomplishing.

I was newly married like Jon and realized how homesick he was. Instead of showing him compassion, asking him questions, trying

41

to make a connection, I was silent. I "sucked it up" and refused to focus on my own feelings of homesickness, much less anyone else's. I thought he should do the same. Sometimes I mistake being calm, which I'm good at, with being passively stubborn.

That's not how a good leader acts. A novice team leader, I did not push myself to get out of my stubbornness and impatience. It's good to let go of little stuff. But when it comes to major conflict or controversy, I needed to learn how to calmly and nonjudgmentally deal with differences between people. I was stuck in thinking that Jon was not suited for the expedition. Perhaps he wasn't, but a bit of kindness and more open communication on my part could have benefited us all. It also could have made a difference in Jon's "fit" in the team. Unfortunately, I'll never know.

A bitterly cold wind kept us pinned in our camp for two days near Thanksgiving. We needed all our strength to stand up and walk through the gale to check on dogs and tent tie-downs. The loud wind overwhelmed all other sound. Trying to put aside our differences, we marked the holiday by huddling together in a tent, smoking cigars, and eating sardines and the seal meat we brought from Tuk. We consumed granola bars and mugs of butter-fortified hot chocolate for dessert while Malcolm read aloud from the book, *The Incredible Eskimo* by Raymond de Coccola and Paul King.

The following day, three of Jon's dogs were exhausted and had to ride in the sled. Alaskan huskies are lanky. They catch the wind. Plus, they have too little fur for this kind of travel. Stocky, low-to-the-ground dogs are best in conditions like this. Jon told Malcolm he might leave the expedition in Paulatuk if another dog wore out or if his homesickness got the better of him. Things didn't improve with Jon's dogs. On November 30, he was forced to carry two of his dogs for 3 miles in the sled. It was obvious they were dying. When Malcolm lifted his rifle to put them out of their misery, Jon was devastated.

That night in the tent we argued over whether we were giving the dogs enough food. Jon was convinced he'd not carried enough food for them. I thought the dogs were getting fed enough, but the next day another of Jon's dogs died. I didn't understand what was happening. I recognized that our hard traveling in the cold and dark was breeding frustration and fatigue, and I wondered if our judgment had become clouded. Had the dogs picked up a bug? Perhaps there was something wrong with the food or with the stink herring we'd picked up in Tuk? Were the dogs suffering from a contagious disease and spreading it among themselves? I had lots of questions, but, no matter how hard I considered the possibilities, I had no answers.

A few days later, another of Jon's dogs died. It was horrible. I took our entire cheese and butter supply and distributed it for the mushers to feed the dogs, as they felt necessary. "The Arctic seems to be sorting the dogs out at an incredible rate," Malcolm mused. I wondered if the other teams were next. I also considered what the outcome would be for the four of us. I thought of something I'd read in Rasmussen's book, *Across Arctic America*: "Considering the rigors they endured, I don't know which is more remarkable, that I came through the three-and-a-half years with the same team of dogs, or with the same Eskimos."

As we pondered the situation, we thought it might be a combination of the dogs eating too little food and being dehydrated. We began to add broth to their food when we could, almost impossible at the moment because most of the snow was salt-laced. Jon was demoralized; he was down to six dogs, and they were fading fast. Our tent was filled with heartbreak and fear.

Because there was little snow, we had to follow the ice of the Horton River. What was to be a short overland journey turned into a long, meandering detour that finally cut through a notch in the Smoking Hills and dumped us into Franklin Bay, back on the Arctic

Ocean. Along the hills, smoke rose from burning sulfur deposits beneath the rock. The steep hills averaged 1,000 feet in elevation and ran for 100 miles to the east. They were gray, dark and uninviting. Even the breeze carried the smell of rotten eggs. We talked about crossing the hills to avoid traveling on the bay with its salty ice, but the hills were too steep and the expedition team too weak. We studied maps, but there was no alternative. We had to cross the bay.

The weather was brutal. The temperature stood at -20°F with a 50-mile-an-hour wind. Better not to know the wind chill. We fought off face frostbite all day. That night, the wind violently drummed the tent walls, and, as we lit the stove, crystals from our frozen breath shifted back and forth in front of our headlamps.

The next day, we left Jon's sled behind. We added his cargo to our sleds and his remaining dogs to our teams. What a waste: all those good dogs, all those days Jon had prepared for this. On December 3, four more of Jon's dogs died, and I lost a dog as well. We were living a nightmare. On top of it all, I realized that my fanny pack—containing my camera, diary, money and expedition credit card—was missing. I retraced our route 3 miles in pitch dark, not something I wanted to do with the prospect of polar bears—and every block of ice looked like one. Luckily, I found the pack laying on the ice.

Still 77 miles from Paulatuk, we were edgy. The dogs were slow, but looked better after we fed them broth from the bit of fresh snow we found. The sled runners dragged as if on sandpaper. The 17 miles we made each day felt like a hundred. We were dehydrated and suffered from headaches. I had frostbite on all my fingertips. Jon had one dog on a leash, and another, limping on blistered feet, wobbled behind him. Every moment I half-expected one of us to stagger and fall. I felt responsible for what had happened.

Days later, I had to shoot one of my most beautiful Inuit dogs after he collapsed into a coma. Crying as I ended his life, I was angry with myself for getting us into this mess. I felt as if we were traveling on a treadmill of death in a world of nothing but bitter cold and utter darkness. At Langton Bay, we cached another pile of equipment to lighten the load for our dogs. I sent Tom ahead to Paulatuk on skis to get help. He could travel much faster than the dogs and would reach the village 24 hours ahead of us. Just 90 minutes after he left, I spotted a light moving in the distance. "Snowmobile! Flare!" I yelled to Jon. We tore through his pack, grabbed the flare and pulled the fuse. At first we weren't sure we'd been seen, so I lit another flare. The machine dipped below the horizon, and its lights disappeared. We waited, but nothing happened. We turned in disappointment and started walking again.

Then, all of a sudden, there he was: an Inuit man from Paulatuk, out hunting caribou. I introduced us and described our situation. He said his name was Steve Illisiak. "We expected you guys about a week ago," he said. "The Mounties are out looking for you now."

We loaded his sled with packs, dogs and cargo. He drove us 2 miles to his hunting hut. We immediately fed the dogs warm caribou meat and broth. With the dogs settled and cared for, I left Jon and Malcolm at the hut, and rode with Steve into Paulatuk, 35 miles away. On the way, he told me he was worried about his brother, who had failed to arrive at the hunting camp.

Soon we were in a full-blown ground blizzard. Halfway to town, we came across Steve's brother, who held up a cigarette lighter to signal us. He'd run out of gas and was walking back to Paulatuk. We were lucky to find him when we did. He was about to dig into a snowbank for the night, without sleeping bag, food or water.

When we reached town, I learned that Tom had been picked up by a Royal Canadian Mounted Police team returning from a Franklin Bay patrol. The next day we retrieved all of our gear and dogs by snowmobile and went into town. Malcolm elected to rest his dogs for another day in the hunting camp. Then he followed the snow machine trail into town.

I was concerned about my lead dog, Al. In the middle of our ordeal, he'd chewed his harness and swallowed a 2-foot length of blue nylon webbing. Dogs die from eating a lot less when it gets stuck in their digestive track. I gave him ample amounts of seal oil to loosen him up, and his belly bloated up as tight as a banjo. Two days later, I was greatly relieved when he pooped out a 20-inch blue pole.

The previous 10 days had been the most wrenching mix of heartache and drudgery in my young polar career, but if I thought things couldn't get worse, I was mistaken. By mid-December, while we still were in Paulatuk, animal rights groups in the United States learned of the dog tragedy and began criticizing us. I was angry to be judged by people who knew nothing about what we'd experienced. None of our critics contacted us to ask what was happening. People asked why we couldn't use snowmobiles or airplanes. The answer was simple, and unacceptable to our critics: We had a different definition of "adventure." It's difficult to get in touch with the land when you are 30,000 feet in the air or going 50 miles an hour on a snow machine. Our Inuit hosts in Paulatuk couldn't understand what the fuss was about. Death from the elements for Inuit hunters and dogs is a given. Finding Steve's brother just in time was the most recent reminder.

In all, we lost 15 dogs, 10 of them Jon's. With his spirit broken and his team gone, Jon chose to leave the expedition. Realizing we still had about 2,200 miles and the coldest part of the expedition to go, Tom decided to leave with him. It was a difficult decision for him. I was sad to see them go.

CHAPTER 6

FINISHING THE PASSAGE WITH
A SLIMMED-DOWN TEAM

The choice confronting me was stark: quit and leave the Arctic defeated, or proceed wiser and strengthened by our difficulties. Malcolm and I agonized over where we had gone wrong. For two years, we had made painstaking plans. If we had made a mistake, it was in starting too early in the season while the sea ice was still thin and salty, and the land was shy of snow. Another October might have been different, but the early start was dictated by the distance we needed to cover between freeze-up and thaw. More determined than ever, we decided to continue.

We met two Greenland Inuit, Jens Danielsen and Ono Fleisher. They, too, were following in the footsteps of Rasmussen, to whom Ono was related. They wore polar bear pants, blue fox parkas and seal skin boots. Their sleds were like those of Polar Eskimos in northwest Greenland, framed with two planks of spruce, 15 feet long. Dog harnesses and harpoon lines were slung over curved upstanders at the back of their sleds.

When I told them in sorrowful detail about our tragedy in Franklin Bay, they looked at each other and then both patted me on the back. "It was not from lack of food that your dogs died," said Ono. "You had enough. Sled dogs can go five days without any food and still work. Starved dogs take several weeks to die. It was salt that killed your dogs. They worked to the end, then suddenly dropped dead from dehydration." It is very difficult to travel in the fall when there is little snow to cover the salty sea ice, he explained. Even with 4 inches of snow covering new sea ice, salt leeches into the snow and the wind picks up salt from the ice, contaminating the surrounding fresh snow. This makes it nearly impossible to find enough clean ice to melt for drinking water. To get around this, the Inuit travel in salty areas for no more than two days at a time. Then they camp and travel in fresh snow areas so the dogs can eat fresh snow. I wished we'd had that option in Franklin Bay, but at least now we understood what had happened.

Paulatuk was a fairly young community, struggling to hold onto its culture, with very few elders to pass on the old ways. Forced like many along the Arctic rim into a western way of life, the Paulatuk Inuit were being pulled apart. Suicide, alcoholism and domestic abuse were common. Only a handful of jobs were available in the village—doing snow removal and housing maintenance, working in the hamlet office or teaching in the school. They were all government jobs. A few villagers made a meager income from carving or guiding outside hunters. Most had lost their native language, and each year fewer hunted and fished, even though food flown in was astronomically priced. A can of pork and beans, for example, went for $4. To pass the time, many villagers gambled heavily and indulged their passion for country and western music.

We rested mostly, spending our days at "coffee-miks," neighborly socials where we all consumed far too much coffee, sugar cookies and cigarettes. These gatherings were the perfect setting for Inuit stories. One day, the conversation turned to Arctic foxes and how they follow polar bears and clean up after them. I asked a hunter, Tony Green, if he had ever seen an Arctic fox swimming along behind a bear. He hadn't, but he told me the story of a young man who, while hunting from a kayak on the ice edge, noticed something swimming in the distance. When he paddled closer, we could see it was a fox, swimming with its fluffy tail shooting straight up to keep it dry. We burst out laughing at the image. "Like a human crossing a cold creek naked, holding long underwear overhead," I said.

After our month-long stay in Paulatuk, Malcolm and I were rested, and our dogs were fattened up, on whale blubber, seal meat and commercial dog food. We left on January 11 at 1 pm. The temperature was -35°F and the horizon was a brilliant orange. We had about six hours of twilight in the middle of the day and longed to actually see the sun. Malcolm had nine dogs and I had eight, the same number Rasmussen had for his Arctic crossing. We were 2,200 miles from Churchill, Manitoba.

We traveled 33 miles the first day, going well into the night, sore as hell but determined to make Pierce Point, the first major headland east of Paulatuk. In the moonlight, we could see smoke coming from the stack of a small hut at the top of the point. It was an old place for spotting bear and whales. We could see for 30 miles in every direction. Inside, our hosts from Paulatuk—Hank, Arnold and Abut—greeted us with coffee. They were hunting bear.

On the trail early the next day, I bruised the side of my foot on a sharp rock and limped alongside my sled for a week. We made good progress anyway. When we faced a ground blizzard at -40°F, we stayed put in camp and rested the dogs. Outside, flesh would freeze in 45 seconds if exposed. Crawling into my sleeping bag was like a wrestling match with myself. The only way to ensure a good night's sleep was to close up both zippers and drawstrings tight.

One night, while Malcolm read aloud from his book, which reminded me of the old Radio Reader program in Alaska, I rummaged through my gear bag. I found two bear-scare firecrackers, similar to cherry bombs. Malcolm stopped reading and started to fill the stove's gas tank. He asked me how they worked. I took the top off one and touched it to the firecracker. "Oh, shit," I shouted. I'd sparked the fuse by accident. Throwing the firecracker across the tent, I somehow managed to hit the softball-sized opening in the tent door. Bang! We nearly blew up the whole expedition. We had a good laugh anyway.

As we continued on, the country was so vast we felt like two ants crossing a plowed field. One day, Malcolm, 100 yards ahead of me, dropped to his knees and bowed to the south. When I caught up to him, I could see that he was gazing down a valley, running south from where we stood. At the end of it, the sun sat, as if in a saddle, on the horizon. I jumped up and down, full of joy. I kept my eyes fixed on it, afraid that if I looked away or blinked, it would disappear. Malcolm and I shook hands.

We'd been traveling with the moon since leaving Paulatuk, but once the sun truly rose again, the light shone on the nearby cliffs and soaked into my raw cheeks. It was January 21. We had gone so long without the sun, 64 days in all, it seemed like a foreign object. We had made it through the polar night. With the light now in our favor, it was time to travel hard. That evening, while I nursed my bruised foot, Malcolm sprained his ankle stepping into a crack in the ice. We were now two slow-moving explorers hoping our injuries would mend at the next village.

When we arrived at an abandoned DEW Line station on Clifton Point, the wind built into a howling blizzard of 60 miles an hour and more. We were lucky to find an old hunting hut. We shoveled out the drift in front of the door, and had a quiet and cozy night in the hut banked on all sides in snow.

Not as much snow falls in the Arctic as one might think. What little does fall is wind-driven, often into beautiful sculpted waves called sastrugi. The people who live here say they don't actually get any snow, they just borrow it from other places.

The next morning, I got up at 9 am. The wind had died down a bit, but it was still too strong for travel. Malcolm went out to check on the dogs while I stayed in the tent and melted snow for water. After about 15 minutes, I wondered where he was. Suddenly Malcolm ran through the door, a look of horror on his face. The wind had shifted during the night and the dogs were buried in a 5-foot snowdrift. One of the dogs was dead.

A cloud hung over the expedition on January 26 as we started out again, crossing the 8 miles of Stapylton Bay. With bad ice and drifts, it took all day. The bay held the worst pack ice of the expedition so far. We inched along over one pressure ridge after another. Lines tangled. Sleds tipped over and wedged between ice blocks. We sweated through the day despite the -30°F temperature. When we were done, the dogs were spent. Malcolm and I were so stiff we could hardly stand, but we managed to rally enough to celebrate Malcolm's 30th birthday.

With Stapylton Bay behind us, the sledding was good. We put in several long days and arrived dead tired at our next DEW Line destination. When we introduced ourselves, the station chief didn't even shake our hands. I said we'd like to stay and rest our dogs a few days.

"No," he said. I suspected he was drunk and "strutting his stuff" in front of his team. I asked if our dog food had arrived. "Yes," was his terse reply. It was dark and windy, so he must have felt compelled to say we could stay the night as long as we left promptly in the morning. We were so tired, we would have gladly slept in the garage with the machinery.

The next morning, we took our time getting ready to depart, and had one last pastry and coffee. It was almost noon when we left. It was bitter cold, so we stopped to put on additional layers of clothing. The dogs were curled up with their backs to the wind, and Malcolm was just ahead of my lead dog. I started to walk to the front of my team when suddenly my hair stood up on the back of my neck. Was there a bear nearby? I peered around through the fur ruff on my hood. I had a strong feeling of a person standing next to me. As I continued to walk towards Malcolm, "this person" walked with me, inches away, first on my left, then passing behind me to walk on my right. I fully expected an invisible hand to touch my face. I wasn't scared. When I asked Malcolm if he felt the presence of someone with us, he said he hadn't. I couldn't explain it. I just knew I had.

Other explorers, such as Ernest Shackleton and Richard Weber, have reported similar "encounters" with the "third person." As I thought about it, I suspected the heightened senses required to survive in such an intense, remote place plays a part in this phenomenon.

In early February, we needed a break and hunkered down for a few days at the Lady Franklin Point DEW Line station. My hip was bothering me from favoring my bruised foot over the last 150 miles. We had had 19 days of -30°F or colder, and we had jogged along-side the sleds to stay warm about one-third of the time since leaving Paulatuk. We were welcomed by the station's conversation-starved hosts. When not talking, we watched all their VCR movies and made a few modifications to our sleds to lighten the load. Unnecessary gear and excess dog food got shipped to Winnipeg to be claimed at the end of the expedition. Every time I thought we'd pared our kit to its essentials, I found additional things we didn't really need. Our bare essentials got even more spare.

On February 4, after our break, Malcolm and I traveled over-land in whiteout conditions: no landmarks, just faded white terrain with no contrast or depth of field. It was like traveling inside a white sphere. The compass was useless this close to the north magnetic pole, the point at which the earth's magnetic field points vertically downward. Unlike the geographic north pole, the north magnetic pole moves over time. We had to rely on prevailing winds and snow-drift formations to guide us. After a midday break, we made one lightening-speed, 16-mile leg when the dogs decided to chase a herd of musk oxen. The hairy beasts looked like something left over from dinosaur days.

The following days dragged as we followed the coast, day in, day out, point-to-point, bay-to-bay. The dogs seemed bored with the white, too, as they darted to investigate every contrasting piece of rabbit or caribou scat they saw. One day they chased a dwarf willow leaf blown by the wind; the next, a rabbit darting in front of them. Sometimes they jerked ahead so hard I was almost thrown from the sled. The sea ice was as flat as we'd seen yet. We made 27 miles in six hours. The temperature was -36°F.

Malcolm and I became very efficient. We had spent so much time together on the trail that we each knew what the other was thinking, so we needed few words. We cooperated, compromised and joked like a married couple. On an expedition, when teammates rely on each other, right down to lifesaving, this is the best kind of partnership, full of respect and humor. Some people are blessed with a great sense of humor. I'm not one of them. Yet I knew the value of humor and I worked hard to develop mine, especially on the trail.

We spent eight days resting and recuperating in Cambridge Bay, where Malcolm received a custom-made fur parka in the mail from his partner, Mary. We both were fighting the cold by combining the warmth of traditional clothing and the utility of modern synthetics. Most traditional fur clothing is extremely warm even when a person is inactive, but if you're moving a lot, such as skiing or pushing a sled over rough ice, traditional clothing is too warm and restrictive. We dressed in layers of synthetic fleece with a nylon wind shell anorak and pants, which allowed us to regulate our body temperature to fit our level of activity and the outside temperature. In extremely cold weather, we wore fur pants made from caribou or polar bear, and mittens made from the leg fur of caribou. The wolverine fur ruff on our parka hoods protected our faces from frostbite.

Wearing fur parkas, along with our other Inuit gear, Malcolm and I resembled Inuit natives more all the time. When we gave a presentation at the Cambridge Bay school, I noticed there wasn't much traditional garb left in this community of about 1,100 people. Nor were there many dog teams. Traditional culture seemed to be disappearing.

We applied new plastic runners to our sleds, so once we left Cambridge Bay, our heavily laden vehicles moved with ease on the south shore of Victoria Island in Queen Maud Gulf. And by now we were acclimated, at least as much as you can be when you're not native dwellers. The longer you're in the Arctic, the less the cold is a problem. You get used to it. If you feel the cold penetrating, you eat a candy bar, swing your arms, flex your fingers and kick your feet to get the blood moving. Wind is always a fearsome enemy though, something Rasmussen noted. "So dense was the whirling snow," he wrote, "the whole of the last day's journey was accomplished with bent backs and bowed heads. We had literally to creep along, following the well-worn sled track with our noses almost to the ground."

But for now, the season was changing and the sun got higher in the sky—up for eight hours a day now. Malcolm and I had to wear sunglasses each day from then on. Umiak, my only female dog, came into heat and my male dogs got unruly. I knew the fighting would start in a few days. I told Malcolm we needed to stop at the nearest 7-Eleven store to pick up some tampons for Umiak. "No problem," he said, "I know of one just 2,000 miles south of here."

On March 2, we arrived in Gjoa Haven, the end of our Northwest Passage crossing. Norwegian Roald Amundsen was the first to navigate the passage, from east to west, in 1906. Twice he wintered in Gjoa Haven, named for his ship, the Gjoa. About 40 people greeted us when we entered the hamlet. They offered us gifts of dried fish and knitted wool hats. Paul Schurke called from Minnesota to congratulate us.

We lived it up in Gjoa Haven. Malcolm called it "a place of good hospitality," and he was right. There were drum dances, square dances and a small feast. We also made the coffee circuit, drinking between 12 and 15 cups of coffee, and eating innumerable sugar cookies as we visited with villagers. The community had a strong, proud sense of its Inuit culture. Unlike Cambridge Bay, many spoke the Inuit language, did traditional drum dances and wore fur clothing. Because of the inflated costs of gas and maintenance, some villagers spurned snow machines and returned to dog sleds.

At night, Malcolm and I planned our overland route to Baker Lake, where we would turn south toward Churchill. Our overland route to Baker Lake would be a good change from traveling on sea ice, although it presented challenges of its own. Some of the worst weather in the world develops in this 350-mile trek through the Canadian Barren Grounds. We were retracing the route of an expedition led by Lieutenant Frederick Schwatka in 1878–80 in search of the remains of the British Franklin Expedition.

Once we left Gjoa Haven, Malcolm and I wore face masks so only our eyes were exposed to the bitter-cold south wind. We longed for spring weather. One night we camped on the tip of Adelaide Peninsula near the bones and relics of Sir John Franklin's lost men, who died on their 1845 trip to find the Northwest Passage.

By mid-March, we had 13 hours of daylight and no longer needed headlamps for morning and evening chores. We ate boiled caribou seasoned with copious amounts of brittle caribou hair that migrated from the tent floor to our greasy cups, bowls and spoons. At first, we skimmed the hair off the top of our cocoa and soup, but after a while we just drank it down. An Inuit child, it is said, eats a pound of caribou hair by the age of five.

A March blizzard kept us tent-bound for 102 hours. So much for the hopes of spring. Malcolm and I shared Walkman ear buds and listened to Aretha Franklin, Credence Clearwater Revival and Bad Company to pass the time. We stayed in our sleeping bags 14 to 16 hours a day to conserve fuel and food. The rest did us good, but by the end, our backs, hips and shoulders ached. Malcolm named us

Tentbagmiut. The Inuit suffix "miut" means "the people of." We were the people of the sleeping bag.

When we emerged, our sleds and tent were completely buried in snow. The sky was clear, but the wind was still blowing hard, obscuring the first 10 feet above the ground. However, we knew we couldn't stay dormant any longer. We stayed close to each other as we mushed along. There were no other people for 350 miles, just caribou everywhere. When the dogs caught sight of caribou, the chase was on. Malcolm and I let the dogs run as long as they were headed in the direction we wanted to go. It took them a long time to realize their efforts were in vain.

A few days later, when travel was back to normal, Malcolm saw a wolf. When he looked at it through his binoculars, it looked right back at him. Moments like this, he said, made it all worthwhile. Hardships were forgotten. This remained one of his most graphic Arctic images: "open country, caribou spotted about like cattle on a range, and wolves trailing you."

After a 36-mile push, we crested a hill and saw Baker Lake, the only non-coastal Inuit settlement in the Arctic, home to the Barren Ground Inuit. The 1,000 residents subsist strictly on caribou, fish and tundra berries. They hunt no marine mammals. Some of the most beautiful Inuit dogs I've ever seen were owned by a respected elder hunter at Baker Lake. At the end of town, a dog with a cut-off tail was wasting away on a chain, no doubt ignored by a drunk owner. To save him from certain starvation, I put him on top of my sled to ride until he was fit to pull. I named him Stubs.

The warm sun softened the snow pack, and the harsh environment teemed with life. Migrating caribou dotted the Barren Grounds, and snow buntings and ptarmigan fluttered above dwarf willow. Finally free of the dark winter, Inuit families headed out to fish and hunt. We were feeling pretty good about our ourselves in the increasing light and warmth, although we were nowhere near finished with our expedition. Traveling by dog team at this time of year is completely satisfying, a welcome reward for surviving the polar night. When we stopped to rest in the mild conditions, Malcolm and I lay on the sleds with our heads pointed toward the dogs and our feet on the upstanders. We soaked up the sun as if we'd never felt it before. We'd averaged just over 19 miles a day during the harsh months of February and March, but in two days of early April, we covered the 71 miles into Rankin Inlet, a hamlet on the Kudlulik Peninsula.

As we came into the village, we ran into a middle-aged man and his dogs. "Where did you come from?" he asked.

"Alaska," Malcolm replied.

"We've heard a lot about you," the man said. "You've come far by dog team. We are proud of you."

We shared lunch with him, gnawing on shavings of frozen Arctic char, as he told us that word of our trek had passed from village to village. It was as if our pilgrimage of insight and knowledge made us part of the Inuit family. It pleased us. We visited a local radio station and staff members there gave me the name Mikilaaq Taussuni, "small one who smells like a seal." I couldn't argue with its accuracy. Given how long I'd been without a bath, even I couldn't ignore the pungent odor coming from my sealskin boots.

In Rankin Inlet, my friend Larry Roepke, who is a Minneapolis freelance photographer, joined the expedition. He would travel the rest of the way with us. The weather continued to warm during the final segment of our journey. It left the snow soft and difficult. We took turns on skis, breaking trail for the dogs in knee-deep snow. From Eskimo Point to Churchill, the flat and featureless terrain offered nothing to take our minds off the cruel work of post-holing (breaking a trail through the snow) in front of the dogs. The slow going left us very low on food, so we reduced our meals to half rations even though this work made us burn more calories. It was the flattest 200 miles I'd ever seen. It reminded me of North Dakota.

By the third week in April 1992, we had been on one-third rations for three days and were always hungry. Following the coast, we ran across a weather-beaten Hudson Bay Company building on the Manitoba-Northwest Territories border. Inside, half-buried in the snow, we found a caribou carcass and half a box of Red River cereal. I guessed the caribou was from the previous fall. Cutting back the hide exposed an outer layer of greenish flesh. Deeper down, the meat looked healthier, so we hacked some off and boiled it in a pot. The pungent smell should have clued us that it was rotten, but Malcolm wolfed it down anyway. Larry and I hesitantly followed his lead. We figured the nutritional value out-weighed the diarrhea, which we all suffered. For the next four days, we ate balls of Red River cereal for breakfast, lunch and dinner, with no milk or sugar to get it down.

As we progressed over the flats, we finally saw a glow from the lights of Churchill, 26 miles away. We were nearing the end. My eyes watered, but this time not from wind and cold. I was overwhelmed by what we had accomplished. After a few miles in the morning light of April 25, 1992, I saw a dark strip on the horizon. It could only be trees. Then they began to take shape, stunted spruce that were a head tall. Malcolm stopped his team, ran off the trail and hugged a scrawny spruce so thin and needle-scarce you could see through it.

Macolm led us for two hours, and then said, "Take us into Churchill, Lonnie." We shook hands. I thanked him for his friendship and for trusting me when things looked bleak. We gave each other a tentative half-hug, the way many men do. Then we crossed the mouth of the Seal River and followed a snowmobile trail through the trees into town. The trail opened up and we drove our dogs down the muddy street lined with trucks and snow machines. We were in downtown Churchill.

I tied the dogs—the real heroes of the expedition—to a stop sign at an intersection, and sat on my sled and wept. Perhaps it was relief that the trip was finally over, that we no longer had to travel each day and steel ourselves to deal with whatever difficulties and dangers we encountered. Perhaps it was knowledge that I finally would see my family and friends again. Only now did I allow myself to feel how much I'd missed them. Luckily, I didn't have to wait long to see Kelly. She was in Churchill waiting for us.

But it was more than this. I would miss our visits with the Inuit. I would miss my exploring partner, Malcolm, and the simple routines we had adopted over the past five months. We had been on the trail 189 days, nine of which were spent waiting out storms and 61 resting in villages or at military stations. We'd learned a great deal about how this Arctic world and its people had changed since Knud Rasmussen's journey 70 years earlier.

The Inuit were losing their culture and identity, and were gaining the afflictions of alcohol and drug abuse—a horrible trade. Fewer and fewer Inuit adolescents retained their native language or learned how to hunt, fish and gather. In all the villages we entered, except Baker Lake, there were no pure Inuit dogs teams left. With the exception of a few mixed-breed teams kept for recreation, dogs had been replaced by snow machines.

The farther east we went from Alaska, the more traditional the communities became. Whale Cove and Arviat had done the best at holding fast to Inuit culture. In all the other villages, in less than two generations, thousands of years of life tied intimately to the land— where everything happened in its own time—had nearly disappeared. I regarded what had taken its place as horribly shallow by comparison—a 9-to-5 job and a money-driven existence. It was happening all across the Arctic, from Alaska to Greenland.

Our expedition was not about conquering the environment, but rather about learning to deal with it on its own terms. We sought to rise above our personal doubts and fears, and to expand our personal limits. I believed we'd succeeded. I had also proven to myself that I was a doer as well as a dreamer. I came away with a deep respect for the Arctic and its people. Insights came hard, some involving tragedy. The Inuit and the unforgiving elements were our finest teachers. I had big dreams and I needed the insights I'd gained—born of hardship and heartbreak—to turn my dreams into reality.

While I was proud of what I'd accomplished, I also felt humbled. We'd started the expedition with a four-member team. At the end it was just Malcolm and me. I'd never know for certain whether I could have kept our team intact, but I had plenty to think about. One thing was clear. My next challenge would be to take the lessons of this expedition into my future expeditions.

As I mused, our dogs crowded around the strange vegetation growing out of the snow—a tree. They sniffed it, chewed it and played tug of war with the branches. Then they peed on the poor thing.

CHAPTER 7

CARRYING AN ENVIRONMENTAL
MESSAGE FOR THE OLYMPICS

I returned to Minnesota and started a new business called Chinook Winds, which offered guided dog-sledding trips in northern Minnesota. However, I soon became bored with the routine and by early 1994 I was ready for another adventure. Norwegian Geir Randby invited me to join the six-person International Environmental Expedition (IEE), a 54-day, 1,000-mile, dog-sled journey that was to begin at the 1994 Winter Olympics in Lillehammer, Norway.

Our mission was to deliver an Olympic environmental message to Nagano, encouraging Japanese officials to incorporate a third element—environmental themes—to the athletic and cultural components of the Olympic games. Norway's commitment to the environment is unequaled. The world can learn a lot from its superior packaging and recycling programs, its use of cleaner power, and its emphasis on efficient transportation. We also planned to spread our environmental message along the route.

I was the only American and was asked to be the expedition's co-leader. Aside from Randby and me, the original team included Anita Fossum and Magnar Aasheim of Norway, Isao Nozaki of Japan, and Stanislav Kostjaskin of the Soviet Union.

I wasn't as worried about our 54-day expedition as I was about our 30-second departure from Olympic Stadium. As we received the environmental message from dignitaries, three of us were to run our dog teams through the stadium during closing ceremonies on February 27. I was afraid my lead dog, Gideon, would take a wrong turn in front of the king of Norway, not to mention the two billion television spectators.

On my first practice run, a television camera operator asked if it was safe for him to shoot video from my sled during the run. I smiled, and he climbed aboard with his gear. At the green light, the dogs bolted towards the center of the arena. The sled clipped the first step on the podium, and sent the camera operator and his equipment skidding across the hard-packed snow. With some difficulty, I righted the sled, still on the move, and headed toward the exit. On the third run, Gideon climbed two rows of bleachers to get at a spectator's hot dog. This practice left me even more worried than before. I later learned that my training runs cost the network $150,000 in equipment repairs.

Finally we had to do it for real. With her usual look of support, my wife, Kelly, was there, holding my lead dogs. I'm sure my eyes were as big as plates as I heard the countdown: "5, 4, 3..." Covered in goosebumps, I adjusted my sweat-soaked long underwear. A guy in a white suit ran over and yelled at me not to forget I couldn't use my brake. People dressed as trolls were hiding under trap doors in the snow for later in the ceremony. Obviously, I was meant to miss them.

"What?" I yelled, in a bit of a panic.

"...2, 1, Go!"

"Hike," I yelled, and we were off. My eyes were fixed on Gideon for any sign of straying. "Just follow the other dogs," I thought to myself. We entered the stadium under intense light and to a roaring crowd. We were supposed to wave at the crowd, but I was too nervous and going too fast to let go of the handle bars. Half-smiling and trying to wave—and beyond caring whether I snagged a troll and dragged him out of his hidey-hole—I applied my brakes. I breathed a huge sigh of relief when Gideon led us safely out of the stadium.

And then we were off. The first leg of the expedition took us north through the Norwegian and Swedish mountains, and across Finland. My most memorable encounters in Scandinavia were our visits with the Sami people, also known as Laplanders, whose stories and way of life charmed us. We could see that traditional travel by reindeer sled had lost out to snowmobiles, although drivers always kept a pair of birch skis strapped to the back of their snowmobiles for rounding up reindeer and getting home if the machines broke down. In the villages, haunches of dried reindeer meat hung under the overhangs of roofs. We took saunas with them and ate reindeer, the staple of their diet, in various forms—fried, boiled, dried, aged and smoked.

We ended the first leg of the expedition on April 22 in Murmansk, Russia, where the spring melt made further mushing impossible. The sights we saw through the dusty windows of a rundown bus on our way back to Norway were depressing. Mile after mile held nothing but dead trees. As we passed the Russian industrial town of Nikel, the ditches on either side of the road were littered with cans, old tires and plastic bags. Toxic smoke poured from large stacks. I wondered what invisible destruction lay below the brown grass and scummy ponds. A bright blue picket fence encased the town cemetery, ironic in so many ways. An old woman on the bus leaned over and said to me, "It's like this for 100 kilometers around Nikel. It's the second most polluted city in Russia, perhaps in the world."

As I traveled home to wait for the next leg of the expedition and earn money as a carpenter, I had plenty of time to ponder what I'd seen. Russia's economic distress was so acute, and its ability to invest in new and environmentally sound factories so circumscribed, that if you spoke to the 40,000 workers in Nikel about the environmental destruction, they'd laugh. They'd not gotten a pay check in four months. How could we make our environmental message heard in a country where many people didn't even have the basic needs of food, clothing and shelter met?

In January 1995, I returned to Russia for the second leg of the expedition and spent a month in a military training camp for dogs, about 100 miles north of Moscow. The dogs were trained for military use, law enforcement, riot control and drug enforcement. I was able to keep my sled dogs in a couple of vacant pens while finalizing the logistics for our travel across Siberia.

I stayed in a heavily guarded compound with uniformed officers, who kept me entertained each day with vodka lunches and sauna evenings. When I ventured into a nearby town, I had a military escort. Bandits from the Russian mafia, dressed in black, stood on prominent corners. Lawlessness reigned in Russia during those days of Yeltsin's rule and economic collapse.

During this time, I found several safety and logistical holes in Randby's plan to go forward. Among other things, the dangers in this

63

lawless and isolated area made it seem foolish for me to continue. I decided to resign as co-leader and leave the expedition. The rest of the team, some original, some new, decided to carry on. I donated equipment and several Inuit sled dogs to the cause.

I later learned that the deeper the team got into Siberia, the more the team's non-motor objective faded. I knew I'd made the right decision. I didn't regret the time I'd spent on the Olympic expedition, because I'd gained valuable first-hand information about how ignoring our environment in one place has both immediate and long-term consequences for people all over the globe. It made me think about how I could help bring environmental concerns to the average citizen.

I also gained valuable insights into the culture and environment of Lapland. And beyond that, my love of the Arctic grew even stronger. It wasn't long before I began to plan my next trip to the north.

CHAPTER 8

CROSSING BANKS ISLAND IN
STEFANSSON'S FOOTSTEPS

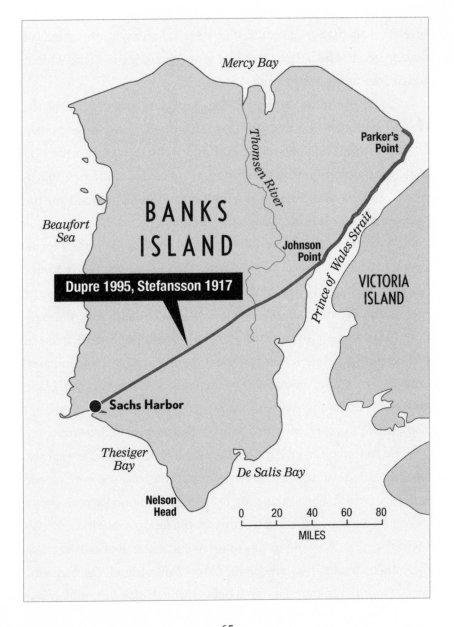

Located in Canada's Northwest Territories, Banks Island is the westernmost island of the Canadian Arctic Archipelago. Banks is 495 miles north of the Arctic Circle. To the east, across Prince of Wales Strait, is Victoria Island. To the west is the Beaufort Sea in the Arctic Ocean. To the south is Amundsen Gulf and the Canadian mainland. Most of this treeless island is less than 200 feet above sea level and is covered with shallow ponds that serve as sanctuary to thousands of nesting geese. The tallest plant that grows there is the Arctic willow, which commonly reaches only 4 inches tall.

Canadian Arctic explorer Vilhjalmur Stefansson crossed the island on foot in 1915 and 1917. He is credited with mapping most of the western Canadian Arctic islands. I wanted to retrace the 1917 route that took him from the northeast tip of the island in a southwesterly direction to the village of Sachs Harbor (Ikhuak) on the southwest coast. It is the island's only permanent settlement.

During the summer of 1995, I embarked on a 250-mile expedition across Banks Island with my wife, Kelly, along with Bert Myers, Mark Connelly and Tom West, all backpackers who helped fund the expedition. We backpacked, with dogs along to help carry the gear. Bert, Mark and Tom were going to photograph the first 85 miles of the expedition before leaving on the resupply flight at Johnson Point, on the eastern coast. Besides traveling with sled dogs as Stefansson had, and thereby increasing my knowledge of these pack animals, I also wanted to experience first-hand summer travel in the Arctic.

We started off from Parker's Point on July 31 in horrible weather: freezing rain, mist and wet snow. By the second day we were soaked and discouraged. The average August precipitation on Banks is only 3 inches, so we hoped the bad weather would let up soon. It didn't. We spent the next 36 hours in our tents. We learned the hard way that there are no "normal" weather patterns on Banks Island. Once moving again, we endured four days of slogging through clay-like mud. It was so heavy we had to stop every 50 feet to scrape the mud off our boots with a knife, no easy feat when you're carrying an 80-pound pack.

Early on, we feasted our eyes on the land's vastness—rolling hills, valleys of grass, moss and tussocks, and clear rivers running swiftly over polished gravel. Up close, it wasn't so enchanting. Tussocks are ankle-twisting, foot-blistering knobs of grass and moss too small to support your weight and too close together to step between. During our breaks, we tended our swollen and blistered feet with gauze, moleskin and duct tape. I had chosen to imitate the Inuit and Stefansson by wearing soft-bottom mukluks rather than hiking boots. Each step reminded me it wasn't a wise choice. Fortunately, the dogs, with smaller feet, moved through the tussocks with relative ease.

We followed the model of the nomadic Inuit people, who moved through the seasons, changing how they used their dogs, from pulling sleds to carrying supplies on their backs. Inuit dogs are able to carry about one-third of their body weight. Males can carry 25 to 30 pounds, females about 20 pounds. The dogs took well to the packs, barely noticing the gear they were carrying. Each day, they ate one pound of dry, concentrated, high-calorie dog food, a significantly smaller amount of food than would be required during an Arctic winter.

We often stumbled upon carcasses of dead musk oxen, usually old bulls or young calves culled by wolves. With 70,000 musk oxen on the island, the wolves were well fed. In this flat land, we spotted the magnificent sun-bleached rib cages and skulls a mile away. The dogs rolled around on the stinky carnage, packs and all, stopping only briefly to gnaw on a bone.

Live musk oxen also entertained the dogs, who were bored with the routine and their surroundings. At the least opportunity, they slipped away to chase the hairy beasts. If the dogs caught an early whiff of oxen, they were in hot pursuit over the low hills. They were oblivious, as we were not, to the dangers of getting lost or being gored by a bull. Because we were taller and could spot the oxen first, we usually had time to restrain the dogs. They wanted to play, we wanted them to work. We needed their precious cargo safely with us. When the musk oxen noticed us, they sometimes ran, but more often they instinctively circled, defensively. The calves went to the center, and females and young bulls formed the circle. The dominant bull patrolled the outside perimeter.

One day, carrying our boots and socks to keep them dry, we made our first major river crossing at the mouth of a large delta. On the other side, we quickly rebooted our clean but freezing feet, and headed across gravel bars to a small knoll in the middle of the delta. On top of the knoll was a cairn stone marker. Four feet to the east, deeply embedded in the ground, were stones forming the initials "EB." The rocks were well set into the soil so the site was clearly old. I suspect they stood for Elias Bow, who was a crew member from HMS Investigator, a ship that searched for Sir John Franklin's lost expedition. Bow was most likely part of a hunting party for the ship, which was abandoned in the Arctic in 1853 when it became trapped in ice.

We also came upon an Inuit camp estimated to be 3,500 years old. Three tent rings made of small stones and four large meat caches made of slab stone stood on the coast overlooking the Prince of Wales Strait. This was the end of the line for Bert, Mark and Tom. We hated to say goodbye. They'd been great teammates.

Shortly after their departure, we shared another common experience with Stefansson's expedition. While sun-drying our belongings, I noticed that the camp cleaning rag used for dishes was missing. After a search of the camp, I found the tag of the rag next to Tigger, one of my veteran dogs. Assuming he'd eaten it and with nothing available to make him cough it up, I gave him large doses of olive oil from our stores to grease the way for the rag.

This very thing happened to Sapsuk, one of Stefansson's dogs.

The caribou suet they used to help him eliminate the rag didn't work. Sapsuk died. A couple of days went by and Tigger, though sluggish from the massive doses of oil, looked no worse for the wear. I was now concerned with Shad, another veteran dog who seemed to be sick. I administered antibiotics and gave him extra food. Ten minutes later he vomited up the dish rag. I think Tigger still holds a grudge.

We were usually on the trail by 9 o'clock in the morning, and typically made 12 to 13 miles a day. We took 15-minute rest stops every two hours, and a two-hour, one-pot meal break at 4:30 pm. Since we were running behind schedule, we kept traveling until about 9:30 pm, which meant we still got eight to 10 hours of much-needed sleep each night. As we got close to Sachs Harbor, with food running low, we decided to cover the last 25 miles in a single day. This required more rest breaks, and constant care of already bruised and blistered feet. Kelly and I were not the only ones with sore feet. I had to slip dog booties on Narpa, the biggest of our four dogs, whose feet were sore from the sharp rocks.

The morning of our last day, we were on the trail by 7:30 am. For food, we were down to six dried apricots. I would have preferred to eat them all at once so I wouldn't have to think all day about the few left in Kelly's pack. Instead, Kelly parceled them out over time, one by one. She was good at such discipline.

More than 14 hours later, in a bit of a stupor, we finally spotted the airport beacon at Sachs Harbor. The lights gave us the renewed strength to make the last few miles. At almost midnight, after 20 days on the trail, we arrived at Sachs Harbor on the same August day that Stefansson had arrived 80 years earlier.

As I left Banks Island, I knew I had a better understanding of the Arctic summer and of Inuit travel with dogs. With my previous Arctic winter experiences, I now had a more rounded Arctic education. I was ready for bigger dreams.

CIRCUMNAVIGATING GREENLAND, 1997–2001

"The difficult is what takes a little time; the impossible is what takes a little longer."

—Fridtjof Nansen,
Norwegian polar explorer

CHAPTER 9

STAGING GREENLAND

Back home near the shores of Lake Superior in northern Minnesota, my favorite time of day was in the evening. Like clockwork, my dogs howled their nightly chorus and wolves cried back from the ridge behind our home. Then all at once, as if on cue, silence. Spooky to many people, it's the comforting sound of camaraderie to me. I longed to be back on the trail with the dogs. I worked during the day as a carpenter and began planning a longer, more rigorous expedition than any I'd taken so far.

My Banks Islands trip gave me the idea of rounding Greenland. It's hard to miss the irony of Greenland's name. No matter the season, most of it is covered in ice. Myth has it that Erik the Red called the island "Greenland" in an attempt to entice settlers to follow him there. For most people, there's no draw to this vast white country at all, but it's been on my exploration radar since 1994, when I was in Norway and heard stories of Norwegian Polar explorer Fridtjof Nansen's 1888 expedition. His was the first east-to-west crossing of the island's ice cap. A century later, Minnesota polar explorer Will Steger crossed the cap from south to north by dog team, a distance of 1,400 miles.

I owed the idea of a Greenland circumnavigation to Wally Herbert, the British polar explorer. He inspired me with his own Arctic journeys and writings in the 1960s. He talked of rounding Greenland, and made several heroic attempts. No one—not even a Greenlander—had ever rounded this island locked in shifting sea ice, awful winds and extreme, unstable weather. I wanted to be the first.

My vision was to travel around the island using traditional modes of Arctic travel—dog teams and kayaks. John Hoelscher, an

Australian fellow adventurer, was to be my teammate. I had met John years earlier when he delivered sled dogs from Antarctica to Minnesota. A native of Queensland, he had spent several seasons in Antarctica at research stations with the Australian National Antarctic Research Expedition. That's where he developed his fondness for dog-team travel. He had considerable adventure experience and loved the Arctic. His competent maturity would serve us well, and his attention to detail was a perfect complement to my "big picture" approach. With his easy-going nature and refreshing outlook, I knew he'd be a good companion in this arduous venture.

There can be strength in numbers on an expedition. Climbing Mount Everest, for example, is generally better with a large team to haul the loads up the mountain. On long dog-sled journeys through the Arctic, however, I consider two to four people the best team. It's easier to raise funds for a small group, but, most importantly, it's easier to manage the dynamics of a small group. With large teams, you are only as fast as your slowest member, and team dynamics become exponentially complicated with each added person. Besides, when I looked honestly at myself, I was gaining confidence as an Arctic explorer faster than I was as a team leader. So for this expedition, it was just going to be John and me.

In September 1996, John joined me and a host of volunteers in preparing for this venture. He took charge of the office and expedition communications. I wanted to contribute to a better understanding of Greenland's indigenous peoples, who, in the face of an intruding modern world, struggle to maintain their traditional way of life with its necessary balance with nature. Via satellite, our expedition would transmit reports, images and videos, and thus provide a unique opportunity to educate people around the world. Kelly's skills as a classroom teacher made her a perfect choice to coordinate the educational component of our expedition.

Greenland is the world's largest island, 1,650 miles from north to south and 750 miles across at its widest point. With no network of roads or railways for land transport, travel is by sea, air or dog sled. Average inland winter temperatures hover around -53° F, and its northernmost point is only 438 miles from the North Pole. Almost 10 percent of the world's fresh water is locked in the Greenland ice cap—about the same percentage, coincidentally, as is held in Lake Superior. If the Greenland cap melted, it would raise the world's seas by an estimated 21 feet.

Rounding Greenland is far more dangerous then an expedition to either the North Pole or South Pole. The Greenland ice cap is ringed by a fence of mountains, and the coast line is heavily indented by fjords that slice deeply inland. Much of the shore is icebound year round. The pressure exerted by the massive ice cap inches rivers of ice through Greenland's coastal mountains and into its fjords, where many icebergs are born. Drowning and hypothermia are the main causes of death among Greenland's Inuit hunters. Either their boats overturn in stormy, frigid seas, or they fall through thin ice while hunting with dog sleds.

Originally conceived as a 15-month, 5,000-mile, non-motorized journey, we had many permits to obtain from scientific and military communities in Denmark, Greenland and the United States, including Pentagon permission to land a chartered plane at the highly restricted Thule Air Base in northwest Greenland. Often in the past, logistical and environmental restrictions had stymied would-be explorers.

In March 1996, during the planning stages of the expedition, I received a curious letter from Sirius Patrol Commander Palle V. Norit of the Søvaernets Operative Kommando in Copenhagen. The Sirius Patrol is an elite military unit, Denmark's version of America's Green Berets. It was formed in 1941 to protect northern and eastern sections of Greenland's coast. The patrol, which travels by dog team, still guards large portions of the Greenland coast, but their main purpose today is to maintain Danish sovereignty.

"First of all," Norit wrote, "I think your expedition is very ambitious, and extremely long. A Greenlander journalist has tried to do Greenland without a motor over many years, and he still has hundreds of kilometers to walk....If you get the permission, I will highly recommend a former Sirius member to take part, or advise you not to do it."

The Greenlander he referred to was Peter Brandt, who tried to round the island by row boat, skis and dog sled, usually accompanied by whatever hunter he could convince to accompany him. Brandt eventually ran out of money, guides and his own youth. I also knew of the Danish architect, John Anderson, who, over a period of 15 years, invested months kayaking and skiing the perimeter. He had yet to travel the whole coastline.

Not discouraged from my goal, I publicly unveiled our Greenland plans before the Great Lakes Chapter of The Explorers Club in Chicago. The projected budget was $400,000, although it eventually was to reach $525,000, including donated equipment and services, in-kind donations, and cash contributions.

On a cold and rainy September day, I traveled to Denmark to learn more about Greenland, secure needed maps and discuss the project with Hauge Anderson, director of the Danish Polar Center (DPC) in Copenhagen. The DPC is in charge of permits for expeditions entering the enormous restricted preserve that includes most of northern Greenland as well as for any travel on the inland ice cap. Separate permits were required for radio communications and for firearms, as well as for crossing Melville Bay and entering Thule Air Base. We also needed search and rescue insurance. While in Denmark, I also discussed equipment and route logistics with former members of the Sirius Patrol.

On my return to Minnesota, I was eager to get on with the planning work. I drew on my 6,000 miles of mushing experience to plan a route and a schedule for covering each segment. Gary Atwood, a good friend with a talent for writing and organizing, helped me develop a fundraising strategy. We sent out hundreds of letters to corporations and organizations asking for money or in-kind contributions of products and services. My explorer friend Will Steger calls the preparation time "the unseen adventure that separates the babbler from the explorer." Putting together an expedition on such a scale stretched me in every way, including financially.

In the beginning, the administrative side of the expedition was supported by my carpentry business in Grand Marais, Minnesota. Then, small donations started to come in from fundraisers like chili dinners and slide-show presentations. We sold T-shirts, posters and hats to cover my phone and postage bills as I tried to drum up support. It took 26 months to plan, organize and raise funds for the expedition. I'm good at organization. It's a lucky trait to possess when you're arranging an expedition. Not only do you need to be highly organized in terms of logistics and budgeting, but once you're on the trail having the right information, the right gear and the right supplies can literally be a matter of life or death.

Traveling in remote parts of the Arctic—and staying alive—takes the best equipment both designed for and tested in Arctic conditions. Nearly everything requires modification. Our small house served as the warehouse for a mountain of supplies, and our basement was the workshop where we modified our kayaks and built our sled. The kayaks were made of polyethylene to withstand collisions with sea ice. We fitted them so we could lash them together into a catamaran, and add small masts and sails. Northern Minnesota and Lake Superior offered the perfect place to train and test our modified kayaks. The lake, right outside the office door, is well-known for the challenges that make it as dangerous and forbidding as most areas of the Arctic.

Our 15-foot-long sleds differed from the light, streamlined dog sleds used for racing and transporting tourists through the north woods. Our sleds were designed to haul heavy cargo on an extended journey over rough terrain. They're the one-ton pick-ups of the dog-team world. During the coldest weeks of the year, John and I trained and camped with dog team and ski. Lake Nipigon in Ontario, Canada, provided treeless conditions similar to those in the Arctic, with driving winds, low temperatures and hard-packed snow. With no trees for traces to get tangled in, we trained in Inuit fashion, running the dogs in a fan-shaped formation with each dog attached to its own 18-foot trace. My Inuit dogs were the same breed as those we planned to purchase in Greenland for the expedition. Importing dogs into Greenland is prohibited to avoid exposing Greenlandic dogs to diseases for which they typically are not vaccinated.

By the time we left for Greenland, we had 80 sponsors, both individuals and corporations. In addition, countless volunteers mixed and packed food, raised money, and prepared gear. Sled dogs are like armies: They march on their stomachs. We knew the dog food had to be something they would be eager to eat day after day. We blended high-quality, nutritious kibble used by mushers in Alaska and Minnesota, then added fish oil, and animal and vegetable fat to boost the caloric content to the level needed for extreme cold. For each 50-pound bag of food, we added in seven pounds of fat, plus Vitamin E as a preservative. In all, we packed 8,500 pounds of dog food.

For the dog-sled stretch, we needed 13 depots of 500 pounds, each containing food, fuel and equipment. Boxed and labeled food was organized into depot locations and transferred to the largest rental truck we could find for the five-hour trip to Minneapolis. There, at our export shipper's facility, we put the supplies on pallets to be shipped by boat to Greenland via Denmark and Iceland. Shipping goods to Greenland is a science. Supplies can only be moved around the coast during the few peak days of the Arctic summer when the ice goes out. We had several lessons in shipping and diplomacy as we worked with Danish authorities to get permits and depots in place. We would be the first expedition allowed to travel through the entire northern Greenland preserve.

Last-minute jobs involved mounting bindings on skis, sewing snow flaps on the tent and putting together a repair kit of the essentials: duct tape, pliers, screwdriver, cloth, spare parts for the stoves, and material for repairing the kayaks and dog sleds. We then disassembled our kayaks and sleds, and wrapped them in reinforced plastic for shipment. Finally, we met with Dr. John Wood, a good friend and local physician, to review the contents of our medical kit. Since we had to do all our own "doctoring" on the trail, having the right contents could mean the difference between surviving and dying. It was an extensive kit, including antibiotics, morphine and hydrocodone for pain, and triamcinalone and ketoconazone for rashes and fungus. And, of course, we also had the usual: aloe, ibuprofen, imodium, antacid, talcum powder, mole skin, surgical tape, knee and ankle braces, band-aids, swabs, thermometers, heat packs and a space blanket.

The main piece of survival clothing worn for kayaking is a one-piece, hooded dry suit made from a waterproof, breathable material. The over suit is outfitted with latex gaskets to seal off wrists and neck, and with latex socks to keep the feet dry. We had thick neoprene-soled shoes to wear over the latex socks. If we capsized, the dry suits would stave off hypothermia, keeping us alive for an hour or more.

We left northern Minnesota on May 12, 1997, and drove to Thunder Bay, Ontario. From there we flew to Toronto, on to Iqaluit in the Northwest Territories and finally to Kangerlussaq, Greenland, where we boarded a Sikorski helicopter for the ride to Paamiut, our starting point on the southwest coast of Greenland.

CHAPTER 10

STARTING THE ADVENTURE BY KAYAK

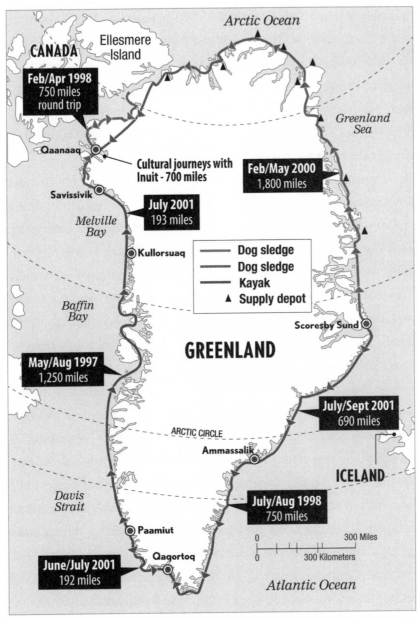

CANADA

Ellesmere
Island

Arctic Ocean

Feb/Apr 1998
750 miles
round trip

Greenland
Sea

Qaanaaq

**Cultural journeys with
Inuit - 700 miles**

Feb/May 2000
1,800 miles

Savissivik

July 2001
193 miles

Melville
Bay

Kullorsuaq

—— Dog sledge
—— Dog sledge
—— Kayak
▲ Supply depot

Baffin
Bay

Scoresby Sund

GREENLAND

May/Aug 1997
1,250 miles

July/Sept 2001
690 miles

ARCTIC CIRCLE

Ammassalik

ICELAND

Davis
Strait

July/Aug 1998
750 miles

Paamiut

0   300 Miles

0   300 Kilometers

June/July 2001
192 miles

Qagortoq

Atlantic Ocean

See Greenland map in color photo section for more detail.

In Paamiut, houses of primary colors with steeply pitched roofs perch on blunted mountains. When we arrived on May 15, snow still covered the valleys and northern slopes. Pans of multiyear sea ice from the Arctic Ocean had drifted more than 2,000 miles to wedge themselves into the bay, a puzzle of 70 percent ice and 30 percent water. I was nervous. Through all the days of preparation, I had been forward-thinking and focused. Now, at the last minute, I was feeling fear and doubt. Had our preparations been thorough enough? Were we ready? What made us think we could do what no one had done before? Would our modified kayaks stand up to the beating they would take from the sea ice? Was this a suicide mission?

I pushed aside my doubts, knowing they would only distract me. John and I left the next afternoon in 32°F weather after lashing our two 17-foot kayaks together to form a catamaran. Unfamiliar with the surrounding seas, we opted for this more stable platform while we tentatively settled into the voyage. An elderly Greenlandic man stopped, scratched his head and asked what we were doing. We explained that we planned to paddle 1,500 miles to Qaanaaq in the north. The weathered wrinkles on his face scrunched into a smile as he wished us luck.

As we pushed off, a cold breeze carried the smell of saltwater and seaweed. We used our paddles as poles to move around pieces of sea ice and small chunks of icebergs. We named them "bergy bits," as though they were a new kind of breakfast cereal. It was a slow start. We made only 3 miles the first three hours. We were just happy to be underway. The coastal scenery was stark and desolate, but we found this gray world amazing. All new to us, it was difficult to imagine I would ever tire of looking at such splendor.

We planned to kayak up the west coast as far as possible before winter set in. We hoped to reach Qaanaaq in Greenland's far northwest corner. We would stop for supplies at native villages. As we made our way north, we paddled through an archipelago of small islands, home to nesting eider ducks, geese and gulls. The islands provided a safer paddle than the open sea and a much more pleasant view than the endless horizon of water and ice, but it made navigation difficult. We paddled a meandering route.

Our biggest problem was paddling into a strong northwest headwind. From Paamiut to midway up the west coast, some 700 miles, we expected the prevailing winds to be strong from the north. We hadn't anticipated how difficult progress would be in our catamaraned kayaks. Strain as we might with our arms and shoulders, we made little headway. We might have made more progress if we paddled separately, but taking the catamaran apart was difficult. Besides, we wanted to play it safe. We were still unfamiliar with Greenland.

On the fifth day out, we stopped at an island to lighten our load. We discarded extra gear and food. We left a note welcoming any hunter or egg gatherer who happened along to keep the stuff. This helped, but we still fell behind. One day, when we'd managed to paddle only 5 miles, despite working our arms and shoulders as hard as we could, John and I talked about the difficulty we faced. We were paddling against time and the change of seasons. Several Greenlanders had warned us we might not be able to make 1,500 miles before September and the onset of winter. We were already behind schedule.

A day later, as if the gods had heard our worried musings, the wind subsided. Under sunny skies, John and I advanced 15 miles on flat seas, passing the notorious Frederickshab Glacier, where the water is shallow and heavy seas sometimes form. The respite didn't last long. Fog and freezing temperatures arrived, dropping visibility to less than a half-mile.

Kayaking in freezing waters, with my butt 6 inches below the water line, I felt on the very edge of life. Slate-colored waves could easily have erased us. The fog and mist played tricks on our vision. We'd be certain we were about to plow into an iceberg large enough to sink a ship only to find it was just a duck-sized bit. Then, actual islands appeared out of nowhere. Knowing what was real and what was imagined required constant vigilance.

One island provided driftwood that had traveled a couple thousand miles across the Arctic Ocean from Siberia. The smell of the wood smoke from the fires we built lifted our spirits and filled our clothes with the aroma of Minnesota. We also found a few seagull eggs to supplement our by-now bland menu. They were like boiled, fishy-tasting rubber balls, but food is food.

One day, during our midday stop, John's speech grew slurred. I realized that from fatigue, too little food, cool weather and soggy clothing, he had slipped into the early stages of hypothermia. It was a signal that we were pushing too hard. It can be fatal if a person's core temperature drops too low. The quickest way to pull someone out of hypothermia and warm up their core is to give them warm soup or a hot drink. That's why we always kept a thermos full of hot liquids with us. It allowed time to set up a tent, get the stove going and change the person into dry clothes if necessary. I poured John a warm orange drink from our thermos, had him eat a bar of chocolate and insisted he put on a dry sweater. He was back to his clear, chipper self within a few hours.

We were supposed to reach Nuuk the next evening, May 28. I was especially eager to reach this next destination because Kelly was waiting for us. However, the village was still 34 miles away, and we had been averaging only 13 miles a day. If we got a headwind, we wouldn't make it. Even under ideal conditions, it would be quite a stretch. The headwind didn't materialize, and we pushed ourselves hard, taking only four short rest stops. We finally made it into the village after more than 17 hours of paddling. Our arms and shoulders were numb.

It was a marathon day we hoped we'd never have to repeat. The good news was that our push had earned us the scheduled week of recovery in Nuuk. We didn't simply lie around, however. We'd learned that the wind was a potent enemy, one that could derail the expedition. It was clear that we needed to lighten our load. We attacked the kayaks and their catamaran attachments, and shaved off six pounds of wood and plastic.

After much discussion, John and I also agreed that we could cut our rations a bit further if we lived off the land and sea. Both locals and a biologist told us sea urchins were okay to eat in a pinch. They would now become part of our diet. A fan of sushi, I didn't think it would be a stretch. Once in the water again, we scooped urchins from bay bottoms at low tide, using the tips of our paddles. Wearing gloves to avoid sticking ourselves with the spines, we split the hard shells with a knife. The insides were a slimy orange-yellow goo. Sushi it wasn't.

Soon after we left Nuuk, we got clobbered by a sudden, nasty storm. We went from a peaceful paddle to life-threatening, 8-foot waves 5 miles from land. The sky grew dark, the ocean darker, and we were pelted by rain. Each wave became a small, wet mountain full of explosive fury that could capsize us. John and I were fit from weeks of paddling, but the wind and waves still strained our ability to keep the kayaks from going over. We were in a fight for our lives. We both knew what it meant if we ended up in the water. Our lips were cracked and raw from constant sun and salt. Our hands ached, and our bodies were numb from the wet and cold. Water seeped through our neoprene gloves and the kayaks' spray skirts. Looking over his shoulder, John called out the approach of each big wave, usually the fifth in a set, and I dug in for another wild ride.

The wind increased, causing the lines and sails to hum. We were right on the edge of losing control, pummeled by each breaking wave, then surfing wildly down the next roller. I thought of Kelly and my son

Jacob, who was now 12 years old. I might be gone for long stretches of time, but he needed me. Would I ever see them again? John had a grim, focused look on his face. I'm sure I did, too. We aimed for the safety of an island 50 yards away, but we had to get around a jagged rock shoal to reach it.

In the trough of a wave, we lost the horizon. The breaking waves above us seemed angry, menacing, determined to beat us. Our little catamaran did a wild dance on the frothy surface of the sea. Then, at just the right moment, a compassionate wave angled us through the sharp rocks to shore. Drained, stunned and soaked, John and I sat in silence, shaking our heads. Our keels rested on solid land. We were safe. The catamaran configuration had saved our lives.

"Dog sledding through a polar night with temperatures at minus 50 looks pretty good right now," I said. We both laughed.

June 13, 1997, was a good day. We paddled 26 miles in 11 hours and crossed the Arctic Circle, accompanied by Greenland white-tailed eagles. We became increasingly familiar with stone cairns erected on little islands and points of land that the Inuit use for navigation. These small markers helped us find safe passages, but they weren't always easy to see. Some were little more than a small rock set on a larger one. I heard dogs as we approached the village of Sisimiut, the southernmost community in Greenland to use sleds. I was reminded of how much I missed dog mushing. Solid ground had special appeal after so many bleak days of paddling.

To save time and distance, we planned to reach the eastern shore of Disko Bay by making two 11-mile, open-water crossings, with a stop at a small island in between. We expected calm conditions, so we didn't wear our dry suits. An hour after we set out, the wind and seas came up, and we quickly found ourselves sitting in cold water. It was major-league discomfort all the way to the island.

During a break one day, we discussed the next leg of the crossing.

In 1983, Roger Pietron and I gill-netted a 72-pound king salmon out of Ugashic Bay near Pilot Point, Alaska. This catch wasn't representative of our overall luck.

My first experience in the "real" Arctic wild involved a lot of snowshoeing, this time on the way to Allekaket, Alaska, on the Koyukuk River near Bettles.

We began the Bering Bridge Expedition in 1989 dog sledding out of Anadyr, Siberia, which was filmed by a documentary crew in the hovering helicopter.

I secured my dogs during a stop in the village of Sireniki, Siberia. Gray whale jaw bones in the foreground were being used as clotheslines.

An Inuit elder gave me advice on the trail ahead in Whale Cove, Hudson Bay.

We met many Inuit children during our Northwest Passage Expedition in 1991.

Malcolm Vance stopped to find Tuktoyaktuk as we crossed the McKenzie River Delta in late November 1991. Temperatures averaged -30° F for the next month.

We came across this 1919 grave on the border between Alaska and Canada. Did the darkest day of the year do her in—or maybe the Spanish flu?

This abandoned Distant Early Warning (DEW) Line site is one of the many sites built every 100 to 150 miles across the Arctic Circle from Alaska to Greenland.

We entered 64 days of polar night in Franklin Bay near the village of Paulutuk.

The Russian mining town of Nikel, 7 kilometers from the Norwegian border, is one of the most polluted places on the planet. There is no living vegetation for several kilometers in any direction.

Sami reindeer herders take their skis with them everywhere in case their snow scooters break down. The Sami (also called Laps) are Europe's northernmost indigenous people.

We discovered this stone marker on the east coast of Banks Island. It was probably put there by Elias Bow, a member of a hunting party from the HMS Investigator, a ship searching for Sir John Franklin's lost 1845 expedition.

With our dogs Shad, Tigger and Narpa, Kelly Dupre and I crossed many cold rivers during our Banks Island trip in the summer of 1995.

Kelly and Tigger checked out a musk ox killed by wolves.

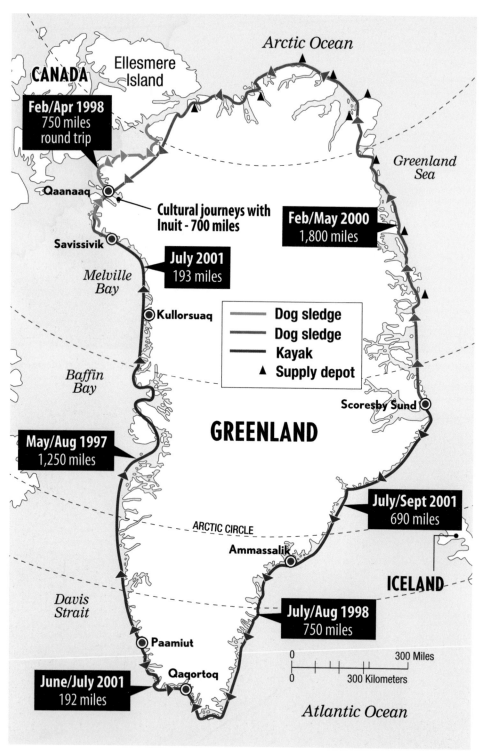

This map of Greenland shows the many individual segments that we traveled to complete our circumnavigation of Greenland between 1997 and 2001.

When kayaking up Greenland's west coast in 1997, we catamaranned our single kayaks. Of the more than 3,000 miles of kayaking, we used our sails for only about 160 miles due to storms.

John Hoelscher and I eventually realized that a double kayak was the fastest, safest and most stable way to travel. It also ensured that we couldn't lose each other!

John held the kayak while I climbed the iceberg to find a route. We did this several times a day at this stage of the Greenland circumnavigation.

Camping on the Blosseville Coast in southeastern Greenland meant finding a level enough spot to camp so we could get a decent night's sleep. It was one boulder beach after another.

We swamped the kayak off Deception Island. Everything was wet and cold, and I mean cold!

Blosseville Coast is about 750 miles of continuous mountains, much of it sheer walls of stone reaching down to the shore.

Storms out at sea shoved the ice toward the shore, packing the sea ice into a nearly impenetrable porridge. Here we rested after 15 hours of constant paddling that still didn't get us to shore.

This Inuit village on the northwest coast of Greenland shows the colorful houses that are typical of coastal villages there.

This hut north of Ammassalik is an example of the huts used by Inuits when they go hunting. Hanging to my right is the solar panel I used to charge my electronics.

From this vantage point overlooking the village of Qaanaaq, Herbert Island is visible. On the left (east) end of the island is the village of Qeqertarssuaq.

In March 1998, we dog sledded on the Kane Basin ice foot in northwest Greenland. An ice foot is a flat, narrow lane of ice along the coast.

In the extreme cold, we iced the runners to reduce friction.

John Hoelscher (left) bundled up in Kane Basin's -57° F weather. We met Ussarqak Henson (right), a descendant of Matthew Henson, one of the six men who reached the North Pole in 1909 with Peary and four Inuits, Ootah, Egingwah, Seegloo and Ookeah.

We packed the sleds in Qaanaaq for one of our many cultural visits to neighboring villages.

Gideon Kristensen chopped up a seal to feed his dogs, who were waiting patiently for their dinner.

Tekumeq Peary (left), a descendant of Robert E. Peary, and her husband, Mamarut Kristensen (center), were fishing for Greenland halibut.

Peter Duneq rested on his sled as we traveled to Thule Air Base, which is where we caught the chartered plane to Greenland's east coast to start our dog-sled journey in 2000.

When we inadvertently placed our tent over a tide crack, a high tide pushed water through the crack and flooded our tent. We had to move the tent and then dig our sled out of the icy mess.

One night four wolves stared down our dogs—and us. At one point, our dog Knud was just inches away from one of the wolves.

John Hoelscher and I flew the National Geographic flag at Kaffeklubben, which is the northernmost real estate on our planet.

Toward the end of the Greenland expedition, we cut excess hair from the 14 dogs' paws to prevent ice balls from irritating their foot pads. Every few days we applied salve to 56 paws!

Our sled dog Ray Charles sat nonchalantly as a storm subsided.

John skijored next to the dog sled around Cape May in northern Greenland. Skijoring, being pulled on skis by dogs, is a common Nordic way to travel over ice and snow.

We collected our supplies from one of the nine depots we'd placed two years in advance of our expedition. The depots were anywhere from 100 to 350 miles apart.

While I did other chores, John collected ice to be melted for drinking and cooking water.

Numerous chores at the end of each day preceded any rest. With smelly wet socks just overhead, John melts ice in the tea kettle while I try for radio contact.

In Peary Land in northern Greenland, John and I followed the ice foot along the shore.

This was our last camp before we ascended the ice cap en route to the village of Qaanaaq in Greenland's Washington Land.

We owed our good fortune of traveling with the dogs we named the "Oak Ridge Boys" to retired hunter Qaavianguaq Qissuk, shown here with John and me.

On May 10, a Russian helicopter took us to Cape Arkticheskiy, Siberia, where we deplaned for the start of our 2005 One World Expedition.

Just two days into the trip, we were navigating our 300-pound canoe-sleds through pack ice. Needless to say: a tough haul!

This polar bear looks more relaxed than we felt during one of our five polar bear encounters.

Ann Possis, the One World Expedition manager, and Dawn Cassidy were among the numerous supporters and volunteers who did anything we needed for expeditions—here, packing food.

On May 1, 2006, we started the One World Expedition again, this time leaving Ellesmere Island and encountering our first tide crack, which we spanned with our skis.

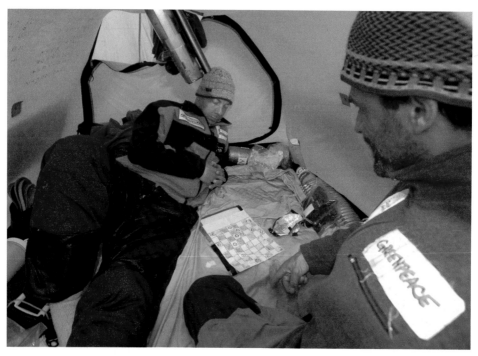

After 21 days on the go, Eric and I took our first rest day during this expedition. We spent part of it playing chess.

On the way to the North Pole, Eric negotiated this particular broken sea ice successfully. On many days, we were not so lucky and fell into the water once or twice.

When we came upon leads that we couldn't get around or that were too wide to traverse, we had to swim them.

By late June, melt-water pools were forming, which accelerated the melting of the ice as the pools absorbed heat from the sun.

Just miles from the North Pole, I rested in the middle of an ice-piece puzzle, which we hopped as we progressed north. Next stop—the North Pole!

Being sick with food poisoning and sharing the DC3 with fuel barrels made for a harrowing flight from Resolute Bay to Ellesmere Island at the start of our Peary-Henson Centennial Expedition.

Stuart Smith stopped for only a moment in the -55° F weather. Our body heat created an ice fog that filled the valley around us as the sun rose above the horizon for the first time in months.

At this stage of the 2009 North Pole expedition, it's obvious from our faces (Max Chaya in background) that the temperature inside our tent was only marginally warmer than outside.

We finally got a break (a relative term) when we found a nearly flat frozen lead we could follow north. Ellesmere Island is faintly visible behind us.

When ice flows came together, the force sometimes popped up beautiful ice blocks like this one that showed us how thick the ice was.

During whiteouts, we had to navigate by a compass, the direction of the wind and the placement of the sun—that is when we could see it through the thick haze.

When pans of ice collide, brash ice is formed. Negotiating the ice boulders and blocks that were left floating in leads was particularly challenging—especially hauling a loaded sled!

For the first time John and I disagreed on whether to continue. I voted to go on; he wanted to stay put. I was the team leader, so we went on. Two-thirds of the way into the crossing, the seas grew into 7-foot swells that made us work extremely hard for every mile, and, truth be told, for our lives. We reached Qasigiannguit at 1:30 am, totally spent. We were paying dearly for my bad judgment. I apologized to John. We used the last of our energy to put up a tent and quickly fell into a desperately needed sleep.

Cold, crappy weather delayed us day after day as we made our way up Nussuaq Peninsula, forcing us to cut back on our rations. We grew thinner and weaker each day. John tried fishing, but only managed to catch a small, paper-flat flounder that wouldn't have satisfied a house cat. The combination of hard work, dreary weather and lack of food was getting to us. After two months of paddling, we were drained and homesick. I'm good at compartmentalizing my thoughts, pushing to the rear of my mind things that might distract me or interfere with our progress. For the first time, I was failing at that. I began questioning my judgment and capabilities, and considering the possibility that this whole trek was a foolish undertaking. If left to run wild, defeatist thinking can be fatal to an expedition. I didn't know what it would take to snap my focus back on my goal.

As often happens, my inspiration came in the form of nature. John and I were making camp one day when I heard a squawk from a nearby hill. I was scheduled for a radio call to Kelly, so I tramped up the hill to get better reception. The squawking grew louder. As I came over the crest, I saw a raven perched on a large rock. Ravens are revered and thought to possess mystical powers in many native cultures. In some, a raven is considered a sacred reincarnation of a great hunter or shaman. The raven appeared to be carrying something in its right claw as it made repeated short flights from one rock to another. As I approached, the raven made no effort to escape. Instead it flew closer, finally landing on the large rock I was leaning against. Now I could see that the bird's right leg was bound to a thin, foot-long piece of driftwood by a wooly ball of musk-ox fur. It was obviously in pain. I approached slowly and spoke in low, soothing tones. Its neck feathers were all puffed out, black and shiny, as it stood awkwardly on its constricted leg and cawed at me. I kept talking, asking the raven's permission to remove the musk ox wool and driftwood. I asked if, in return, the raven would give me the strength to find safe passage and complete my journey. The raven's dark beady eyes met mine. It dipped its broad, wedged beak and picked up a pea-sized stone. I took it as an offering, a trade.

I picked up the raven and set it in my lap. With the scissors in my Swiss Army knife, I cut the wool and stick from its leg. The bird pecked at me as I worked. It took 20 minutes of careful effort to free the leg without injuring the bird. Then, with an upswing of my arms, I set the raven free. It made a tight circle and settled on a rock a few yards away. It stared at me, squawked again, took flight and disappeared over the hill. A feeling of renewal washed over me. Gone were my doubts and negative thoughts. My interaction with the raven linked me even more intimately to Greenland, to nature and to our purpose. I was ready to take up our challenge once again.

Despite insulating the inside of our cockpits with foam pads and wearing insulated footwear to protect us from the frigid waters, our feet, blood-deprived from long hours bent in the kayaks, were cold and wooden by the end of each day. The coastline in most spots prevented us from approaching shore. We often could not stop within hours or miles of the best place for a break or camp.

One July day we had to keep pushing long past our desired stopping point. Finally, we found a sandbar created by a small river. When we climbed out of the kayaks, we were so stiff and sore we were hunched like old men—grumpy old men to be precise. Our mood

changed abruptly, however, when we spotted mushrooms growing nearby. Research had told us all wild mushrooms growing in
Greenland are edible, so they became delicacies in our tiresome menu
of oats, rice, soup mix and dried fish. We consumed about 3,500 calories in "warm" weather. In winter, we would eat approximately the
same number of calories as the dogs did—5,600 a day.

By late July, the beginning of the Arctic fall, Greenland's western coast started getting colder. In the mornings, a thin film of ice
formed on puddles and in the protected bays. These hints of winter
concerned us, and we reviewed our plans. We knew we needed to be
out of the water in Qaanaaq by September 1 to risk getting pinned
down by ice or storms. When we did the math, we discovered we'd
been averaging 16 miles a day. In order to make Qaanaaq on schedule, we needed to average 21 miles a day for the next five weeks. This
required the unlikely combination of calm seas, no wind and little ice.
It seemed impossible, but we had no choice. We picked up our pace.

John and I had to be especially alert when we paddled near unstable, newly formed icebergs. Our greatest fear was ending up in the
bone-chilling water. One day in early August, we were paddling separately near Upernavik when a piece of ice the size of a ship exploded
off an iceberg to our left. John, who was ahead of me, shouted, "Damn!
Watch out for the wave!" We pushed our paddles into the water and
strained our shoulders to turn our kayaks bow-first into the brunt of
the wave. Up and down we went, over the first wave and through a
burst of smaller waves that followed.

We were congratulating ourselves on our quick reactions when a
second ice chunk, this one the size of an automobile, exploded off an
iceberg to our immediate right. We came about quickly to confront
its waves, which caused another large piece of ice to calve from the
iceberg to our left. We were caught between the two bergs in a chain
reaction of ice explosions and unruly waves. For five minutes, feeling

as if we were on the inside of a giant washing machine, we were in a fight for our lives. A minute later, gazing at the sunny sky, we sat on calm water as if nothing had happened. How swiftly our lives might have ended.

Most evenings we were so exhausted, almost any campsite would do. One morning we woke to find that the high tide had come within 8 inches of our tent. We laughed at how well we'd slept. Later the same day we rode up and down 7-foot gradual swells. It wasn't much to worry about. We actually enjoyed the ride. But then, the light winds turned into major gusts of 40 miles an hour. In no time, we went from enjoying ourselves to once again paddling for our lives. The wind turned the rollers into steep, black walls. We fought for hours through oncoming waves, colliding with backwash surging out from nearby cliffs and icebergs. Finally we spotted a pebble-covered beach, a place to pull in—if only we could reach it. With a tremendous effort, we surfed the kayaks onto the beach. We got wet in the process, but we were safe, at least for now.

As we made camp, the wind grew more intense. Gusts broke two of our aluminum tent poles. We duct taped them together with splints and weighted the tent corners with large boulders. By the time dinner was done, the wind had climbed to 75 miles an hour. We heard a crack. A guy rope had pulled a brass eyelet through the tent fabric. We couldn't hear each other talk in the screaming wind, which turned to a dull howl when we put earplugs in to sleep. We spent the next 18 hours in our sleeping bags, unable to accomplish anything until the storm let up.

On August 7, 1997, we paddled for 17 straight hours, not hauling the kayaks out of the water until 11 pm. We didn't find a flat spot big enough to erect our tent, so, fully clothed, we dozed against rocks near our kayaks that night. The next day, as we paddled through an iceberg-clogged channel towards Kullorsuaq, we met three small boats carrying families out for a hunt. They must have radioed back because when we reached the small dock at Kullorsuaq, a crowd of about 50 people—a quarter of the village—celebrated our arrival with rifle shots. Kullorsuaq is the Inuit word for thumb. The village is named for the 300-foot thumb-like rock that towers over the village.

The villagers were bemused that John and I had willingly paddled 1,250 miles up the Greenland shore. An elder smoking a greasy cigarette said it was the longest kayak journey he had heard of. Since Greenland is the home of the kayak, we were especially pleased with our accomplishment. We met Nikolai Jensen, a retired hunter of local fame called "the compass of Melville Bay" because he had made several crossings of the notoriously treacherous body of water just to the north. He and John were both celebrating birthdays. John turned 34. There was no birthday cake, but there were sweets, coffee and tea, as well as boiled seal, polar bear and narwhal, which is a medium-sized Arctic whale with a long, straight helical tusk. Nikolai gave John a traditional Greenlandic drill made from wood, bone and sinew. John gave Nikolai a gold-enameled, emperor penguin stickpin, a symbol of his association with Antarctica. In this simple act, John linked the world's two largest ice caps.

Nikolai and his sons reported that 150-mile-wide Melville Bay was blocked by sea ice. The only open waters were 15 to 25 miles out to sea, too far for us to risk kayaking. Had we been caught in a storm that far from the coast, we would almost certainly have perished. Two days earlier, a trading ship headed for Kullorsuaq had to turn back because of sea ice. We knew what this meant. We arranged for passage on a boat to the Qaanaaq district with local hunters, and left our kayaks for shipment to southern Greenland and then home through Denmark. Three different hunters, fearing the danger, refused to take us even as far as Savissivik, well short of Qaanaaq. Ultimately, the father-and-son team of Gabriel and Martin Olsen agreed to take us.

Shortly after reaching Savissivik, we realized it would be impossible to achieve the entire circumnavigation in a single, continuous effort. With ocean currents running in one direction and prevailing winds coming from the other, along with unpredictable fluctuations in the weather and sea ice, we needed to choose the very best window of time to travel each long section. That was the only way to succeed and remain alive.

John and I had finished short of our paddling goal for the first segment of our expedition. To keep our commitment of rounding the entire island in non-motorized craft, we knew we would have to come back and make up the missed miles between Kullorsuaq and Qaanaaq later. Yet we were happy with what we had accomplished. We had seen more of Greenland's coast than most people who live there, and we had done it one stroke at a time. We had also lived to tell the tale.

CHAPTER 11

WINTERING IN QAANAAQ

To travel the uninhabited northern part of Greenland during the winter, we needed to switch to dog sled and skis. While we waited for the right weather to start on this next leg, we settled into Qaanaaq from September 1997 until January 1998. Qaanaaq is a collection of colorful houses with steep-pitched roofs, all in various states of repair. The village rests on a rocky hillside at the mouth of Ingelfield Bredning and is home to 600 people.

A couple of days after we arrived, I bumped into Jens Danielsen, whom I had met in Gjoa Haven on the Northwest Passage Expedition. Jens had just returned empty handed from a narwhal hunt. "Winter," he said, "has come too early this year." It was only the third week of August, and big storms were hitting the village already. I shivered at the thought that John and I might still have been kayaking our way north. Later that night, the winds reached 180 miles an hour at Thule Air Base 70 miles away. It was the second strongest wind ever recorded there.

I couldn't immerse myself in Inuit life totally because I needed to go back to the United States to deal with dwindling finances. In the fall of 1997, I flew to Washington, DC, to meet with National Geographic Society's Expedition Council, which covered a portion of our costs and supplied film for cameras. While there, I got a call from Malden Mills, makers of Polartec fleece. We were recipients of a Polartec Challenge Grant, which brought us money, clothing and invaluable publicity. Other organizations soon came on board: Australian Geographic Magazine, Scandinavian Airlines and Iceland Air.

Even though such support affirmed our mission, I suffered a crisis of faith while I was away from Qaanaaq. I wasn't sure I wanted to complete the expedition. For the first time in 15 years, I worried that I had lost my spirit for Arctic adventure. I was discouraged. It would take so many legs to accomplish our circumnavigation goal, I was overwhelmed by the logistics required to maintain the effort.

Greenland's harsh winters, shifting sea ice and difficult currents meant that on the northwest, south and east coasts, marginally safe kayaking was possible for only 30 to 45 days between the middle of July and the end of August. On the west coast, the window was a bit longer, between the first of June and the middle of August. We faced similar problems when we shifted to dog sled. Thin ice, lack of snow, blizzards and the long polar night restricted mushing to four months. We couldn't start until February and had to stop before June. Long story short: We couldn't embark on long journeys by either dog sled or kayak between the middle of August and the middle of February, a full six months of each year. Therefore, the only way for anyone to complete this circumnavigation without using motorized vehicles or vessels was to break it up. I knew some people would dispute our accomplishment—even if we were successful—because we hadn't circumnavigated Greenland in one continuous journey. However, since that was virtually impossible, I steeled myself against the criticism by reminding myself that nowhere in the definition of circumnavigation is the requirement that it be one sustained effort. I believed our journey would have no less integrity because of its many legs and extended timeframe.

On my final flight back to Greenland, on a helicopter, I gazed down at the fjord ice. The full moon's illumination created fanciful shadows of icebergs and hills. My doubt was gone. I remembered why I loved the Arctic and why I was returning. I got back to Qaanaaq in the last days of December of 1997. In my absence, John had assembled our dog teams. Picking a dog team is tricky. Jean Malaurie, the first European to reach the geographic north pole, was nearly killed by his sled dogs. As he walked in front of his team one day, he stumbled and fell. The team, sensing his vulnerability, attacked. He was saved only by a thick parka and fur pants.

We spent six weeks taking training trips from the village. On a two-day, 90-mile trip, we traveled through the polar night without even the moon to guide us. In this dark season that begins in late October, the land seems to sleep, waiting for the sun to bring it back to life in mid-February. Our Inuit sled dogs needed no lessons in how to pull a sled; they were born with the instinct. However, we needed to put some miles on the dogs to build their muscles for the long journey ahead and get them to work as a cohesive team. That meant letting them work out their aggression and establish a pecking order. Although John had kept the dogs in good shape during my absence, they were not responding well to commands. Receiving commands in English, Danish, Australian and Inuit confused them. They were smart, but not multilingual. We decided to stick to basic, easy Inuit commands already familiar to the dogs: aquitsit (lie down), huck-huck (go), hookwa hookwa (run fast), et-et (turn right), harku-harku (turn left), ah-ah (come) and aee-aee (stop).

During a training run to Herbert Island, I saw my good friends Mamarut Kristensen and Tekumeq Peary. Tekumeq's father was Tetilinguaq Peary, a grandson of explorer Robert E. Peary. Another day, I ran the dogs 45 miles down Ingelfield Bredning to the village of Qeqertat, which has a dozen small houses, a church and a tiny store. Standing in the snow outside a cabin devoted to meat storage were several frozen seals, their heads buried, their rear flippers pointing to the heavens. Inside was a pile of Greenland halibut. These flat fish would be excellent food for the trail. There is so much fat in the meat that even at -40°F, fillets can be easily carved off with a knife. I bought two seals and six halibut, food for both dogs and explorers.

CHAPTER 12

DOG SLEDDING FROM QAANAAQ
TO CAPE JEFFERSON

On February 15, 1998, as the polar night came to an end, we mushed out of Qaanaaq with 21 energetic dogs. I admired these dogs for their wild nature, endurance and distinctive personalities. They had the heavy fur and the weight, about 75 pounds, needed for the extreme conditions of Arctic travel. I prefer traveling with dogs to kayaking. When we made the switch, I was more than ready.

This portion of the trip from Qaanaaq would take us more than

3,000 miles over the incredibly rugged terrain of Greenland's north-west, north and east coasts. Our 13 supply depots had been placed for us by air and icebreaker. When weather wouldn't permit either kayaking or dog sledding, we planned lengthy breaks, living among the Inuit, training our dogs, absorbing the culture and contributing to Kelly's educational program.

Our goal was to travel 1,800 miles up Greenland's north-west coast, across the northern tip and down the east coast to Scoresbysund. We aimed to complete the trip before the spring melt in June. Each sled was 13.5 feet long, 34 inches wide and carried 1,000 pounds. We planned to travel from seven to 12 hours and aim for 18 miles a day. We intended to rest every sixth day. On paper, we knew that seemed simple enough, but unpredictable Arctic weather could pin us down in camp for several days at a time.

We also knew what lay ahead: 100 mile-an-hour winds, temperatures falling to -60°F, storms and rough seas. Being out in these elements for an extended period would bring us face to face with a multitude of hardships. We had to be prepared, anticipate problems and, as important, work to maintain an optimistic outlook. We would be our own worst enemies if we fell into mental sink holes.

Luckily, by now I was a much more seasoned dog driver than I had been on my earlier trips. I'd mushed thousands of Arctic miles, faced bitter cold and wind, and learned from the Northwest Passage Expedition when our dogs lapped up salty ice and died from dehydration. That was a mistake I would not repeat. Even in the coldest, most alarming conditions, I knew how to care for the dogs. Traveling with them gave me an intense connection to the Arctic land and Inuit culture, and to the great polar explorers of the past.

It was cold and windy as we reached Siorapaluk, the northern-most village in the Qaanaaq district. Nearly a whole village of wide smiles and bronzed faces greeted us. The children played on our sleds while the adults examined our equipment. We settled our dogs and bought a supply of walrus meat. Then, over tea and cookies, we had a long night of stories. The major topic of discussion was the coming polar bear hunt. As the daylight stretched, hunters with dog teams planned to head out for weeks at a time to track bears. Hearing stories of how frenzied, howling dogs can keep a 10-foot-tall bear trapped until a hunter is close enough to shoot amazed us. The most prized possession of each hunter is his polar bear pants. Exceptionally warm, they're a proud symbol of a successful hunter.

When we left Siorapaluk, Aaron and Asiajuk Duneq, and Asiajuk's wife, Benigne, joined us. They planned to travel with us until they reached an area where they could hunt bears. Benigne was decked out in a stunning blue-fox parka, the legendary symbol of the polar Inuit. Our caravan of three sleds and 49 dogs moved north.

At noon, stopping for tea and a short rest—as all Inuit hunters do on the trail—the sun appeared for the first time in four months. Even though the temperature was far below zero, my face imagined warmth. I was excited when we started up the Clements Markham Glacier. I knew Knud Rasmussen and another great Arctic traveler, Peter Frenchmen, had been over this territory. Halfway up, we iced the sled runners to reduce friction. This is a time-consuming process. You start by melting ice so you can soak cotton fibers in the water. The icy cotton is applied to the runners and scraped smooth with a knife. Then water is applied with a piece of bearskin. When done right, the water instantly freezes and creates a surface far more slippery than any plastic I know.

We planned a two-day push over the glacier, but a blizzard arrived and 100-mile-an-hour winds kept us in camp. I tried to crawl out of the tent to check on the dogs. It was impossible to reach them. I managed to put 45-pound bags of gear on the tent's snow flaps, but the violent wind blew them off. With snow in every crevice, collar, cuff and pocket, our world was defined by howling wind and driving snow.

For the next five days, as snow piled up foot after foot, pushing the walls in on us, John and I sat in the shrinking, claustrophobic space with our backs against the walls. With feet against each other, we pushed back against the tent and tried to keep it from collapsing. On the storm's third day, the wind was so loud we could only communicate by leaning close and yelling. That night the lantern swung so wildly it fell to the floor in pieces.

When we were finally able to go outside, we discovered that just 100 yards away, the poles on the Duneqs' tent had broken during the storm. As they lay under the fallen and torn canvas, their fur clothing got plugged with snow. Even though they were wet and freezing, they began to construct an igloo. On the fourth day, a lull in the storm allowed them to complete the job. Retreating down the glacier and away from the storm's intensity would be extremely dangerous, but our Inuit friends were freezing to death in their damp clothing. They'd exhausted their kerosene supply and were unable to dry their clothes. By now the dogs had ice balls on their coats, which made them susceptible to fatal exposure.

Weathering the storm was no longer an option. During a slight lull in the wind, John and I consolidated our essentials onto one sled, hooked our 21 dogs to it, looped rope brakes over each runner, and gingerly eased the dogs down the glacier. Heading for a hunting hut at the glacier's base, we followed the tracks of our Inuit friends' sled. We could only see a few feet ahead of our lead dogs. We stopped our team, and searched on our hands and knees until we spotted Aaron's sled tracks, then continued slowly down the glacier along a moraine ridge.

Darkness swallowed the day. With their ears cocked backward to our commands of "eh, eh" to slow down, our dogs picked their way down the treacherous slope of ice and rock. Jogging at the rear, we held tight to the upstanders and constantly shifted our weight to steer the sled. The hunting hut suddenly came into view, along with Aaron's team. Protected from the wind by the gravel moraine, we staked the dogs, rubbed them down and gave them each a double meal of kibble and fat. Then we joined Aaron, Asiajuk and Benigne in the hut, and collapsed with exhaustion.

The hut was 12 feet square, and stank of kerosene and walrus fat. Everything's relative. It felt like a four-star hotel to us. The drifts burying the building softened the noise from the wind. When the storm ended a day later, the Inuits decided to turn back. They'd been badly shaken by the storm. John and I would miss their company.

The day we left the hut, we passed the remains of our original camp. Things were scattered everywhere: broken tent poles, snow blocks and hundreds of piles of dog poop. We couldn't have chosen a worse location for our camp. The glacier there was so sloped the wind had scoured it clean of snow.

We divided the dogs into two teams and picked up John's sled. For the remainder of the day, we pushed and hauled our heavy loads. At one point, using my whip to keep the dogs away from a crevasse, I lashed myself in the eye. Howling in pain, I fell to the ground and dropped the seal skin whip. Holyfield slurped it up like a piece of spaghetti. I fell into small crevasses twice because I couldn't see. Eventually John treated the eye with a salve, and we covered it with a gauze patch. It was a reminder of just how vulnerable we were. What if one of us broke a leg or got appendicitis? Some things couldn't be fixed in remote Greenland.

I was relieved when my vision improved a bit the next day. The temperature stood at -36°F, and, for the first time in nearly two weeks, the sky was clear enough to see the mountains of Canada's Ellesmere Island, 70 miles to the west. While we were packing to depart, two of our dogs, Aten and his brother Alingmik, came over, rubbing and pushing against my legs like cats. I wondered how they could be so content and happy in such difficult circumstances. I drew energy from them. The traveling became easier—except, that is, for the large, sled-swallowing crevasses. Some were clearly visible. Others were partially covered by a layer of snow. What gave a crevasse away to the trained eye was the spot of concave surface, where the snow dipped a bit under its own weight. Each time we came to one, we stopped our dogs and walked ahead gingerly, poking the snow with basketless ski poles, testing to see if it was sturdy enough to carry the weight of the dogs and sleds.

At the end of each day, we faced an annoying reality of Arctic travel. Everything gets damp from sweat and snow, so even getting undressed was a production. First we knocked the ice and snow off our fur clothing with a stick, and stored them under the sled covers, where they'd be safe from the dogs. When hungry, the dogs will eat almost anything—nylon harnesses, skin clothing, boots, pieces of rope. When John left his cherished caribou fur mitts hanging on the back of the sled, Holyfield gnawed the thumb off one of them. They even eat their own poop. It's a form of recycling and a means of surviving famine. Even when they're not hungry, they gnaw on their frozen poop, evidently just for the fun of it.

Then, before entering the relative warmth of the tent, we removed our outer anoraks, shook away most of the frost that had accumulated between the layers, and brushed the frost from each other's back and arms. Once inside, we hung frozen neck gaiters, boot liners, socks, gloves and mittens on a drying string attached to the tent ceiling. The product of all our efforts was less than great because the tent never got warm enough to completely dry our clothes and gear. At night, when we put out the stove and crawled into our sleeping bags, we had to kick our arms and legs for half an hour to get warm. This was polar bear territory. Often when we heard noises outside, most likely just the dogs settling in, we imagined bears.

Bears weren't our only worry. As March began, I worried about whether our food and fuel would last, and whether the caches left for us were safe. John kept saying that everything would be okay, but I worried that our depot at a hut on Tek Bay might have been rooted out by polar bears. John was right. When we arrived at the hut, the supplies were fine. After three days of rest, we moved on, carrying 800 pounds of new supplies for the 300-mile journey to the next depot. It was -45°F again. Even our bottle of Canadian whiskey froze solid.

Getting going and starting a stove in these temperatures each morning was as hard as setting up camp the night before. The biggest problem was rolling out of bed when it was -50°F. Then we had to get the stove going. The normally thin Coleman fuel was as thick as corn syrup, and ignition required a tepee of match sticks ignited over the flooded burner. I cooked breakfast—oatmeal mixed with dried milk, brown sugar and raisins. That was followed by a multivitamin. We washed it all down with a cup of instant coffee.

We crossed Kane Basin, headed overland through the area known as Washington Land and worked our way down a riverbed that eventually narrowed into a gorge with sheer rock walls. My heart sank. The rock-strewn landscape stretched as far as we could see. We would ruin the sled's plastic shoeing for sure, which would make it impossible for the dogs to pull.

Our only option was to travel along the coast up the Kennedy Channel. Our route originally had been selected to avoid the Kennedy Channel, which separates Canada's Ellesmere Island from Greenland. The Kennedy Channel had been well-documented by many earlier expeditions as an extremely difficult place to travel. British polar explorer Wally Herbert called it "that horrendous channel." Storm-blown winds and sea currents drive ice onto the coast and create a landscape of misshapen, pressured sea ice that is nearly impossible to cross. John and I dreaded going even a short distance there, but we had no choice. As we approached Cape Jackson at the head of Kennedy Channel, we traveled on rime ice that was perfectly flat, thin and laced with salt. I was wary and tested every step by plunging an ice chisel into the surface. Often, the chisel pierced the ice and ran into black, cold water. That meant changing our route. Where there's thin ice, there are seals, because it's easy for them to make breathing holes. What's good for seals is good for polar bears.

That explained all the bear tracks we'd been seeing. Inuit hunters use their dogs to pursue bears, but we weren't Inuit hunters. John and I weren't eager to see bears. We had no desire to risk our team in a fight. Our dogs, however, felt differently. As soon as they picked up bear scent, the dogs bolted. I was thrown off the sled and John held on desperately. I chased after the sled, and when it got stuck on a pressure ridge, I was able to latch on. Between us, John and I were able to hold back the dogs, but about 300 yards away we spotted a menacing-looking, 10-foot-tall, yellow-colored polar bear. If it noticed us, it didn't want anything to do with us. It seemed to "know" hunters and dogs. It ran the other way.

That night, after many attempts, we made radio contact with Siorapaluk. We talked to Peter Duneq, a hunter and dog driver from Qaanaaq, who happened to be monitoring the universal radio system most hunters use. We asked him to let our friends and families know we were okay.

As John and I climbed the side of Cape Jefferson—at N 80 20—a killing north wind funneled down Kennedy Channel. With eyes watering, tears instantly froze on my cheeks. An even worse sight confronted us. We faced miles of pressure ridges and pack ice that extended all the way to Canada, 50 miles to the west, and as far north as we could see. That's where we were headed. I was so discouraged, from weariness and cold, that I yelled at John for the first time. I told him he was the slowest person I'd ever met, adding that I was sure glad to get that off my chest. He responded that I was impatient. Our exchange, of course, was actually a bit more colorful, but it resulted in no lasting wounds. We both knew we were stressed and overwhelmed. Not unsurprisingly, the dogs took their cue from us and promptly pitched into their own scrap.

March 21, 1998, the first day of spring, proved to be one of the most difficult days of my life. We were blocked completely by pressured pack ice and our pick axes were not up to the task of forging a trail. It would take a bulldozer and all the time in the world. It was clear we couldn't continue on our planned route. After climbing a 50-foot chunk of ice thrust against the shore, I broke down and cried.

We were 125 miles from our next depot in Hall Land, and we were running short of fuel and food. We had to find another way forward. We were tempted to take a high path away from the sea, over the ice cap. But the Danish Polar Center prohibited travel across the cap before April 15. Even if we were willing to break the rule, we would waste a lot of time finding and skirting dangerous crevasses. Besides, there was no guarantee we would make it, and we didn't want to anger the Danish authorities who had authorized our trip.

We considered radioing for an airplane pickup. We could be flown to our next depot, pick up supplies and go on from there. But that would cost $6,000 and violate the basic premise of the expedition—to circumnavigate Greenland using only kayak and dog sled. Before we left, we'd agreed to seek air rescue only if our lives or those of the dogs were in danger.

If we couldn't stay where we were, couldn't go forward, couldn't make a detour and couldn't call for an airplane pickup, what could we do? We had only one option. We had to turn around and backtrack 325 grueling miles to Siorapaluk. And we had to race to make it before our food and fuel ran out. I thought of the Japanese proverb: "Fall seven times, stand up eight." We began our journey back.

It seemed we couldn't catch a break with the weather, with the temperatures still running in the -40°F range. We smoothed the sled's plastic runners with a carpenter's plane so they'd slide more easily over the granular, abrasive snow. We hoped they'd hold up over the rocks. We scheduled a rest day to rebuild the dogs' muscles and began rationing their food. By my calculations, we'd reach Siorapaluk before running out of supplies, but just barely.

At the Rensselaer Bay hut, we ran into Peter Duneq and his family, who were going north to hunt polar bears. They were glad to see us. We were glad to see anyone. As Inuits do, they made good-hearted jokes that we were going back the way we'd come and made light of our supply problems. They had plenty of walrus and gave us some for ourselves and for the dogs. During our layover at the hut, I cooked up a storm of spicy things like walrus fried with butter and coated with Cajun seasoning, and Cajun pemmican patties. They were a welcome departure from our usual fare.

John and I also indulged in a bucket bath, our first real cleaning in a month. Some of my dry, calloused skin, the result of frequent, low-level frostbite, peeled off. We looked a little haggard and thin, but relatively okay. The dogs lay on their sides, big round bellies attached to thin frames, appearing as if all memories of past hardships were erased by two days of "all-you-can-eat" walrus and stale hut rations. Aten, warm, overfed and curled up in a wax-coated depot box, was in dog heaven.

When we arrived back in Siorapaluk, the community turned out to say hello again. The snow was so deep only the roofs of the houses were visible. We bumped into Peter Duneq's wife, who reported that the hunters had already killed three polar bears.

On April 3, 1998, we came into Qaanaaq—the end of the road for now. The locals told us a rabies-distemper outbreak was ravaging non-vaccinated dogs. Some 450 dogs, 65 percent of those in the district, had died. We were relieved that our dogs were inoculated, but it was still depressing news. We spent the next three weeks mushing through the region, making videos and taking photographs of local life. We wanted to document a lifestyle that was under siege by the modern world. We also visited several villages and traveled south to Thule Air Base. That way we were able to travel additional coastline in our rounding of the island.

Then it was time to say goodbye to our dogs. They had served us well over the past seven months. Caring for our dogs day after day, putting their welfare on par with our own, made us extremely attached to them. I was especially fond of Egileraq, who would accompany me back to Minnesota when I finally headed home. He rarely caused any fights among the other dogs and would be a good addition to my Inuit dogs at home. He was cool, calm and collected, which is probably why I liked him so much. I pride myself in having the same temperament. Egileraq's nature suited him for the flight. Not so the other dogs, who were still quite wild. Flying would cause them stress, perhaps even death.

After traveling more than 1,250 miles by dog sled, we were done exploring northwest Greenland. Rounding Greenland's north coast would have to wait for another trip.

CHAPTER 13

WAITING IN AMMASSALIK FOR KAYAK WEATHER

We flew from Qaanaaq to Ammassalik to gear up for our last leg by kayak to Paamiut. When we arrived on May 27, flags were flying at half-staff—in honor of Kali Peary, son of Robert Peary, who had died that day in Qaanaaq at the age of 92.

The melt season in Ammassalik had begun a month early. Summer was coming fast. The sea ice had begun to melt and the coastal pack ice was breaking up. Small Arctic flowers were blooming and tundra grasses were turning green. As summer temperatures reached close to 50°F, berries grew in the fjord valleys. The rivers gushed with melt water from the ice cap and from the heavy snows that accumulated during the winter. The 6,000-foot-high mountains, 2 miles to the north and west, provided an incredible backdrop to the little community. Occasional patches of dark granite on the south-facing slopes broke through the past winter's snow.

Built on the steep hillsides like most Greenland settlements, Ammassalik was beautiful in a rugged way. Most of its 400 residents were native Greenlanders. A smattering of people considered themselves Danish. Similar to west coast and northern residents in many ways, Greenlanders who live in the eastern part of the country are also distinct. Isolated as they are by geography, their language is unrecognizable to those in the west and north. Because of deeper snows and slightly warmer seasons, their hunting, fishing and sledding techniques are slightly different from other parts of Greenland.

While we trained for our 930-mile kayak journey, set to begin on July 9, we absorbed the local life. This time of year, a typical morning in Ammassalik began around 6 o'clock. The sun quickly dispersed the morning chill. Most days, after a quick breakfast of instant coffee, toast and jam, I wandered outside to watch the hunters leaving from the harbor, only a few hundred yards from where we were staying. More and more men were going out in their small open boats now that the ice had melted in the fjord, the ammasset were spawning and the seals were drifting down with the polar ice.

Local hunters couldn't travel very far because pack ice still blocked the mouth of the fjord. Later in the summer, they could take longer hunting trips by boat for seal, whale and polar bear, and visit friends and family living in other villages. Already, families along the coast were netting small ammasset by the thousands from the shore, much like the smelt we catch in Lake Superior. They dried them on the rocks, to be eaten later, like fish jerky. They also fried the fish while they were still fresh. John and I netted and dried 300 finger-sized ammasset to supplement our food supply for our kayak journey. This would be a welcome addition to freeze-dried, vacuum-packed food. While kayaking, we ate more carbohydrates than when we were dog sledding. We supplemented our kayaking meals with berries, mussels, ducks and fish we found along the way.

At the Royal Arctic Line dock, workers shifted large shipping containers. They were getting ready for the town's first ship of the season. Ammassalik is visited by three ships a year, all during July. The cargo ships come from Denmark and carry the food and material Greenlanders can't get from the land and sea—fuel, building supplies and miscellaneous hardware. Because of this, living in Greenland is very expensive. Although stores stock a wide range of goods, from fishing nets to baby diapers, supplies are limited, especially in smaller communities.

Up from the harbor at the local store, people gathered to buy food for the day. Others people-watched and socialized. The front of the town grocery store is a gathering place for news of the day in all Greenlandic towns. On these steep slopes and hills, you need the legs of a mountain goat. Unaffected by the steep hills, children play and run. The adults are also accustomed to the inclines, but the elderly and disabled struggle, and there are few resources to help them.

Many communities in Greenland have no plumbing or running water at all. Often, people gather water by hand from the nearest freshwater stream. If they have a water-storage tank, water is delivered by truck. In the winter, they collect glacial ice from the fjord and put it on kerosene heaters to melt for drinking water. In places like

105

this village, only about 25 percent of the homes have plumbing and flush toilets. The usual toilet system is a vented bucket that is emptied by hand when it's full.

One morning, I watched as Gert Ali, an Inuit elder, departed for a day's hunting. He was outfitted with a small day pack containing his lunch, an extra pair of warm gloves and shells for his guns. With a shotgun and rifle slung over one shoulder, he held a thermos of coffee in one hand and a pipe filled with Sweet Dublin tobacco in the other. His hunting boat was anchored away from shore on a 75-foot line attached to a buoy, an old plastic juice jug. The air carried the harbor smell you find all over the world: fish and boat gas. Gert pulled on one side of the continuous circle of rope running through a pulley on the buoy, drew the boat to the dry rock and hopped in. The floor of his white fiberglass, 16-foot boat was stained with old fish slime and seal blood. Inside the boat were a long-handled ice chisel, ammasset scoop net and long broom handle with a large fish hook attached to the end by two hose clamps. The latter served many purposes. He would use it to catch seals and big fish, to snag boat ropes, and simply to hold the boat next to the ice edge.

A small gill net rolled up in a burlap sack was for catching polar cod and Arctic char. For the deeper fish, a large spool with monofilament line was secured to the boat with a series of baited hooks a few feet apart. A weight would send this to the bottom of the sea with the hope it would be rolled back a few hours later with halibut or cod. The wind created by the swift pace of the boat could make even a good day a chilly, eye-watering experience. Warmly dressed, with a bent-up baseball hat holding down his gray hair, Gert's high-cheeked skin was tanned almost black by days of hunting. During the long hours of summer's sunlight, fishermen are often out all day, searching with their binoculars for bears and seals from their small open boats.

When Gert returned at low tide, he threw me the line to his boat.

I dragged it to the landing through the sand a few inches below the water. Eight seals were draped across the hood and rear of his boat. He passed me the seals, which I staked at the top of the ramp. Nearby was the hunters market, a small open-air structure with a table for placing the catch of the day. Hunters gathered around throughout the day, smoked their pipes and told stories of the day's hunt. On the table were ducks, sea weed, dried ammassets and pieces of cut-up seal ready for the pot. The hunters traded some of their catch for boat gas, repair materials and hunting supplies.

Gert told us he had never seen this much "big ice" from the Arctic Ocean choking the water this late in the summer. He had heard that the icebreaker, which supplied the village three times a year, would not arrive that day because it was caught in the ice 10 miles off-shore. Because of the year's warm winter and early summer, more ice released from the Arctic Ocean and glaciers drifted toward us. With more than 700 miles to paddle before fall storms shut us down, we would have our work cut out for us.

CHAPTER 14

KAYAKING FROM AMMASSALIK TO QAQORTOQ

Finally, at 6:30 the morning of July 9, 1998, we left Ammassalik in our new kayak. As we paddled, we skimmed through a thin layer of ice. We had switched to a 19-foot, tandem kayak that was fast and stable. We chose a durable plastic kayak for hauling across sea-ice when open water would be scarce. The first 518 miles of this third and final 930-mile leg crossed a desolate, uninhabited coast. It was fitting that so much of our expedition was by kayak. It was the Inuits who invented this boat. In fact, kayak is the Inuit word for "hunter's boat." We had to carry all the supplies we needed for at least 40 days: 175 pounds of food, fuel and equipment. We didn't know if the weight would turn us into our own icebreaker or sink us to the bottom of the fjord. This time there was no place to resupply and no depots waiting to replenish us. If we reached the village of Qaqortoq in mid-August before the fall storms started, we planned to continue on to our original starting point of Paamiut, 180 miles farther up the west coast.

As we set out, a narrow paddling lane of clear water opened up along the coast. Before long, passing the village of Isortoq, we left behind the last community for hundreds of miles. On this stretch we could expect no help from the cold, rock-bound, mountainous land. Soon after we passed Isortoq, we heard our first rumblings from calving icebergs. It was a sound we knew well from our kayak trip up the west coast.

Two days into the trip, we got stopped by pack ice. However, during the night the ice shifted so we were able to squeeze between chunks of ice across Ikertivaq Bay. The passage was so tight we couldn't actually paddle. We pulled our way through with homemade gaff hooks. Progress was excruciatingly slow.

One night, John and I made camp close to a centuries-old Inuit stone grave. The skull of the occupant was visible through the rocks. It made for an eerie night under the orange glow of a three-quarter moon. It occurred to me that if John and I met the same fate here, perhaps a stranger would stumble across our remains one day.

Heading south, mere specks on a sea of ice, we spent as much time pulling the kayak out of the water to haul it over ice as we did paddling. Occasionally, as we hauled, ice broke beneath us and we found ourselves in water up to our armpits. At every step, we had to be on constant alert to guard against errors in choosing our route, especially near icebergs and active glaciers. Even then, we were often caught by surprise.

One day, in the middle of a fjord, a sudden strong wind threatened to capsize us. We made a hurried decision to turn around and paddle 3 miles to safety on the nearest shore. Having a healthy dose of fear is essential for an explorer. If you become complacent, you risk being reckless. I believe the healthy fear John and I had of the unknown kept us alive many times. Another mandatory trait for an explorer is patience, and I learned a lot about that from John. Sometimes progress is measured in feet, not miles. "One step at a time" and "one day at a time" are sensible sayings for everyone. For us, it was often one boat length at a time.

About a week after leaving Ammassalik, we reached Fridtjof Nansen Halve, an ice-capped peninsula in the Denmark Strait. Named for the famed Norwegian explorer, this was where he and his team began their 1888 crossing of the ice cap on skis. It was where John and I started to bicker, picking at one another over everything and nothing. We were pushing so hard our bodies were constantly overworked. We had to take aspirin and cod liver oil as well as food each time we had a meal. On the dog-sled segment, I'd been the morning person, getting up early to cook breakfast. On this leg, it was John's turn. However, he slept with such good earplugs he often didn't hear the alarm. Constant oversleeping was a problem. We had to stay on a strict schedule to reach southern Greenland before the fall storms hit. Each day, we needed 11 hours of paddling, four hours of camp time and nine hours of sleep. The sensible thing was for me to take over cooking and for John to gather fresh water at each camp.

Along this route of coastline, we were out of radio range for 22 days. How easy it would have been to simply disappear. I worried that John and I would get killed in this empty land of ice and rock, and no one would know. It wasn't until July 30, standing atop Kutsit Island, that we were able to make contact with the outside world. When we raised a man at the VHF station 52 miles south at Prince Christian

Fjord, he couldn't believe we were transmitting from the east coast. We were the first to do it. He relayed messages home for us that we were okay. Buoyed by this contact, we built a 3-foot stone cairn, one of three we erected during this expedition, and I renamed the knob of sea rock Jacob Island for my son. We placed a note inside the cairn explaining our expedition.

I also tucked in a note expressing the wish that someday I might entice Jacob to come to this cairn even though I knew I was wise not to attach too much hope to it. My son and I were brought up in different worlds, in different times, with different skill sets. I was brought up on a farm and taught how to live off the land—literally. Jacob's early life was urban. The survival lessons he learned had much more to do with society than nature. We had different dreams.

Mostly, I was conscious of that and tried to steer him away from choices he might later regret—tattoos for instance. But sometimes, I forgot how different his childhood was from mine. When Jacob was young, I took him dog sledding. I wanted to show him my world. What he remembers of the adventure is how cold his feet were. But on this day, once again far away from him physically, all that mattered to me was that even if he never shared my passion for the north, which was likely, and even if he never saw this spot dedicated to him, he would always know that I carry him with me wherever I go.

Paddling through a thick fog on August 3, 1998, John and I reached the manned weather station at Prince Christian Sound. We'd come more than 500 miles from Ammassalik, all without seeing another human being. We were lucky to find the weather station in the fog, and did so only because of the noise the generator made.

The Danish station consisted of several green shacks anchored to bedrock by cable. When we beached the kayak, we climbed a long flight of wooden stairs to the door. As we approached, the station chief came out and questioned us closely: Who were we? Where had we come from? How had we traveled? When we explained our expedition, he said, "You must be hungry." They were astounded that John and I had kayaked from Ammassalik in 26 days. The Danish crew fed us well. They were glad to see new faces and hear our stories. Hard to say who was happier for the company: them or us.

This location had been chosen for a station because the weather is horrible, similar to Cape Horn on the tip of South America, where several weather systems converge. Sure enough, a day after we left the station, we made only 9 miles because of a stiff headwind blasting down the sheer sides of the fjord. As an added aggravation, mosquitoes and gnats came at us in swarms. Putting up our tent was torture. Two days later, a 30 mile-an-hour wind kept us camp-bound for three days. It kept the gnats down, too, so we picked blackberries and mushrooms.

On August 10, we reached Appilitoq, a village of 40 people on a small island. It was the most beautiful village I saw in Greenland. Mountains rising to 6,000 feet formed a bowl for the cluster of brightly painted red, yellow and blue houses. Once again, we created a stir when we paddled in. An elder and his wife greeted us and asked where we'd come from. When we told them we'd paddled 32 days from Ammassalik, he smiled and asked, "Ammassalik?" He pointed in the direction of the ice cap.

The villagers made us feel right at home. Once we'd settled in, we snacked on dried fish, shared a smoke and received an update on ice conditions. The supply ship that was scheduled for May had just arrived, three months late. Conditions from here to Paamiut were bad. Fearing we would be forced to stop short of our goal once again, we quickly moved on.

One night in a camp pitched on a puny ledge, we were buffeted by gale-force winds that heaved sea spray onto our tent as icebergs swayed in the heavy seas. In mid-August, John and I made only 5 miles in four days and spent nine out of 13 days on shore, unable to travel. We were running out of time. We set the alarm clock to ring every six hours so we could check the weather, but the wind just kept on howling.

Eventually, we made it to Nanortalik, but it had become obvious to both of us that we needed to end this leg of the journey at Qaqortoq, short of our goal. The open coast between Qaqortoq and Paamiut contains some of the most violent waters in the world, which can only be paddled in the best of conditions, and even then with great caution. The leg to Paamiut would have to wait.

As we left Nanortalik, the mornings were getting colder. Local women were picking the last of the abundant blackberries, and the tundra was starting to show faint signs of rust color, indicating the onset of autumn. Waterfowl could be seen massing for their journey south. A thick fog obscured our route during the morning hours and for the first time we were forced to paddle by compass and GPS. We made 20 miles the first day out of Nanortalik and were exhausted.

Shortly before heading to a piece of shoreline suitable for a campsite, we ran into a pod of four fin whales feeding on small shrimp concentrated between a large iceberg and the shore. The whales swam almost directly under our kayak, boiling the water with their enormous fins as they worked together to round up the shrimp. Once they had a number of the crustaceans encircled, they took turns surfacing in the middle, their huge mouths gaping to the sky.

We finished this leg at Qaqortoq on August 20, 1998. We had paddled 750 miles from Ammassalik in 43 days. Since the start of our expedition in May of 1997, we had covered 3,200 miles of Greenland's coast, all by dog sled or kayak. Still short of our ultimate goal, John and I bounced between feelings of exhaustion and exhilaration.

CHAPTER 15

STAGING THE NEXT TRY

Back in northern Minnesota, I spent five months decompressing. The long months of planning, and the hard physical and mental work of the expedition had taken its toll. Not long after I arrived home, I received an email from the Danish Polar Center. Lone Madsen, a Danish kayaker and journalist who was also trying to circumnavigate Greenland, had died while traveling along the east coast. The skeptics said John and I were just lucky. Experienced Arctic travelers from Denmark and the United States said flat out that our kayak journeys would be impossible to achieve.

John stayed in Minnesota for a while, then returned to Australia. He signed up for another season with the Australian National Antarctic Research Expedition. I worked at my carpentry business, but found it hard to adjust to the daily routines and obligations of life. After being gone so long, I was slightly depressed and felt reserved in the company of friends. That's the downside of a life of adventure. After the high of living on the edge, feeling joy and pleasure in everyday life back home becomes a feat in itself.

As always happens, as time passed, I forgot the hardships of the expedition. Instead I remembered only the challenge of survival and the simple pleasures of my life on ice. I recalled our experiences with the Inuit and dreamed of returning to Greenland. Going back required days working by phone and computer, as well as traveling to line up sponsors and support, which in turn meant little outdoor time. Eventually, things came together. Frisby Technologies agreed to come back as our lead sponsor and fund one-third of our budget. This prodded me to seek the remaining funds we needed.

In September 1999, I flew to Washington, DC. I met with the Smithsonian about the possibility of our filming Polar Inuit string games, and I met with the National Geographic Society about funding. After admiring Robert E. Peary's sled and a 6-foot spinning globe in the National Geographic lobby, I was taken to the office of Peter Miller, expeditions editor for the magazine. Peter came in and we talked about the expedition. An hour later we walked down the hall to a conference room. Feeling intimidated, I choked out my plans to a group from various divisions of the society. I passed out proposals, showed video taken of our first 3,200 miles of travel, and rolled out a map of Greenland while pointing to key points of interest. I feared I wasn't entertaining the group very well and scolded myself for not bringing my slides.

Afterwards, I was sure the meeting had gone poorly. I was afraid I had blown my chance at convincing them this was a notable project. Three months passed and I had all but given up hope when I received a call from the National Geographic Expeditions Council. We had received all we asked for.

A few days later, I got a call from Malden Mills, makers of Polartec fabric. We had been chosen as a recipient of the Polartec Challenge Grant. I'd applied several months earlier and had almost forgotten about it. I even had support from two of my hometown resorts, Caribou Highlands and Bluefin Bay. John and I would be able to go back to Greenland for the second stage of the expedition.

When Christmas of 1999 arrived, I broke an unwritten rule: to never leave for an expedition at Christmas. It's too hard on a family. Unfortunately, the most convenient time to leave Minnesota was Christmas Day. I had to catch a once-weekly flight in Greenland, and I needed six weeks to assemble and train a new dog team. On the drive from Grand Marais to catch a plane in Chicago, Kelly and I talked about everything except my departure. Finally, we both started to cry. I told her I knew I was a jerk for going and promised her I would not be gone so much in the future. She rolled her eyes. She'd heard it all before.

"Pretty soon I'll be too old to do these kind of things," I insisted.

"Great. Then I can take care of an invalid for the rest of my life."

This was not the first time I put being a husband and a father behind my life as an explorer. And no matter what I told myself—or them—it would probably not be the last time.

CHAPTER 16

PICKING UP THE TRAIL WITH NEW DOGS

I flew into the polar night on the last day of the year 1999. Silhouetted in the twilight, mountain peaks grew out of a gray-white frozen sea that was dotted with icebergs. At a latitude of N 77, at this time of year the stars shine even at noon. Later, in pitch dark, I caught the weekly helicopter flight from Thule Air Base to Qaanaaq, which was to be my training ground for the next six weeks. As we landed and the prop kicked up snow, we were greeted by Danish friends from our first trip, Torben Diklev, an anthropologist and curator of the small Knud Rasmussen museum, and his wife, Tine Lisby Jensen. They had put together a solid base for our team: eight dogs, including Knud and Quick from the previous year's trek along the northwest coast.

I pinned a note to the hamlet bulletin board announcing that I was looking for dogs. I planned to pick 15 but wanted to see at least 20. I was looking for 70- to 75-pound dogs. Experience had taught me it was more efficient to have 15 dogs of that size than 10 large dogs. Smaller dogs are faster and easier to handle. Besides, one dog out of 15 getting hurt is less problematic than losing one of 10.

I managed to get four dogs from Qaavianguaq Qissuk, a small man in his seventies with tiny, worn hands. His clothing was tattered and shiny from dirt and seal fat. He lived near the shore in the older section of the village in a one-room, one-window house with peeling red paint. In the 10-foot by 16-foot room was a bed with a bare mattress, a miniature oil stove and candles for light. Rusting rifles, harpoons and fishing nets were tucked under the bed, and old sealskin kamiks stood at its foot.

Qissuk was too old to handle a dog team, he told me, so his hunting days were over. "If I can't go hunting, there's no meat to feed the dogs," he said. The younger men of Qaanaaq wouldn't take him out, fearful he would be slow or get hurt. "I have a lot I can show and teach them," Qissuk said, "but they won't take me." He and I formed an instant strong bond. We walked over to the dogs, and he handed me the traces. He seemed to know we would take good care of them.

On January 11, 2000, I made my first run with the dogs, 15 miles to Herbert Island and the semi-abandoned village of Qeqertarssuaq. A handful of my friends were staying in its weather-beaten sheds. After I secured the dogs, I walked to the center of the village. A lantern burned in the window of a house that was three-quarters buried in a snowdrift. Smoke poured from the chimney. I knocked and opened the door, announcing myself by my Inuit name, Mikihuaq Americamiut, which means little American.

Tekumeq Kristensen saw me first and squealed. Mamarut Kristensen patted my belly and then his own ample midsection, which he called his bank account. He invited me to make a deposit in my account by staying for a dinner of walrus meat and raw seal liver. Smelling of boiled meat, the small building was humid, full of half-clad bodies, and polar bear pants and seal skins drying on frames. A few guests were missing fingers. One had lost a hand to frostbite. Hunting seals and other marine mammals is dangerous work.

The wind whipped the snow into a ground blizzard and forced everyone to stay put. As the storm raged the next morning, we drank our coffee to a chorus of wooden beams creaking overhead and nails tearing off the roof. When the storm subsided, I mushed back to Qaanaaq, refreshed by my time with these good people.

At -18°F, moving along in lunar light almost bright enough to read a book by, the only sounds I heard were panting dogs and gliding sled runners. Eerie shadows cast by the bright moon made me feel as if I were wandering across a beautiful black-and-white photograph.

Shortly before I left Qaanaaq, I hosted a dinner for the Sirius 2000 Expedition, which was led by a stern man named Steen Broen Jensen. They were to produce a documentary commemorating the 50th anniversary of the Sirius Patrol work in Greenland. They planned to dog sled the north coast as we were, only in reverse order and on a shorter route of 1,350 miles. The party included four former Sirius Patrol members, as well as Crown Prince Frederick of Denmark. Adventurous and easy to be around, he is about as popular in Denmark as Princess Diana was in Britain.

With royalty expected for dinner, I pulled out all the stops. My Danish friends Torben and Tine rolled their eyes when they saw the entrée, good-ole Minnesota tuna casserole. I made up for the casserole by serving an ice cream cake (far past its use-by date though) and Danish beer. After dinner, we hovered over detailed Russian defense maps of northern Greenland, marking places that were dangerous or where navigation was tricky.

John arrived with my photographer friend Larry Roepke on February 4. I hadn't seen John in 18 months, and I was looking forward to traveling with him again. Larry hadn't traveled with me since the Northwest Passage Expedition nearly a decade before. We celebrated our reunion with Cuban cigars and a jug of Irish whiskey.

CHAPTER 17

TRAVELING GREENLAND'S NORTHERN SHORE

Accompanied by our old friend Peter Duneq, John and I left Qaanaaq for Thule Air Base in -20°F weather. It was a good chance for John and me to mesh again on a dog sled. At Thule, we had two days of rest before a charter flew us across the ice cap to a remote gravel airstrip at Constable Point, near Scoresbysund on the east coast. From there, the plan was to go 1,800 miles by sled around the north shore of Greenland and back to Qaanaaq before the end of May.

Inuit dogs can handle just about anything, except airplanes, so we sedated them to calm them down. In blowing snow, it was a rough three-hour ride to Constable Point. A nervous flyer, I held tightly to the arm rest and looked around at the dogs. They were dead to the world. By the time we landed, I was drenched in sweat. I wished I'd taken some of what we'd given the dogs.

When we arrived, I met Benny Musinski, the Constable Point station chief who had been only a voice on the phone for two years. He'd stored the supplies we'd shipped in 1996. I was curious about how the four-year-old food had held up. Looking and smelling just like it did when we packed it, the dog food had come through just fine. The dogs wolfed it down as if it were fresh sirloin. The human food was not as fresh. Lunches, drink mixes and supplements were fine, but the breakfasts and dinners were somewhat stale. I'd added oil to raise their caloric content, and the oil had started to turn rancid. The meals were still edible, just not very tasty.

As John and I packed the sled for our estimated three-month trip, the station phone began to ring. Representatives of the Danish Polar Center and Royal Danish Navy, 1,100 miles away in southern

Greenland, were calling to ask about our gear, wish us luck and fax us our travel permit. Palle V. Norit, the commander at Sirius Patrol headquarters, tried one last time to scare us out of continuing. He told us that two of his men and their dog teams had died a few months earlier on a training run. The dogs fell through thin ice into the water. The men jumped in to save them, but the panicked dogs dragged them down, and they all drowned. Even this story didn't deter us.

The small crew at Constable Point cheered us as we mushed north into a slight wind on February 18. The new sun, still low over the horizon, filled us with excitement. We traveled 15 miles on the first day of our 1,800-mile journey. We expected to be on the trail for 14 or 15 weeks and come within 436 miles of the North Pole. Our first depot was at Daneborg, 272 miles away.

These statistics knicked into my excitement. On the second day out, I was filled with doubt. We were alone on a long, arduous journey in a desolate landscape. The last thing I had loaded on my sled was a duffel bag holding an envelope from Kelly. Each time I went on an expedition, she gave me a packet of cards—Easter and birthday cards, and then a bunch for days when I needed cheering up and reminders that she loved me. They kept me connected to home. But now, on the trail, I needed to accept my reality and push aside gloom and doubt, and, in a way, thoughts of home. Anything less than full concentration on the present put my life, and John's, at risk.

We skijored (being pulled on skis by our dogs) along with the sled, holding the upstanders with one hand and poling with the other. The bindings on our skis were designed for mukluks rather than cross-country boots. When our arms got sore, we awkwardly switched sides on the move.

On the last day of February 2000, a dog fight broke out just after we got on the trail. Dancer started it by running from the far left side all the way to the right side to bite Kiao on the rear leg. They rounded on each other and quickly merged into a ball of flying fur and gnashing teeth. The 13 other dogs kept pulling, and the two fighters were pulled under the sled runners with our 1,000-pound load. It took me about 100 yards to bring the team to a stop. Kiao ran off on the pack ice, scared and bruised. Dancer ran ahead, crying in pain. Because the snow was as hard as concrete, they had both suffered the full impact of the sled's weight. I had seen this same thing happen numerous times, even with the best Inuit dog drivers. It always happens too fast to do anything. I knew Dancer was seriously hurt; the sled had run directly over his midsection. I took him back to the sled to examine and comfort him. Kiao came back, shook off the fight and rejoined the team. We made 22 miles, carrying Dancer on the sled.

At camp that night, I made a soft bed for Dancer, but he grew weaker by the hour. I worried that he had suffered internal injuries. "Poor devil," I said to John. "Why'd he have to pick that fight?" The next morning, Dancer couldn't stand and was barely conscious. His teammate and brother, Dorian, came over, sniffed Dancer and nudged him, as if to say, "C'mon, let's get going." We were devastated when Dancer died. His character and boundless energy had inspired and motivated us even on the bleakest days. When we started out on the trail in the morning, our sled dogs were always eager, even when we weren't. More than once, their boisterous energy adjusted my attitude when I most needed it. Dancer, especially, had excelled at this.

Later that day, an Arctic fox trailed us. It was light on its feet and was seemingly all hair. Foxes sometimes follow polar bears to clean up what the bears leave behind when they kill a seal. This fox was no doubt hoping for stray dog food, food scraps or frozen dog poop to gnaw on.

The coldest times on the trail were the morning, rest breaks and the end of the day, when we were exhausted. In the morning, our metabolism was still shut down from sleep, and we burned energy simply digesting breakfast. It took an hour of being on the move before our hands and feet warmed up. Each day we scheduled three 15-minute trail breaks to rest and eat, but the cold got to us within five or 10 minutes of stopping. Our bodies stole heat from our hands and feet to digest frozen chocolate bars, nuts and dried fruit. It took half an hour of hard skiing, arm waving and running before circulation was fully restored.

If we pushed ourselves too hard, we used up our energy reserves and worked up a sweat that left our clothing damp. If that happened, we were nearly hypothermic by the time we made camp, which made feeding the dogs and putting up our tent almost impossible. Add a sudden storm at day's end to the mix, and the danger increased. A year earlier, three Finnish adventurers had died on the ice cap at the end of a long day while trying to erect their tent in a storm.

John and I were camped 62 miles from Daneborg when we ran into a ground blizzard. I slept in all of my clothes, including three sets of head gear and insulated camp booties. Our North Face VE 24 tent was made of bright yellow, rip-stop nylon, chosen to make it feel a little sunny and cheery inside even when outside was gray and gloomy. This well-tested geodesic expedition tent has been used for decades by mountaineers and expeditioneers. A sheet of half-inch, closed-cell, foam padding stretched wall to wall to insulate the floor. The padding, sandwiched like an accordion, fit neatly on the sled. For additional insulation, John and I slept on individual three-quarter-inch pads. We also strung parachute cord from five points on the tent ceiling to dry clothing. Light came from two small candle lanterns, chubby camping candles held in spring-loaded sleeves with glass tops. They looked like tiny kerosene lanterns.

The next morning, we followed a shallow river bed of gravel and snow that eventually brought us back to sea ice. The smooth ice allowed us to make 34 miles that day. We clipped along at 4.5 miles an hour. The going was so good we stowed our skis and rode the sled for the first time. One day, Knud did a great job leading. It was almost as if he had a GPS in his head. He knew just where to turn and which land feature to aim for.

Remote Daneborg serves as headquarters for the Sirius Patrol. The men who patrol the north and northeast coasts—by boat and plane in summer, and by dog sled in winter—are selected from elite Danish commando units. They serve two-year stints. It is lonely, challenging duty. The Sirius men stationed at Daneborg welcomed us. They knew we were coming but were surprised to see us so soon. We were pleased that we finished with eight days of rations left. At dinner that night, the men pulled down a wall map of Greenland and gave us advice on the best route forward. They also warned us of places to avoid. A note was passed to us from Palle Norit, the Sirius commander, officially welcoming us to Daneborg and wishing us the best on the remainder of our journey.

By mid-March 2000, John and I reached Monstedhus, a hut named for Otto Monsted in 1932. This was the main station for his Nanook Trading Company, which supported hunters and trappers who went after bear and fox pelts. The hut, with its vertical shiplap siding, reminded me of a photo I'd seen of Robert Falcon Scott's hut in Antarctica.

We heated the hut with 68-year-old sacks of coal we found there. The walls were varnished black from years of accumulated soot. I found an old steel frying pan and put together enough ingredients to make pancakes. I'd always wanted to cook on a real coal stove just like in the old days. I was in heaven standing on the creaky wood floor, flipping pancakes in the air, showing off to John as he ate his fill. It was a treat to be in a heated space. We were 65 miles shy of our depot at Danmarkshavn, a six-man weather station that provides meteorological data for European and international flights. In the morning, the wind tapped out a clear message: stay inside. To help pass the time, I made poor man's fish chowder by mixing leftover sardines, anchovy paste, vegetable bullion cubes, potato flakes, dried milk and butter. Compared to our usual fare, it was tasty.

Travel was marginal when we started out on March 18, but we hoped for an abating wind. Pushing the dogs and the sled sideways despite deep snow that reached the dogs' bellies, the wind was our constant enemy. We finally gave in and were stormbound three hours short of Danmarkshavn. Our basic contact with the outside world came in twice-weekly radio calls—one to Sirius headquarters and one to Thule Air Base. We gave them our location, described the status of the expedition and our planned route. John had brought a pocket-sized shortwave radio. Mostly we got static, but occasionally we got a fuzzy signal from BBC in London, something to anticipate when nightly chores were done.

After a while, you get used to the difficulty and inconvenience of most daily tasks on an expedition: erecting the tent, cooking dinner, feeding the dogs. But there's no way you get used to going to the bathroom in a storm. Three rules apply: find a high spot so the wind blows past you, pee sideways to the wind and make it snappy. The truth is no matter how quick you are, cold snow blasts any skin that's remotely warm and spindrift fills your shorts.

One night, in the blinding snow, we unwittingly set the tent on a tide crack. Where sea ice meets land, the rising and falling tide creates a crack. When the tide is higher than usual, it pushes water through the crack, where it mixes with snow and creates pools of slush. At 2 am, John woke me to tell me there was ice on the tent floor. Sure enough, the tent was floating in a 6-inch pool of slush. With a gale-force wind blowing, we risked losing both the tent and our lives if we tried to move it. To make matters worse, the full moon, obscured by clouds that night, produced a high tide.

Fortunately, the tent had a waterproof floor sewn 8 inches up the sides to protect against flooding. By morning, the water was breaking over the top of the waterproofing and coming in through the seams. The whole tent floor felt like a water bed. It was time for an emergency camp shift.

The wind was still blowing hard enough to damage the tent if we tried to move it, but at least it was getting light out. The sled was also sitting in a pool of slush. We had to dig them both out before the mess froze. Otherwise we'd be left without shelter or transportation. First, we relayed the sleeping bags and ground pads out of the tent, and put boxes of dog food on top of them. The stove and personal gear came next. Then we began shoveling. My feet got completely soaked. Finally, with death grips on the flapping tent, John and I pulled it out of the hole and moved it 10 feet to a snow ledge behind us. We quickly staked the corners with our skis and shoveled dry snow onto the tent floor to soak up the water. Then we turned to the sled. The slush had created a suction around it, like a boot stuck in mud. After two hours of digging and prying on the runners with our ice chisel, it finally popped loose. We went back to the semi-dry tent and were pinned down again as the storm raged for a third day.

The next morning marked the first day of spring, which to most people means warm weather. In the Arctic, early spring is usually the coldest time of the year, with warmer weather at least six weeks away. We woke to a tent that looked like a science experiment run amok. Caribou hair from our mitts was stuck to greasy bowls and cups. Wet, smelly gear hung everywhere, and added to the already-strong odor of our bodies, urine and dog poop. I began to dream of the Danmarkshavn depot, just hours away. I planned to really live it up: change my long underwear and have a sponge bath, which would be my first in five weeks.

When the wind subsided into a brisk ground blizzard, John and

I decided to make a dash to Danmarkshavn. The horizon was a harsh pink filtered by blowing snow, but the snow surface was good. We made a remarkable 15 miles in three hours. The Danmarkshavn station chief welcomed us warmly and said a plane had landed just the day before with some boxes for us. Our depot was safe. Work could wait until the next day, he said. Now it was time to eat, celebrate and drink beer with the men. It was the best offer we'd had in weeks.

The chore of melting ice to keep the small base supplied with fresh water was laborious, so John and I took short, hot showers. They did the trick: thawing our aching bones and removing layers of calluses and dead skin from frostbitten toes and fingertips. The clear water turned to gray scum as it swirled down the drain. Stepping out of the shower, I caught sight of myself in a mirror. I was a skinny runt with new pink skin. We had each lost 18 pounds in the 41 days since we'd left Qaanaaq.

We left Danmarkshavn with a fully laden sled and covered a good 29 miles along the coast of Germania Land. Our next depot was at Lambert Land, 126 miles away. We made good time, in part, thanks to fresh tracks from a polar bear that just happened to be going in our direction. There was blood in the track, and the dogs eagerly followed the trail. I wondered if the wound had been inflicted by another bear. As the scent grew stronger, the dogs grew increasingly excited. When they started to run, I knew we had to be close to the bear. I yelled at the dogs to stop, and once we had anchored the sled, I jumped on top of it for a better view. There, 200 yards away, was a polar bear, quickly moving away over the chaotic pressure ice. We were delighted to see the bear and even more delighted that he was running in the other direction. We did, however, sleep uneasily that night, knowing a wounded bear was in the neighborhood.

March closed with temperatures hovering around -45°F. The Arctic was living up to its reputation of extremely cold weather at the beginning of spring, even as the days grew longer. We had a hard time keeping the waxy yellow circles of frostbite off our noses and cheeks. Steam rose in the crisp air from the dogs, silhouetted against the snow by the low-lying sun. Listening to the swish of our skis, I daydreamed about my mom's barbecued ribs on a warm summer evening.

We arrived in Lambert Land in -30°F temperatures on April 17, 2002. More than three years had passed since the food at this depot was packed in Minnesota. Some of the volunteer packers had followed Kelly's lead and put little notes in the packages to encourage us or simply give us a laugh. One of my favorites said, "Fritz was here." At Cape Drygalski, a peninsula of Lambert land, we came upon a wooden cross sticking out of a pile of rocks. It was the final resting place of Jorgen Bronland, the last surviving member of an ill-fated 1906 Danish expedition. He'd died when he was returning from mapping the north.

We left the Lambert Land depot and crossed a glacier to Dijmpha and Hekla Sound. Resupplied and toting heavy loads in extreme cold, we limited our travel to six or seven hours a day. We needed to be careful not to wear the dogs' foot pads down on the cold, abrasive snow. As we crossed the 20-mile-wide glacier, it was -35°F. A stiff wind blew straight into our faces. The glacier surface was like a giant washboard of blue ice moguls. Crevasses snaked across the ice, making mushing treacherous. We couldn't ski alongside the sled because it lurched right and left with the undulations. I wondered if the sled was going to snap like a match stick. As we passed the halfway point, John nervously probed snow bridges with his ski pole before crossing three monster crevasses with the dogs. When we finished the crossing, nearly every muscle of our bodies ached from trying to balance on the slippery surface, but we were delighted with the crossing given Sirius Patrol's warnings. We camped 50 yards back from the vertical face of the glacier. Thirty feet below us lay the flat ice of the sound.

We spent the first two hours of the next morning lowering the sled and dogs down the glacier face. We ratcheted in two ice screws, and John belayed the fully loaded sled over the edge. I watched nervously as the titanium screws bent. To my relief, they held. I descended the rope with each petrified dog. Some resisted being suspended in mid-air while others leaped from the edge on their own. Caught by the rope, they landed on all fours in the snow below.

By noon, two sets of feet and 56 paws were running down Dijmpha and Hekla Sound in the most impressive yet forbidding landscape I had ever seen. The frozen waterway was surrounded by tall, dark, intimidating mountains. Between the peaks, turquoise glaciers ran down steep valleys. We left the coast and journeyed overland, following a narrow river valley with hopes of stepping on the polar shores of the Arctic Ocean by mid-April. Our goal now was a depot 100 miles away at a glacial lake named Romer Sø.

This area had so little snow that John and I had difficulty scooping up enough for melting without also collecting sand. The result was fine grit between our teeth at dinner. The lack of snow made it impossible to drive the sled directly overland. We had to follow the shallow river of aqua-blue glacial melt. The riverbed meandered over sled-punishing gravel beds. On several occasions during this rocky obstacle course, precious pieces of plastic peeled off the sled runners. I kept a small carpenter's plane handy to shave the plastic smooth each time it happened. The river ice, clear and polished from blowing wind and sand, was slippery. The dogs hated it.

On April 4, John and I reached N 80 24, matching the northernmost point we had reached at Cape Jefferson on the northwest coast. It was -30°F, and the wind chill was fierce, perhaps -90°F. Any exposed flesh froze immediately. Our fingertips, cheeks and noses took the worst of it. The wind blew directly into our faces, and even with fur hoods and face masks pulled tight, our eyes watered and our eyelids froze together. We made 22 miles on glare ice. The dogs were stressed to the extreme, exhausted from trying to keep their footing on the slick surface. At times all the dogs were spread-eagled on the ice as they tried to regain their footing. Tonto threw his shoulder out struggling to stay upright. He had a tendency to panic more than the other dogs on smooth ice. I put him on aspirin for a few days and prescribed ibuprofen for us.

For three days we fought through the worse elements of polar travel, quickly going from traversing an Arctic desert to swimming thigh deep in snow. We spent at least five hours post-holing up to our britches in soft snow as we struggled toward the supply depot. Sometimes being on the short and wiry side is an advantage on expeditions, but not always—in deep snow, for example. As we left the hut at Romer Sø, my short legs were next to useless in the deep snow. After a few hours, we put the dogs in a modified fan trace, dividing them into three groups, one in front of the other, with space between. That provided more power close to the sled and helped keep us moving. Traveling by dog sled is like fine-tuning a guitar. It requires continual tweaking.

Our 3,000-foot ascent of a glacier out of Romer Sø was up a narrow corridor between a 75-foot sheer wall of blue ice on one side and a granite mountain face on the other. As we rose, a panoramic view of the valley spread before us. We could see for 70 miles in all directions. To our east lay Elephant Foot Glacier. On the horizon to the north we could see the Arctic Ocean. Once again, the hardships of circumnavigating Greenland were eased by endlessly spectacular scenery.

We were just under halfway on this segment of our rounding. As John and I headed out for the Arctic Ocean, I felt renewed and I was inspired to complete the next 950 miles. However, we almost immediately fell off course when a storm forced us to set up camp on the glacier. It was 11 pm. High on the glacier, exposed to high winds and low temperatures, we were not in a good place to be stormbound. I was angry with myself for getting us off the track for the second time in the trip. John took the brunt of my crabbiness, which he, of course, did not deserve. By now, we'd been on the move for almost 12 hours, and our reserves were running low. It was incredibly cold at this elevation. Our fingers were frozen as we fought to set up the tent in the horrible winds. I feared the poles would snap and the tent would blow away. The wind blew fine snow into our clothing, filling every void, pocket and cuff.

Our energy was fading fast, and I worried that I was going to begin losing fingers. Waxy yellow spots of frostbite had formed on our faces. We managed to flip the sled on its side as a wind break for the tent. We finally got the tent up. I ran in circles, wildly waving my arms to bring up my core temperature and force warm blood into my throbbing fingers. As they thawed, the pain was excruciating. This was our most dangerous camp yet, and we'd paid a high price getting it set up. The dogs were clearly done in, too. They immediately lay down, backs to the wind, and for the first time on the expedition skipped their dinner.

Once we were ensconced in the tent, I reminded myself that we were doing pretty well and that being hard on John or myself wouldn't solve anything. The best thing I could do was to focus on the tasks at hand. That's essential when you're leading an expedition. Not for the first time, I wished I were more like Ernest Shackleton, who was expert at keeping his men calm and optimistic when they faced seemingly insurmountable challenges.

We spent two days waiting out the storm. Once we could move again, we had a wild ride down the glacier and through a river gorge in spots as narrow as the sled. Full of twists and turns, it was like a bobsled run. After a bumpy five hours, the river dumped us out on the Arctic Ocean. It felt great to have the sea ice under us again, but the soft snow turned to 3-foot sastrugi, wavelike ridges of snow, the closer we got to the next depot, the Station Nord depot. It was nearly impossible to ski, but a jarring ride in the sled was no better. After 32 miles of this horrible travel, we were met with handshakes and sandwiches at Station Nord.

Aside from the Canadian Arctic station Alert on Ellesmere Island, Station Nord is the northernmost outpost in the world. The station is a symbol of Danish sovereignty and serves as an emergency landing spot for military and rescue aircraft. It is only accessible by a long flight from Spitzbergen or Thule Air Base—and now, clearly, by dog sled. A six-man civilian team maintains the airstrip, mainly keeping it free of snow.

While we were checking on our supplies in the station storeroom, I spotted a hilarious "7-11" sign nailed to the door, as if this were just another neighborhood convenience store. We used the station radio to contact the Sirius Patrol 2000 Expedition and Crown Prince Frederick. They were two days away, coming from the opposite direction. We hoped to rendezvous on the trail.

We left Station Nord in heavy fog. After six hours, we spotted the Sirius expedition about 2 miles off to our right. I yelled at the dogs to shift course, and we bounded across the sea ice toward the three dog teams on the horizon. As we came to a stop, Frederick ran over, hugged us and shook our hands. Expedition leader Steen Sorensen said they'd shot off several flares to attract our attention, but we hadn't seen them in the dim fog.

"You've been traveling fast and well since leaving Constable Point," Frederick remarked. It was clearly a compliment.

"Yeah," replied John. "We like to travel light, like the Inuit. We call it getting down to our running weight."

Standing by the sleds, we shared lunch: our Italian salami, and their fruit drink and chocolate. We pored over maps, sharing route information and warning each other of dangers ahead in both directions. As we waved goodbye, they mushed toward Daneborg and we headed for Qaanaaq, almost 1,000 miles away.

CHAPTER 18

WEIGHING THE ODDS, AND NOT JUST FOR A SMOKE

By mid-April, the sun never goes down in the Arctic. By noon each day, the sunlight reflecting off the snow is so bright, snow blindness is inevitable after about 30 minutes. We knew the cold was about to ease up. We'd been carrying eight days of emergency rations and fuel. Expecting more stable weather, we cut it to a two-day supply.

We arrived at the Sirius hut on Cape Clarence Wycoff on April 17 after a 42-mile run. We searched the cape in vain for the 1900 stone cairn that explorer Robert Peary had built on a coastal high spot. We eventually concluded it had been buried in snow or dismantled by polar bears. Still, I could imagine Peary here. He'd have known he reached the northernmost part of Greenland a few days earlier. Short of provisions, he returned to Canada and his ship, which was frozen in a bay of Ellesmere Island.

This day, April 17, marked the fifth birthday I'd spent on an expedition. We'd saved a small ration of whiskey for the occasion, and John had a mother lode of old pipe tobacco he found under a bunk. Sadly, we had nothing to roll the tobacco in. "How about a piece of your Bible?" John urged. "It's about the right feel and thickness."

Our only remaining reading material was a copy of Nelson Mandela's *Long Walk to Freedom* and the Bible I'd brought along, not because I was religious, but because I'd never finished reading it, and I knew it would keep me occupied over many hours and many storm layovers. Besides, it was a good opportunity to better understand people whose faith was tied so firmly to these words. I was torn. Should I really use a page of the Bible to roll a cigarette? The superstitious part of me worried that if I smoked a Bible cigarette, it would come back to kill me.

"C'mon, Lonnie," John pleaded. "It's basically just a book."

I paged through the Bible uneasily. I'd already removed the heavy cover to save weight. At the back of the book I found a blank page. I smiled. John tore it out. With our Primus stove roaring, we sat, bare-chested, on bags of dog food in the overheated hut, sipped whiskey and smoked roll-your-owns like two kids in a fort.

Because the dogs' pads were developing thin spots and cracks from our long days on the trail, we eased up, rested more and gave them time to heal. I concocted a foot ointment from seal boot wax, Dermatone skin protector, antibiotic ointment, cod liver oil, vitamin E and lard. We rendered it all down and put the mixture in an empty cocoa container. Each time, it took us two hours to apply the salve to all 56 dog pads.

Most days, we now traveled on the ice foot—a narrow lane of flat ice along the coast—to avoid the Arctic Ocean pack ice, which was pressured into a chaotic mess of huge blocks. Walls of rubble had piled 30 feet high against the steep shoreline, often leaving only enough ice foot to squeeze through with the sled.

At camp on Cape John Flagler, just southeast of Frederick E. Hyde Fjord, John nudged me awake at 2 am. "There's a bear in camp," he said. Each night, we parked the dogs in three separate groups to cut down on squabbles and spread them out for better polar bear alerts. Now I could hear the dogs' unusual yipping. When I unzipped the tent door, I was shocked to see four white wolves just 40 feet away, two of them within inches of Knud and his gang.

These were the northernmost wolves in the world, most likely surviving on musk oxen, lemmings and the occasional seal pup. They had scruffy white bodies, lanky legs and large snowshoe-like paws. They looked demonic, with jet black eyes and noses in white-furred faces. They were all business: intense, cunning, deliberate in their moves. Knud stood up in front of his group, proud and prepared to defend his position as the alpha male. Showing their teeth, the two closest wolves approached him in a hunkered down stance, tails between their legs. I didn't believe they were really being submissive. They were trying to trick Knud so they could get close enough to jump him and kill him, but Knud held his ground, kicking snow backwards like a bull ready to charge. These wolves were accustomed to taking down 700-pound bull musk oxen. Knud had no way of knowing the wolves could take him easily, although it probably would have made no difference if he had understood.

The nearness of our other dogs, however, made the wolves cautious. They didn't like the odds. Then Quick stupidly decided this was the time to move off on his own to take a dump. Immediately, the wolves made a run for him. True to his name, Quick jumped swiftly back to his comrades. Wolves have been known to kill sled dogs in their traces, and if our dogs had been staked out in single file, I'm sure we would have lost one or more of them before we could have intervened. Evidently deciding there were just too many dogs grouped together, the wolves settled for eating leftover dog food on the ice, plus a few dozen piles of dog poop. As I took photos from the tent door, John whispered, "We're probably the first people these wolves have ever seen." Our presence didn't bother the wolves in the least. When they were finished, they walked away nonchalantly, carrying themselves with great poise.

When we broke camp, John and I made it down the coast to a Danish geological expedition cairn made by J.P. Koch in 1906 and on to Kaffeklubben (Coffee Club) Island, which is half a mile south of

Oodaaq Island, once considered the northernmost piece of land in the world. Oodaaq's exact location is N 83 40.565, W 30 39.511, a little more than 379 nautical miles from the North Pole. Many, like me, don't really consider it an "island" because it's really just a large gravel bar, 28 yards long, 14 yards wide and 3 feet above sea level. In summer, when the sea ice melts, a bit more of the "island" is exposed, mostly basalt shale, with a few pieces of quartz thrown in, but sometimes it disappears altogether.

We camped on the sea ice at the shore of Kaffeklubben Island and walked to the top of a gravel hill. We faced wind chills of -60°F. It was no place to stand around drinking coffee. In the distance, we saw a coast of snow-capped mountains, unvisited valleys and glaciers. We flew the flag of the National Geographic Society, but the wind was so strong we had trouble holding on to it.

Twenty miles to the west, where our next depot was located, was Cape Morris Jessup, which in Peary's day was believed to be the northernmost point of land. However, in 1969, Kaffeklubben was surveyed and found to be about a mile farther north. We arrived at Cape Morris Jessup, named for a Peary benefactor, in late afternoon, found our depot and located Peary's northernmost cairn. I could envision Peary's cold, weathered hands placing rocks on the pile, then scribbling a hasty note before yielding to the urgent need to keep traveling.

It warmed up on Easter Sunday, April 23, the very first day of this leg that John and I didn't have to work hard every minute to keep our hands warm. Typically, they numbed up at lunch and every time we untangled the dog traces. Even with the temperature at -15°F, it felt balmy to us after the truly extreme cold we had endured. I joked that the sun was so powerful we could bake potatoes on the sled. If only we had tin foil. Or potatoes for that matter. Summer was on the way.

Our course turned south for the first time at Weyprecht Fjord, and I felt we were finally headed home. Flat-topped mountains with sheer sides and narrow veins of glacial ice dominated our views to the east, west and south. The scenery was so magnificently pure I felt as if we were skiing in nature's cathedral. The dogs were less inspired with the surroundings; their focus was on getting through the deep snow. Fights broke out hourly, forcing us to stop at one point and stitch up wounds to one front leg and one scrotum—not easy medical procedures on the trail, especially the latter.

We were swimming in snow. Even with long skis, John and I sank to our knees. I felt sorry for the stubby-legged dogs we called the Oak Ridge Boys, and especially for Puff Ball, who was built very low to the ground. Days passed, and our only news that the outside world still existed came from John's small, static-impaired shortwave radio. We picked up English language programming from Kuwait, Russia, Canada and the BBC in London. We heard a lot about a Cuban boy being held in Florida while his relatives battled over him, and about ethnic fighting in a place called Chechnya. From our spot on the planet, everything seemed foreign and far removed.

Our high-frequency radio schedule was built around evening contacts on Mondays and Fridays. Each conversation with Sirius headquarters lasted about five minutes. We relayed our position, our condition and our route. At each depot and on rest days, I tried to relay information via satellite phone to the Web sites covering our project. I also got to speak with Kelly, who was back home in Minnesota. By now, she had found her own passion—art. She was doing linoleum cuts, illustrating books and working as a graphic designer.

April 27 brought the first real sign of spring. White snow buntings appeared, flapping their black-tipped wings. Buntings are a cheerful, energetic little bird, flitting about in tight little flocks. It was like seeing the first robin after a long winter. After weeks of traveling in a void, with not even animal tracks on the snow, the dogs were as captivated as John and I were. They ran after the birds flying close to the ground. Then one afternoon, John shouted, "Those boulders are moving." He wasn't hallucinating. Through our binoculars, I made out half a dozen dark brown, almost black, musk oxen. Their outer guard hair is 18 to 24 inches long, and they survive the most extreme wind and cold by foraging on moss and lichen. Their ancestors saved both the Peary and Rasmussen expeditions from starving.

As we mushed into May, the sun was so strong my eyes burned at night even with regular sunglasses. The UV rays reached my eyes from the sides. John had a pair of glacier glasses with side shields. I made a note to myself for the next expedition. We kept moving as quickly as we could toward our next depot at Frankfield Bay. Our main worry was escaping the deep, snow-filled fjords before warm weather slowed travel to a crawl, or, worse, stopped us dead in knee-deep slush and melt water.

The sled was light, and we were moving well. We were down to absolute necessities. We rounded Cape May in Wulffs Land on the first day of May. To the far west, I saw the mountains of Canada's Ellesmere Island, which felt like an extension of my backyard in northern Minnesota since I live so close to the Canadian border. Oh, how I missed trees.

It was a mild 23°F when we crossed Newman Bay and found the hut that contained our depot in Hall Land. We'd spent an exhausting 12 hours on the trail that day and were glad when the hut came into view. It was near the center of Polaris Lake, a dry, flat, gravelly glacial lake that stretches for miles above sea level. Through the last three days, gravel had played havoc with our plastic runners. We expected four more days of plastic abuse near Humboldt Glacier before we reached the ice cap. All we cared about was preserving enough plastic—an eighth of an inch or so—to get us across the cap and down the Tugto Glacier to Qaanaaq.

Now that it was warming up, the nasty aromas held at bay by the cold hung in the air, particularly the smell of dog poop on our gloves and clothing. Our stinky bodies, damp crusty socks and pungent long underwear were hard to take in the confines of the tent. Even outside, when the wind was just right, whenever we caught a whiff of ourselves, we yearned for a bath and clean clothes.

We'd traveled 1,422 miles since leaving Constable Point in February and had a 17-day push to make the last 368 miles to Qaanaaq. We pampered the dogs, feeding them from what amounted to an all-you-can-eat smörgåsbord of dried fish, lard and two varieties of pemmican. We also applied salve to their feet twice a day, clipped their nails and snipped off hair between their toes, which tended to collect snow and ice.

When we spilled onto the shores of Kennedy Channel, the majestic mountains of Ellesmere Island stood out across the pack ice, about 50 miles away. The channel created a nasty, cold north wind like the one that nearly killed us in 1998 when we stuck our heads around Cape Jefferson in search of a route north. Fortunately, the wind was now at our backs.

For the first time on the expedition, John and I came across old Inuit tent ring sites. Both were on the coast, at the mouths of small rivers dumping out of Hall Land. They were made of large stones, placed to hold down tent skins in circles about 10 feet across. This was a particularly desolate area of rock and gravel, barren in every way. I marveled again at how difficult life must have been for these most-northern nomads.

One day, a 40-mile-an-hour channel wind created a ground blizzard. I left the tent to retrieve our map case from the sled. With the case in one hand, I held up a map to confirm it was the one I needed. The wind snatched it from my grasp. Shock, then panic, washed over me as I watched the map fade away into white oblivion. I ran after the map in my camp socks, hoping it would snag on a piece of ice or something. It was -27°F. Camp socks are like bedroom slippers with nylon covers. Leaving a tent at all in that kind of weather was foolish, let alone wearing camp socks. Visibility was 50 feet as I ran unsteadily in the slippery socks. I bruised my feet on the hard ice. I slumped to my knees and wondered how long I could survive at -27°F wearing only light gloves and a flimsy wind shirt. I checked divots, cracks and overhanging slabs of pack ice for the map, but found nothing. I stood for a while, sadly pondering my options, before finally stumbling back into the wind.

I guessed our camp was about 200 yards away. No matter how tough it was to face directly into the raw wind, I dared not veer off if I hoped to find the tent. My camp socks gave me no traction. I grabbed pieces of pack ice to pull myself along. Fearful of passing the tent, I looked right and left every few paces. Finally, I spotted a ski, then a dog. I came into the tent bitterly cold and ready for the ass-chewing I deserved. We had another map of the area, but it was on such a small scale it was only slightly better than looking at a classroom globe. We needed details of river beds, lakes and their surrounding terrain to avoid rock fields and impassable gorges as we crossed Washington Land—the place that stopped us in 1998.

"Everything come out okay?" John joked, assuming that I'd gone to the bathroom.

As I told him I lost the map, his smile turned into a blank stare. Then the smile reappeared. "Not to worry, little buddy," he said in a patronizing tone. "Two days ago I entered all the critical areas of our route across rivers and frozen lakes to the ice cap as way points on our GPS." I could have kissed him. We checked the GPS and, sure enough, all the coordinates were there. John's attention to detail saved us perhaps a week of needless toil over uncharted ground.

On May 13, 2000, we camped at a latitude of N 80 20, a few miles from the northernmost point we'd reached in 1998 at Cape

Jefferson. We had completed the link, tied the knot and covered all of Greenland's north coast. But our happiness at this accomplishment was short-lived. Ahead of us was the most dangerous and challenging portion of the expedition. Rather than spending a small fortune airlifting our whole expedition 216 miles to Qaanaaq, we planned to pioneer an ambitious new route up an unnamed glacier to the ice cap, cross the Humboldt Glacier and then descend the Tugto Glacier half a day's journey north of the village. Crevasses were our biggest worry.

We camped on a frozen lake at the base of a glacier we called "the ramp" because the route up it looked gradual and crevasse-free. John and I decided to give it an Inuit name: Manighug, which means flat or smooth. On the map, it seemed the only feasible spot in the area to climb the ice cap safely. Taking extra care, I shaved the sled runners smooth for the last time. I wanted to make it as easy as possible for us and the dogs to climb the 4,600 feet to the ice cap plateau. The dogs watched me curiously as they gnawed once again on their frozen, nutrient-rich poop.

We informed Qaanaaq and Thule Air Base of our status and our estimated date of arrival. We planned to drive hard the last 216 miles, with the Tugto Glacier descent our last major objective. The slope up Manighug was so gradual we probably could have made it in a four-wheel drive vehicle. Soon we were onto the 65-mile-wide Humboldt Glacier, Greenland's largest. For safety, we were only skiing now. At one point, we crossed a snow bridge across a deep, blue crevasse. Luckily we reached the other side before we realized it. The white, empty expanse of the plateau was jarring after all the scenery along the coast. It was mentally challenging to push into miles of nothingness. The only thing that kept us from daydreaming into a coma-like state was the fear of coming across the occasional, hidden crevasse.

When we crossed crevasses, the dogs' legs sometimes poked holes in the snow bridges, exposing a dark abyss, while John and I glided over, supported by our skis. Further on, we confronted the more visible but equally dangerous melt-water crevasses, caused by torrents of water streaming off the plateau during past summer thaws. They were slick-sided and large enough to swallow large earth-moving machinery. Most gapped 40 feet wide and ran for miles, interrupted periodically by thin snow bridges. My heart pounded when I approached one of these crevasses and peered over the lip at the polished aqua blue walls. I backed up a step, then moved forward again for a better view. I could see no bottom.

The dogs were accustomed to seeing John and me dressed in thick, insulated fleece and fur clothing. One night, I stripped for a quick snow bath. It confused them. I no longer looked like a fur-clad Inuk, but some sort of pale, scrawny, hairless thing. They bolted up. I laughed and began imitating an ape, walking around in the snow, with one hand hanging limply over my head, and grunting. They cowered and gave me a chorus of growling barks. Such silliness broke the tension of our rugged journey.

Three days from Qaanaaq, I wrestled with a strange fear that came over me—of dying before we finished. I thought that it would be tragic to come all this way, overcome so many obstacles and see so many wonderful things, then not be able to share the experiences. The fear wasn't entirely baseless, because the most dangerous part of the trip lay just ahead, when John and I descended the Tugto and crossed its crevasses.

As we approached one melt-water crevasse, John led on skis to find a safe passage, while I stayed with the dogs. He probed with a basketless ski pole, looking for thin spots. The bored dogs had discovered it was fun to run after John or me on the ice cap when one of us got ahead, but now was not the time for that. I was putting away lunch and the thermos when the dogs bolted, trying to reach John on the other side of a deep crevasse.

I frantically threw myself on the bouncing sled and tried desperately to get the rope brake off the upstanders, all the while knowing we were getting close to the edge. At what point, I wondered, do I bail to save myself? That, of course, would have left John and me alone without dogs or supplies. A death warrant either way.

After struggling, I managed to slip the brake over the elusive runner, and the sled slowed enough for me to race ahead of the team, crack the whip and stop the dogs just a few feet from the crevasse. I couldn't help but imagine the dogs and sled lying at the bottom of the deep crevasse, with John and me standing on the lip looking down and knowing we would die of exposure or starvation barely more than 100 miles from Qaanaaq.

Back on the trail, our view of the glacier's base and Bowdoin Fjord was obscured by fog. Over the fog, we could see, 35 miles away, familiar landmarks around Qaanaaq. The sight was breathtaking. I could visualize people outside, taking advantage of the spring warmth, hunters pursuing game and seals sunning themselves on the fjord ice. The view from camp was daunting. Between black granite escarpments lay slippery blue ice. Distant ice falls and crevasse fields spread across our line of march. Halfway down, Tugto split in two around a point of land; the two spurs descended another gradual 4 miles to the base. We hoped to find safe passage along a strip of gravel and boulder-strewn moraine running down the middle.

Our map told us it was possible. The route would probably be no big deal for an experienced mountaineering team, but it was a far different challenge for a sled being towed by 14 dogs. We followed the moraine down the gradual descent, with the rope brakes kicking up snow and bits of gravel. John was ahead on skis. I controlled the sled.

Half-way down, to my astonishment, the moraine crossed a convergence of seemingly bottomless crevasses. We backtracked 200 yards, and John skied to reconnoiter what looked like a possible route.

He returned an hour later and reported that the steep, polished ice bottom made it impossible for proper footing. We had no choice but to cross to our right through a field of undulating, polished crevasses. The going was slick and hazardous.

At last we reached the western edge of the glacier. Between the glacier and land was a steep drop to a snow-filled corridor. I unhitched the dogs from the sled and passed the traces to John. Then I slipped a rope brake over the nose of each runner, grabbed the upstanders of the sled and teetered it on the lip of the drop. John was shaking his head as though I was nuts, but then gave me a thumbs up. I went over the edge like a bullet, trying frantically to dig my feet into the ice to slow down. By jerking on the right bystander and shifting my weight, I dodged a large boulder at the bottom and avoided an explosion of flying wood. With a margin that felt no thicker than a fox hair, I went from terrified wimp to Olympic gold medalist in the course of a 10-second run.

Wrapping the traces around his hand, John coaxed the dogs to the lip while I called to them. They began to pussy-foot near the edge, looking down at me and testing their footing. John scooted over the edge and slid down on his butt. The dogs followed, all ending up at my feet in a ball of snow and fur and rope, but apparently enjoying this new way of getting around. A mile down the corridor, we ran into a chasm in the ice that was 125 feet deep, 100 yards wide and 200 yards long. A huge flood of melt water apparently had eroded all the ice before us. Our jaws dropped as we surveyed the pit that was blocking our route.

"It's a canyon," I said, as John climbed a rocky outcropping to get a better view.

"Only thing we can do is climb out of this corridor and bypass the chasm along that slope," he yelled.

"Are you sure there's no other way," I yelled back.

"I'm positive," he said.

We pushed the sled from behind and shouted at the dogs to pull. John and I and the dogs, all sweat-soaked, inched our way back up out of the ice corridor and onto the face of the glacier. Carefully, we picked our way along the lip of the chasm and followed the only snow patch that offered any footing on a sea of polished blue ice. We were at such a steep angle I had to use a rope brake and steer the sled from the back to keep it from sliding sideways and dragging the whole works over the ice cliff. I gave a huge sigh of relief when we reached the edge of the glacier.

After 12 hours of heart-pounding work, we finally covered the 9 miles to the glacier's base. Our last camp at the top of the glacier had been at -20°F. At sea level it was 32°F. We thought our troubles were over when we realized we had to cross thin ice over a series of small melt-water lakes and a stream. Three-quarters of the way across, the ice broke and the dogs went for a swim. The sled rolled from one side to the other like a boat about to capsize. Only the air in our stuff sacks kept it afloat. John and I tried to maintain our balance as we stood on the last dry inch of the load as the swimming dogs pulled the sled toward shore.

Elements and accidents had regularly destroyed our cameras—we went through eight of them—and I contemplated a leap to shore to save my current one. Just then the sled sank deeper and John called out, "Where's Puff Ball?"

I took a quick head count. "My God, he must be under the sled," I yelled. John crawled to the front of the sled and leaned over between the runners, partly in the water. Finding a trace, he yanked on it. Coughing and sputtering, Puff Ball popped up between the runners.

"Poor bastard," John said. "His legs are too short for swimming. He must have held his breath for 30 seconds."

With a struggle, the dogs pulled themselves, and then the sled, onto thicker ice. We stood clear as they shook themselves dry. The dogs looked fluffy and renewed. Even Puff Ball looked as though he'd been groomed for the Westminster Dog Show. As much as John and I needed baths, we opted to wait until we reached Qaanaaq.

An hour later, Bowdoin Fjord opened before us, and on the western shore we spotted the sleds and tents of our friends Torben Diklev, Tine Lisby Jensen, Ooqaaq Duneq, his wife, Putu Kivioq, and their son. We had a glorious reunion: hugs, handshakes and rifle salutes. Tine commented on how well the dogs looked, and John volunteered with a straight face that we tried to bathe them regularly.

When we neared Qaanaaq on May 27, 2000, Qaavianguaq Qissuk was the first to greet us. With pride, he grabbed the traces of his four old dogs, Floppy, Puff Ball, Ray Charles and Doc—the ones we'd named the Oak Ridge Boys—patted them and tethered them to their old spots with the rest of his dogs. John and I had completed our 1,800-mile sled journey in 95 days, a giant step toward our goal.

We couldn't have done it without our dogs, in ways far beyond the obvious. They provided an endless source of inspiration and entertainment. Just trying to figure out what was going on in their brains was amusing. On one hand, they're as wild and beastly as any polar wolf, yet on the other hand, they are capable of a form of companionship—with conditions, of course. If you're walking ahead of a hungry team without a whip and fall, they will devour you, clothing, boots and all, then cough up the indigestible synthetic stuff later and wonder what happened to the sled driver. On the flip side, they'll defend you with their lives against a charging polar bear.

We had a little feast with Torben and Tine, eating auks, still in their feathers, boiled in a large iron pot. After dinner, Torben handed us a message from Rear Admiral Axel Fiedler of the Royal Danish Navy. The note welcomed us back to Qaanaaq and said, "Bravo! Well done! Furthermore, I wish to recognize your safety attitude and good communication during your speedy travel. Professional expeditions like yours will always be welcome traveling in Greenland."

Such good will was lucky for us, because we'd be coming back. John and I had not yet completed our goal of being the first to successfully circumnavigate Greenland.

CHAPTER 19

TACKLING A COUNTRY WITH A MIND OF ITS OWN

Greenland sets its own schedule. We had long downtimes waiting for the snow and ice we needed for dog sledding, and for the open water we needed for kayaking. It gave us the time we needed to rest from the rigors of this expedition. Even with our careful research and preparation, our Greenland expedition had morphed from a planned 15 months into a fourth year.

In the spring of 2001, while we waited for the weather we needed to return to Greenland, Kelly and I gave presentations in libraries and schools back home. We spread the word about our findings, and the dangers today's climate change poses for us all, but most especially the native people and animals of the Arctic. I used to talk about global warming. Now I talk about climate change. Even though the climate is warming at an alarming rate, shifting weather extremes can cause both abnormally cool periods and record-breaking heat waves. For many people, thinking of this as global warming is confusing. I find that the term "climate change" is more easily understood.

The earth's carbon dioxide levels remained fairly constant for 400,000 years. With human progress and the industrial age came fossil fuels, which caused atmospheric carbon dioxide levels to climb significantly. Carbon dioxide traps solar radiation from escaping through the atmosphere, thus increasing the earth's temperature. This higher temperature causes the polar ice cap and glaciers to melt, which in turn raises sea levels all over the planet. More than 100 million people around the world live within 3 feet of mean sea level. Scientists believe this disruption will eventually displace millions of people living on the world's coastlines, increase disease and result in even more severe weather all over the globe. Throughout Greenland, we had seen the results of climate change firsthand.

In late March of 2001, a full year after we left Qaanaaq, we returned to fill in the gaps. I flew into Thule Air Base and connected to a 45-minute helicopter ride to Qaanaaq. Once again, my friends Torben and Tine picked me up. My immediate task was to put together a fresh dog team. We had to sled from Qaanaaq to Savissivik, then across Melville Bay to Kullorsuaq, a distance of 400 miles. It took me three days to gather 12 dogs and three weeks to get them ready.

Three months earlier I had been contacted by Paul Schurke, with whom I had gone on the Bering Bridge Expedition. He was working on a project with the National Geographic Channel and asked me to guide some of his clients. That entailed lining up several Inuit hunters and dogs to haul them around. Their goal was to produce a half-hour documentary on Ussarqak Henson, the grandson of Matthew Henson, who accompanied Robert Peary to the North Pole in 1909. At first I was hesitant. I knew how rude and demanding film producers could be as they cope with deadlines and budgets. They also would have little knowledge of Inuit ways. The Inuits I knew did things in their own way and in their own time. And they weren't very good at taking orders. Despite my reservations, I agreed and met the group's Twin Otter when it landed on the fjord ice at Qaanaaq.

Out hopped John, six of Paul's clients and Kelly, who was traveling with us for 200 miles, as far as Savissivik. I wanted her to experience traveling by dog team with the Inuit. While I was involved with my Greenland expedition, Kelly had developed "Arctic Challenge," a Web teaching tool about our expedition. She had also written and illustrated a book based on my experience with the raven. *The Raven's Gift: A True Story from Greenland* had just been published.

On April 16, 2001, we set out for Savissivik: eight sleds, 108 dogs and several Inuit drivers dressed in polar bear, caribou and fox fur. One of our Inuit companions, my friend Mamarut Kristensen, was renowned as the area's greatest hunter. He was 325 pounds, mostly muscle. His weight, along with that of his wife, Tekumeq, and one of Paul's clients, plus their gear, required a 20-dog team and a wide 16-foot sled. Mamarut's pride required him to ride the sled every inch of the way. Tekumeq lived as a hunter's wife, sewing skins into beautiful fur clothing, skinning the 80 or so seals her husband dragged home every year in addition to ducks, walrus, narwhal and the occasional bear. Tekumeq was dressed traditionally in polar bear pants, seal-skin boots and a blue fox parka.

The star of the documentary, 63-year-old Ussarqak Henson, with his taut, bronze skin, appeared young for his age. His African facial features, inherited from his grandfather, were distinctive. He was a pleasant man and enjoyed mimicking our English. It's lucky he had a good sense of humor because the film crew and Paul's clients kept mispronouncing his name. They kept calling him "Ussagaq." Since that's the Inuit word for "big penis" there was no end to the enjoyment of Ussarqak's friends.

From Qaanaaq, we headed due south across the Ingelfield fjord to the hut at Itivdeleq, near the base of Politken Glacier. We set up camp and began chipping out 18-inch holes through the 6-foot-thick ice to fish for cod. Dripping sweat from chiseling through 5 feet of ice, I stopped what I was doing when Mamarut motioned me back and told me to cover my ears. He pointed his rifle into the hole, tilted his head to the side and fired off two shots. The sound echoed off the walls of the fjord and I expected to see an iceberg break loose from the reverberations. I looked into the hole but still couldn't see water. Mamarut grabbed the chisel and thrust it into the hole forcefully. Sea water gushed up like a fountain. "Yeehee," Mamarut shouted, as if he had just struck oil. We cleared the hole of ice chips and lowered heavy, spoon-shaped lures with treble hooks into the water. The lures were attached to several hundred feet of monofilament fishing line spooled on 2-foot boards with a notch in each end. We dropped them 140 feet to the bottom, raised them 2 feet, and jigged up and down. When we felt a fish strike, we ran away from the hole until the fish flew out. The constant jigging kept us warm in the crisp evening chill. By morning, we had caught 70 cod from 14 to 20 inches long. We cleaned them, and threw the heads and guts to the dogs.

On April 17, I celebrated my 40th birthday. Kelly whipped up an "instant cheesecake" in the hut. I'll never forget the view—an aqua-blue iceberg frozen in place just offshore, a small glacier to our left and friends fishing on the ice.

We hitched up the dogs again and moved west around Steensby Land, where we turned south. We crossed over thin ice at Camp Radcliffe and eventually were forced to leave the ice for a short, overland route across the Sermipaluk Glacier into Booth Sound. We headed toward Thule Air Base across Wolstenholme Fjord. The sun's strong rays reflected off the snow, and fried my nose and lips. It was odd that you could cook on the outside and freeze on the inside. I noted that all along the coast to the south, as far as Crimson Cliffs and on to Kap York, there was open sea. The Inuit said it opened more each year, a sign of climate change. So much open water along the coast had been unheard of in mid-April. "It's not supposed to be," Mamarut muttered.

Once-reliable sled routes were disappearing, and we were forced onto an alternative route along a rocky river bed to the ice cap, just south of Thule Air Base. Ussarqak spotted our first seal, sunning itself on the ice. I loaned my skis to Mamarut. He glided quietly forward, crouching behind a kamotahut, a miniature hunting sled that held his rifle. A white, canvas screen in front of the sled served as camouflage. Every 30 seconds, the seal lifted his head to see if a bear was around. Each time it looked up, Mamarut crouched low and was still. When the seal lowered its head and resumed its sun bath, Mamarut moved. It can take up to an hour to close on a seal. A head shot is needed for an instant kill. A wounded animal will lunge back down a breathing hole and disappear.

Mamarut advanced to within 50 yards of the seal. Through binoculars, I saw him take aim. His dogs' ears perked up. Even at that distance, they recognized what was about to happen. Bang! The seal's head flew back in a spray of blood. Not even a flipper twitched. There was no suffering. Mamarut held the skis in the air and shouted, "Skis namato." Skis good.

When we reached him, Mamarut was fishing out the small intestine through a hole in the seal's abdomen. Several yards of the pink innards were piled at his feet. He made a slit in the intestine every 6 inches and then ran his fingers along it to squeeze the greenish brown contents into the water. Mamarut stripped the skin and fat, laid the seal on the bottom of the sled, and placed a tarp over it to keep the greasy fat from getting all over everything.

Underway again, we struggled through thigh-deep snow in Deads Fjord, following a peninsula that brought us to Cape York. By late afternoon, a storm moved in just as we reached land's end. Just a few hundred yards from this point, land-fast ice met drifting pans of sea ice heading north with the current. Perched on a steep hill were two hunting huts and several century-old Inuit dwelling sites, from which I could see for miles in a 180-degree arc. It was easy to understand why this place was chosen for a camp. A hunter could spot bears, seals, narwhal and belugas miles away. We huddled in the huts and waited out the storm, playing cards with the hunters and eating our new "delicacy"—seal intestine cut into 3-inch lengths and boiled into chewy little sausages. I dubbed it "Eskimo rigatoni." In reality, it tasted like al dente fish noodles.

When the weather cleared the next morning, we set out for Savissivik, 25 miles away, stopping halfway on the sea ice to fish for Greenland halibut. Hunters from Savissivik had left a large spool of fishing line on a hand-cranked transom. We cut a 3-foot-square hole in the ice, baited hooks with Arctic squid and sent the line, with hooks 15 feet apart, into the hole. A heavy piece of sheet metal shaped like the bill of a baseball cap was hooked to the end. Once under the ice, it was designed to pull the line horizontally away from the hole along the sea floor. We drank tea and napped for three hours, then pulled in the line, which took an hour and a half. We removed the fish, baited the hooks again, and sent the line back down.

Halibut are flat, with both eyes on the same side of their head. One side is milky white, the other dark and scaly. As we pulled up the line, fresh halibut joined their cousins on the ice. Some hooks were empty, but others had caught a small type of Arctic stingray. Once the dangerous barb was removed from its tail, it became dog food.

For fun between fishing sets, Mamarut made a small target on a piece of wood and stuck it in the snow 50 yards away. The prize for the best shot was a harpoon head and a knitted wool cap. When my turn came, I pulled the shot and missed the 3-by-8 inch target completely. Before Kelly even aimed, the rifle went off; she was unfamiliar with the hair trigger. The shot missed the target by several feet. Mamarut fell over face first, then rolled over with his feet in the air. Everyone laughed hysterically. I joined the play by doing a low crawl, keeping my head down, to retrieve the rifle. John nailed the bull's-eye on his first shot, winning the prizes and a round of applause.

Three miles from Savissivik, one of my dogs put his leg through the thin ice. Sitting on the sled, I nervously surveyed the area. Fortunately, it was an isolated thin spot; the rest of the ice looked stable. I wondered though about ice conditions to the south. It was only late April. The ice should have been at its thickest.

At Savissivik, we staked the dogs on the sea ice in front of the village. Polar bear hides were stretched over a frame atop meat racks, and old, scarred-up bear dogs were tied to its base. As I walked through the village, I could see how it had changed since our visit nearly four years earlier, in August 1997. Two houses had been added, and the village looked cleaner, with several feet of snow covering the garbage that accumulated in the summer—cans and bottles alongside the bones of seals, narwhal, walrus and bears. The people behaved as they had for centuries, discarding their garbage on the tundra, some of which decomposed and fertilized moss, grass and Arctic flowers.

Over tea, at a house high above the sea ice, the hunters agreed that we had to hunt seals if we were to cross Melville Bay. They said the snow between Savissivik and Kullorsuaq was too deep for us to carry enough food in the sled. Even an average sled load would be too difficult to transport. I looked out the window and considered the idea. I counted five seals on the ice. They were everywhere. Maybe we could do it.

We heard the hum of an airplane and ran outside. The arriving plane carried Paul Schurke and the film crew. Soon my Inuit friends would be working for these "invaders." Hoping it would work out for the best, I consoled myself with the idea that the Inuit could use the income to buy items that would make their lives easier.

John and I traveled on alone, and as soon as we left Meteorite Island, we confronted knee-deep snow, riding on 8 inches of water overflowing the sea ice. We waded through the snow and pushed the sled to help the dogs. We were soon drenched with sweat in the heat

151

of the sun. The exhausting work was made even more difficult by our efforts to keep the water out of our mukluks. When it began to snow so hard we could no longer navigate, we called it a day. We'd traveled only 4 miles.

Thinking we might make better time in cooler air that would firm up the snow, we packed up camp after a five-hour rest and tried traveling at night. John broke trail on skis. Waiting by the sled, I felt the overflow soaking into my newly dried mukluks. I shifted around, trying to find a patch of snow that would support me, but to no avail. It was just too soft. John was out only 300 yards when, to my horror, his poles sank to mid-shaft through thin ice. Backing up on his skis, he desperately tried to keep from plunging into the cold water head first. He looked at me and put his hand over his heart, as if to signal its frantic beating. Then he poked his poles through the ice six more times as he moved around trying to find a safe route.

"It's thin ice everywhere!" he yelled. We seemed to be on a small peninsula of ice capable of holding us, 4 miles out at sea. Icebergs towered around us like skyscrapers. The nearness of the floating crystal monoliths concentrated the sea current, undermining the ice until it was paper thin. As we gingerly backtracked to Meteorite Island, I watched in fright, my heart pounding, when the dogs put their legs through the ice. It was incredibly difficult for them to get any traction. I had no idea what kept us from sinking. At times it seemed as if the tension of the snow alone kept us suspended above the water. We only managed an agonizing mile an hour.

It was the morning of April 29, 2001, and while we still hadn't made it around Greenland, we had nearly rounded Meteorite Island in our effort to seek a safe way south. East of the island, two of my dogs broke through the ice. I yelled to them to pull with all their might. As I helped them move the sled, I broke through with one leg and thought we were all going down, but the ice ahead was slightly firmer, and we

152

managed to escape. Discouraged again, we pushed back toward shore. Three miserable days without progress was enough. We needed to return to Savissivik and regroup.

A mile from the village, the ice broke under the dogs and sled, and two dogs plunged into water that was deeper than I would have thought possible so close to shore. We ran up and yanked them out by their heads. The two dogs scratched for good footing, and the remaining dogs jumped to safe ice. We entered the village late in the afternoon. It was not a triumphant return. "Siqu iorpoq," I said. The ice was no good.

A storm blew in that evening. Hunters in Kullorsuaq called Savissivik and told us not to come because of an extremely dangerous combination of deep snow, thin ice and overflow all the way across. John pushed hard to continue, which is why he was such a great companion on this expedition. He didn't want Melville Bay to beat us for a second time. No one wanted to cross the damned bay more than me, but we had to make realistic plans based on the information available to us. The storm intensified, which kept us hunkered down in the village for 48 hours. The hunters from Kullorsuaq called again to tell us that the wind had broken up all the ice on Melville Bay and moved it out to sea.

On the bright side, it was shaping up to be a good year for crossing by kayak. Once again, Greenland gave us no choice. The sledding season was over. We would have to return, paddles in hand, to Melville Bay in July. I was also grateful we weren't out at sea when the ice broke up.

When the storm died out, we spent another five days hanging around the village enjoying the company of its Inuit residents. The view from the village was as breathtaking as those from most Greenland communities. We could see for miles in the clear air. A panoply of icebergs adorned the sea, and snow-covered mountains graced the coast. The 24-hour sunlight spread a warm hand over everything.

At the end of the first week of May, the first auks arrived, another sign of spring. When the first 12 birds showed themselves, the hunter Apalanguaq went out with a long-handled net and caught them. His mother, perhaps 80 years old, squatted as limberly as a child next to the oil stove and began parting the feathers. Inuits use every part of the bird. Hundreds of thousands of these little waterfowl arrive from the sea and nest in the rocks behind the village. The locals catch tens of thousands, a few at a time, in modified butterfly nets. What they don't eat, they sell to people in other villages.

Lifting off in the weekly helicopter to Thule, we asked our pilot to fly around Cape York and along the coast to the air base. Nothing but open sea water lay where we had sledded two weeks earlier.

CHAPTER 20

REGROUPING FOR ANOTHER TRY

I returned to Minnesota and John went home to Australia. We realized it would be a logistical hurdle of the highest order for us to finish the three remaining legs of our circumnavigation—about 1,100 miles of untraveled coastline—but we were determined to try. Through the rest of May and early June 2001, I worked on developing a fresh plan with a strict schedule. Our window of opportunity was from June 27 to August 21, 2001, the start of the storm season. We would chopper to Paamiut in June and kayak our remaining 200 miles south to Qaqortoq. Two Minnesota friends were joining us on this leg. Buck Benson, from Grand Marais, is a skilled paddler, mountaineer and supporter of our Greenland undertaking. Brian Bergeron of Duluth is a marathon runner and family practitioner who would serve as our doctor for this leg. They would also help with photography. After that first leg, we would fly northwest to Kullorsuaq and try, once again, to cross Melville Bay. Finally we would head for the east coast and kayak 690 miles from Constable Point to Ammassalik.

When I left, I wasn't sure we could complete the rounding in this single sojourn. Gazing out the helicopter window as I returned to Greenland, I was encouraged to see a relatively ice-free sea with icebergs floating lazily in the fjords, and the colorful pitched roofs of Paamiut's houses. Our contact, Birger Knutsen, greeted me when the helicopter settled on the pad. He'd been in Greenland for two decades and made his living as a jack of all trades. He drove me to the docks to collect our supplies from one of our sponsors, the Royal Arctic Line. We loaded the kayaks, food and fuel, and dropped them off at the exact same spot from which we had departed in 1997. I was glad to see John when he arrived that night. "Deja vu all over again," I said as we shook hands.

"Let's knock the bugger off," he replied. He was as eager as I was to finish rounding Greenland. We unwrapped the kayaks and packed them with gear, food, fuel, a shotgun, communications equipment, first aid materials and a new set of cameras. It was time to begin paddling once again.

On the sunny morning of June 27, 2001, Brian, Buck, John and I slid our kayaks into cold, clear water. I relished the familiar scent of salt water and seaweed as we paddled out of Paamiut. Only the occasional bobbing piece of ice interrupted the surface. We were pleasantly surprised by the great weather, which was not very common in this part of Greenland.

The first night, we camped 30 feet above the rocky coastline on a few square feet of grass and moss. During that night's rain, we discovered our first mistake on this leg. The new single-wall tent we'd chosen for lightness worked about as well as a plastic trash-can liner.

Forty-five miles south of Paamiut, we negotiated heavy ice as we came into the abandoned village of Narsilik. When we paddled up to a rundown dock in the center of the village, we could see stinky, pale carcasses of seal and fish floating half-submerged in the water. A family on a boat outing from Sisimiut was staying in the only painted and well-kept building, which they maintained for hunting trips. Wet and cold, we were happy to be invited inside for cookies and coffee.

Beautiful, clear days showed off the peaks of Greenland's mountains and the clean lines of the coast ahead. The sun was warm. At times there wasn't a ripple on the water. One day as we glided along, we spotted something in the water a few feet ahead of us: a young seal, suspended in the water with its head tilted back. Only its whiskers and nose broke the surface of the water. The pup was so still I wondered if it was alive. When I gave it a light nudge with my paddle, the seal looked up at me, focused its sleepy eyes into a look of fright, and, spraying us with sea water, dove into the black oblivion, That night, our tents were nestled in the middle of a small cobblestone bay facing the open ocean. Two icebergs guarded the entrance. Behind our camp, two Greenland eagles, much larger than the American bald eagle, flew against the backdrop of a mountain amphitheater.

As the calendar turned to July, we paddled south into a sound within sight of the interior ice cap. This narrow inland waterway, far from the rough seas of the outer coastline, was the safest route. We spent most of July 4 with our heads down and arms burning as we bucked 3-foot seas into a 25-mile-an-hour headwind. Finally, the white caps and driving rain shut us down. We were tired and chilled.

"Lonnie, let's get camp set up quickly," Buck said. "Brian is really cold." I could see right away by Brian's slow movements and slurred speech that he was hypothermic. We got busy erecting the tents and warming something to drink. Brian recovered within an hour of getting hot liquid and dry clothes. As the wind and rain continued through the night, we became human sponges in our sleeping bags, soaking up the puddles on the floor. We spent the next 48 hours in the damp sleeping bags, with cold, soggy air aggravating our achy joints.

It was still raining on July 5, but we set out in damp clothes anyway and paddled headlong into the weather. We just couldn't take the wet camp any longer. After a few hours, we were stiff and hypothermic, and our joints felt as if they were glued together. We pitched the tent and cooked a large bowl of afternoon oatmeal, fortified with brown sugar and butter, washed down with mugs of butter-fortified hot cocoa. In 45 minutes we were back to normal. After a short nap we were back in the kayaks. By the end of a very difficult day, the clouds lifted and we glided into Qissaqniut under a full moon. We ate our fill of energy-rich whale meat that night and slept comfortably for the first time in three days.

On July 8, we paddled through dense fog. By afternoon, the sun had eaten through the mists, revealing a fox scavenging for carrion in the dry seaweed along the gravel beach. Its white winter fur was shedding into a summer gray. Like us, the fox was searching for a meal. In a small bay, we stopped to boil and eat mussels. The busy village of Qaqortoq was just 2 miles ahead.

It felt good to have completed this leg of the expedition, where we'd been stopped short in 1998. This dangerous section of coast, known for its convergence of currents and notoriously bad weather, had been kind to us this time. Brian and Buck left us at Qaqortoq, and John and I thanked them for their companionship.

This was the end of our time in southern Greenland. It was time to shift our focus to Melville Bay in the far northwest. We took a chopper from Qaqortoq to Narsarsuaq, and from there we took a twin-engine plane to Upernavik, where we got another chopper to the northwest, to Kullorsuaq. We had heard that hunters from Savissivik and Kullorsuaq had been hunting narwhal in Melville Bay. That meant land-fast ice had broken away from shore, which should make the remaining ice navigable.

Still, it was difficult to know what lay in store for us. Melville Bay is a desolate, uninhabited body of water, normally full of ice, and exposed to the inland ice cap. The bay always harbors the potential of high winds. It is 190 miles wide, with Kullorsuaq at the south end and Savissivik at the north end. If a straight line were drawn between the two villages, it would intersect a series of very small weather-scrubbed islands, roughly 15 miles from the coast and 14 to 24 miles apart. We chose that route to avoid the dangerous ice-filled coastline with calving glaciers and few places to pitch a tent. Our worst fear was being caught in a storm between islands. If that happened, our bodies would wash up lashed to a broken kayak on Canada's Baffin Island about 500 miles to the west. There would be no stopping. We had to push through to each island—no matter how long it took, no matter what kind of weather we encountered, no matter how much ice we had to cross.

Locals watched as John and I stuffed the kayak with food, stove gas and other provisions. We started our facing high waves, and after 11 miles of early evening paddling, set up camp near an old hunting hut on the same island where Knud Rasmussen had erected a trading post. The hut still stood there, a short walk from our camp. Throughout the night, icebergs exploded, throwing chunks of ice skyward and into the sea. The vibrations shook the hut and kept us awake most of the night.

The next day we pushed for 13 hours and made 28 miles to a lonely island. All rock, except for a few blades of grass and mounds of seagull droppings, this speck in the vast bay rose only 20 feet above sea level. It provided no fresh water, no food and no shelter from the beating winds, just security from a potentially hostile sea.

Each morning, we looked forward to getting underway. The euphoria of moving—and realizing that with each stroke we grew closer to the culmination of our dream—kept us motivated for about two hours. For the rest of the day, we just toughed it out. With no chance to stretch or take a break, a 10-hour day of paddling tested our wills. Still, with water as smooth and clear as a mirror, one day we made 24.5 miles, our longest single crossing so far. Ibuprofen helped.

Halfway into our paddle to Thom Island, we landed on an unnamed group of islands. I named them Kelly in English, after my wife, and Mikisoq, Small Islands in the Inuit tongue. Their position is N 75 32, W 59 45. We discovered another unmarked Thule Inuit site. From the pile of bones—from sled dogs and poar bears—we could tell that these rock-and-sod dwellings, like those at Kupeqarlik, were the winter camp of Inuits who hunted with dogs near the floe edge. With nothing to hunt in the summer, they could not have been here any other time of the year.

The water shifted from dark gray to fluorescent green, a result of microscopic algae absorbing the sunlight. Miles out to sea, we sometimes thought we saw the bottom of the ocean, but it was only layers of bright algae. Heading north, the sun was our clock: hot on our backs at noon and straight west by 6 pm. Although the sun never set, it dimmed and a cool breeze marked the start of night. We Velcroed our pogies—neoprene waterproof mittens—to our paddle shafts to keep our hands warm in the evening. By this time of day our legs were numb and our backs were stiff from a full day bent in our kayak. The joy of peeling off our damp dry suits and walking around at the end of each day was just slightly tainted by the odor that escaped our suits' latex neck gussets: a mixture of crusty sock smell, body odor and urine. A neat pee was nearly impossible from a stiff, waterproof relief zipper, especially after a 20-mile crossing.

Two-thirds of the way across Melville, we were forced to push, pull and gaff-hook the kayak over thin ice on the last half of our jump to Brant Island. Steep, it offered no flat place for a tent. We finally settled on two narrow ledges 50 feet above the water that were just wide enough for our sleeping bags. Tight against the cliff, I placed flat-sided rocks between my bag and the edge of the cliff in case I rolled over in my sleep. We had neighbors, but not welcoming ones. Between mating rituals, nesting guillemots and gulls squawked and dive bombed us all night long.

The ice pans became denser and more concentrated as we got closer to Savissivik. We gaff-hooked to get around them. Always nervous that the ice would delay us for a day or more, or force us to drag the kayaks, we climbed as high as we could on our last island to assess the conditions ahead. Peering through binoculars at the ice floe, I heard what sounded like a motor.

It was an umiatsiaq, an open boat with an outboard motor. Two of them, in fact. I grabbed the shotgun and fired off three greeting shots, a traditional Inuit way of communicating. The boats turned and headed towards us. Soon, our friends Peter and Markus Hansen, plus three other hunters, tied up their boats. We celebrated our meeting with a feast of chocolate, dried fruit, cheese and crackers, which we ate while lounging on the sun-warmed ledge rock. We washed the meal down with the customary Inuit tea. Our friends were well-stocked for a long boat journey to hunt narwhal and then visit relatives in Kullorsuaq.

When we finally reached the north end of Melville Bay, we saw—on a large south-facing slope of the mainland—the first significant green vegetation we'd seen since Upernavik. A nesting auk colony had deposited enough guano to provide a platform for moss and other Arctic plants to flourish. A storm was brewing to the south, bad weather that would probably catch up to us the next day. As we paddled around the cape and the water grew rougher, we rode high on the waves. We were nervous that conditions would worsen before we reached the safer ice pans. When we made it safely to a pan about a mile in diameter, we put on our harnesses and pulled the kayak past a thousand-pound bearded seal too busy scratching itself to pay any attention to us.

The pan ended at a large concentration of massive icebergs pushed tightly up against Meteorite Island behind Savissivik. We nervously threaded our way through this city of ice, fearing we would be crushed by falling ice any second. By 8 pm, we rounded the last bend of the island to Savissivik and saw people gathering on the beach. Auks flew overhead on their way to their nesting rocks behind the village houses. Our third attempt to cross Melville Bay was the charm. Just short of the village, John and I stopped paddling long enough to shake hands.

CHAPTER 21

GATHERING REINFORCEMENTS
FOR THE FINAL LEG

Only one leg of 690 miles remained in our quest to round Greenland. There was good reason to leave this leg on the Blosseville Coast for last. We didn't expect it to be kind to us. On July 24, I looked out the left side of the plane from Kulusuk to Constable Point at the most stunning mountain vista I had ever seen. Layers of crumbling basalt stair-stepped in contours until the peaks disappeared in the clouds. Rivers of ice, moving at a snail's pace to the sea, covered valleys below. To my right, sheer mountains rose 3,000 to 4,000 feet from the sea for almost 700 miles. This was the Blosseville Coast, beautiful but uninviting and uninhabitable.

Station Chief Benny Musinski, whom we'd met during our 2000 dog-sled journey north, greeted us but also brought us bad news. The ship with our kayak and supplies couldn't get through the ice to deliver cargo. We panicked as we watched the ship turn around and head north out of the fjord. It wouldn't return for another three weeks, and we couldn't afford to wait that long. John headed for the communications room to plead with the captain. I paced the end of the runway, watching the ship drift out of sight into the fog.

"Lonnie!" John shouted, a positive note in his voice. The ship had stopped because of the fog. If the fog lifted, the captain promised to load a chopper with our supplies. An hour later, a chopper descended out of the fog with our loaded kayak slung underneath. We were so delighted to get the kayak and our supplies, we celebrated with the station crew until 4 am. What I remember, dimly, is taking turns dancing with the cook and receiving a bath of sorts. It was really just a rinsing with some kind of Danish liquor. Later that morning, with thick heads, we packed up the station's old Toyota pickup, and Benny gave us a ride to the beach. Everyone else was too hung over to see us off. We traveled just 6 miles before we let ourselves be enticed by a flat patch of soft tundra on the shore. We camped and let our bodies recover from the celebration.

The next day we left the entrance of Hurry Fjord and passed in front of the village of Cape Hope. From a quarter-mile out, we could see villagers feeding dogs and throwing wash water out of their modest shacks. Even from a distance, the place looked dirty and greasy from all the garbage and seal fat. The villagers waved, and we waved back. We knew they were the last human beings we'd see for a month and a half.

The wind picked up, and so did my worries about the unknowns ahead. The section of coast we were about to travel deserved great respect. When we camped at Cape Tobin, I looked south across 16 miles of Scoresbysund's fjord to Cape Brewster. At 6:40 on the morning of July 31, the skies were cloudless, with a slight breeze from the south. It was a sign of stable weather, exactly what we'd hoped for to make this crossing. Even though the weather was good, the waves were fairly large as we approached the center of the fjord, the largest in the world. With heads bent, we leaned forward at our waists to get purchase with our paddles. We bucked the wind for several miles before making camp on a narrow gravel beach. This was the last big "have-to" crossing of the expedition, and we were happy to put it behind us.

On August 1, we faced a heavy frost, and I wondered whether we would make it to Ammassalik before the ice-up. John and I pulled on almost all of our clothing. Given the cold, we'd probably only last 30 minutes in the water, even in a dry suit. We paddled close to shore whenever we could. We watched as guillemots and appats, fat from the summer abundance, bounced their bellies off the waves and kicked hard as they made several attempts to get airborne. Farther out to sea, two bearded seals patrolled the edge of the ice pans as they searched for ducklings.

From our cockpits, we looked up at tall, gray, blunt headlands that stretched for miles along the coast, one after another, like soldiers guarding the inland ice. Three narwhals showed themselves between ice pans during our lunch break on the ice. The wildlife viewing was a treat, but we still had to face the headwinds, which we just could not beat. After a week of paddling our guts out, we switched to night travel, from 9 pm to 6 am, when the winds were less severe.

Our minds were completely focused on the simple task of paddling and on how much closer each stroke took us to the end of our journey. On August 5, we spent almost 12 hours in the kayak. On August 6, we saw three sets of fresh polar bear tracks crisscrossing the snow near the waterline at Cape Barklay. The bears had been transported to the area from the north on the polar ice that surrounded us. They'd hopped ashore to hunt seals. When we camped, we erected a trip wire around the tent and slept with the shotgun at our feet. The flare pistol was in the tent pocket near our heads.

By morning, skim ice about a quarter-inch thick had formed in the bay where we were camped. We launched our kayak, breaking the clear ice into jagged plates. We jammed down hard with our paddles, cutting into the ice. I saw more bear tracks in the snow 50 yards to our right and, with my eyes, followed them up the slope. Two bears stood high above us. They had dug a shallow cave in the deep snow to lay down and cool off. Unaware of our presence, they swatted their massive paws at each other in play, and rolled and slid in the snow. They were large, 800 to 1,000 pounds each, and to our relief, they looked fat and satisfied. They appeared to be a mother and her three-year-old offspring. When the mother bear heard our paddles thwacking the ice, she rose to her haunches, trying to catch our scent. "That's a big animal," John whispered.

The mother bear dropped to her belly and slid down the long slope like an otter, heading in our direction. For the first time, I felt extremely vulnerable strapped in a kayak. As the mother drew closer, she disappeared into a dip in the hill. We were trapped between the ice pack and land in a narrow band of water 50 feet wide. John fumbled for the flare gun. I reached for the shotgun.

There she was, huge and intimidating, right at the water's edge. Her muscles rippled under fur that was more yellow than white. I dug frantically in my pocket for a shotgun shell while John paddled gingerly ahead through the lead of open water. I knew the water provided us no safety. This bear could swim like a seal and peel us from the cockpits in seconds. We were easy prey, but we were still downwind so she didn't yet know what we were. Maybe a walrus or a large, frolicking seal. Gradually we came upwind, and she caught our scent

164

with her swinging nose. She retreated, racing down the shore, clearly not attracted to unbathed humans. "I didn't think we smelled that bad," John said. "Didn't we use a scented wet wipe a week ago?"

After a night's sleep dreaming of polar bears, we found ourselves in a fog, 2 miles offshore, push-poling the kayak with our paddles and gaff-hooking our way through the ice. Eventually the fog grew too thick to go on. The hard going frayed our nerves, and once again we bickered and contradicted each other, over almost everything—the weather, the route, the ice, our campsites. If you're well-suited on an expedition, you end up behaving like a long-married couple. John and I had been "tied at the hip" for long enough to know that these were trivial matters, and that the tension would dissipate soon enough. Both stoic by nature, neither one of us wanted to talk about our feelings. So we didn't.

It was August 8 and we'd pushed hard since we'd left Paamiut in late June. We still had a long way to go, and it was becoming difficult to find the drive and motivation day after day. John had been unusually quiet the past three days. It was the first time on the expedition I had seen him in such a melancholic mood. We saw bear tracks in the snow and sand around our camp before we went to sleep. In a dream during the night, bears rolled around in my head until I bolted upright, sweating. Half asleep, I shouted, "John, a bear!" Sleeping head to toe, with a door at each end, we both grabbed for a window zipper and searched our camp for signs of a marauder.

"There's no bear," John snarled, irritated at being woken from a sound sleep.

"Well, better safe than sorry," I said meekly.

By morning, the wind had compressed the sea ice tightly against the coast. It looked almost impossible to get through to Cape Dausey. We worried that we might be stuck for a long time. That night, we woke at 2:30 am to check the pack ice. Looking through binoculars,

I saw nothing encouraging. "Everywhere is still a jam sandwich," I shouted to John.

At 5 am we poked our heads out again and this time saw that the ice had started to release its grip on the land. It was time to move again. A raven had been following us for two days, seemingly curious about what we were doing. At times, I fantasized that it was "my" raven, the one I freed on Greenland's west coast. High tide brought more water, separating the ice pans as we set out at 6 o'clock the morning of August 11. We were upbeat again. The wider lanes of open water meant less wiggling and gaff-hooking through tight passages. Farther out to sea we had fair going, at least until we needed to return to land. That required us to manhaul the last mile, jumping from ice floe to ice floe, all refrigerator-sized bobbing chunks of ice. Often, the edges of the ice broke and we ended up in the water up to our armpits. Thank goodness for the dry suits.

The first half of the next day we dragged the kayak over ice pans and hop-scotched from ice chunk to ice chunk. At times, we chose pieces too small and ended up in the drink. Other times, we made leaps that would have done an Olympian proud. Hampered by the bulky, inflexible dry suits, we sometimes landed with arms out, seeking a hold, while our legs dangled in the water. The obstacle course made the day exciting, but it also strained our arms and shoulders.

The next morning, I was so tired I put on my dry suit backwards. Morning fog forced us to spend half the day in the tent. It was John's birthday, his third in Greenland. I gave him one of my cameras as a gift because his had gotten pulled off the kayak by a passing piece of ice. I passed the time writing in my journal and reading Neale Donald Walsch's *Conversations with God: An Uncommon Dialogue*. I was looking for an antidote to fog.

With supplies dwindling and ice compressed firmly against shore, we elected to wedge our way 4 miles out to the open sea. After several hours fighting our way through the band of floating crystal, we rested on the last floe. Clear paddling lay ahead of us. We ate our last energy bar, and watched a seal swim around the perimeter of the ice pan while it, in turn, checked us out.

August 15 was our first day without coffee, our only luxury, and that left me a bit ill-tempered. We also ran out of sugar, which did nothing to improve my mood. I was really looking forward to our Soldalen depot. We'd covered 324 miles from Constable Point, a little less than halfway. I shot three guillemots, seabirds that taste like wild duck. We boiled them in a pot and drank the greasy, calorie-rich broth off the top. We needed the fresh protein to help repair our worn muscles. Warmed by the broth, we grabbed the carcasses and ravenously picked the meat from the bones with our teeth.

As we paddled into Mikis Fjord, we passed two magnificent veins of copper in the mountain wall leading down to the water. It was turquoise, like an old copper-roofed parliament building in Europe. I wanted to dig out a loose chunk with my knife, but it was a couple of feet higher than I could reach from the kayak.

Our Soldalen depot was at an uninhabited Danish geological outpost, 3 miles up Mikis Fjord. A back-up depot had been placed at Aputiteq Island, which we would reach with a few more days' paddling. We had to pull our kayak the last mile up a shallow stream. Nestled in this steep-sided fjord, protected from the open coast, this warmer ecosystem boasted low tundra grasses and purple saxifrage. After weeks of seeing nothing but ice and scoured rock, we welcomed both the warmth of the air and the colors of the vegetation.

We were also grateful for the 6-mile, round-trip hike we needed to take to get our supplies from the depot. We needed the exercise for our atrophied legs, which looked more like whooping-crane than human legs. Kayaking provides an excellent workout for the upper body, but doesn't do anything for the legs. We headed up a small valley and found the outpost where our depot was sheltered: two red, 10-foot by 16-foot, plywood huts assembled on a flat, dry riverbed left by a receding glacier. Next to the modular huts was a gravel landing strip with red plywood markers every 100 feet. Inside the hut, we found an old can of Danish curry and a box of rice on a shelf. We heated it on our mountain stove and washed it down with cups of thick, hot coffee. Back at the kayak, we erected the tent and celebrated once again the feat of staving off starvation. We drank our eight-day ration of medicinal whiskey in one sitting.

Out of Mikis Fjord, we went south, rounding Cape Hammer, and passing the couple-thousand-foot rock face that guarded the mouth of Kangerlussuaq Fjord. It was the most stunning of all the fjords we saw in Greenland. On both sides, shark-toothed peaks extended from the sea 40 miles inland to the ice cap. A third of this land is occupied by massive glaciers. Laced with deep blue crevasses, frozen rivers the size of the Mississippi River fell to the sea. The sun was out, and a group of harp seals played in the waters around us. All of it seemed otherworldly. I knew the calm was deceptive. Winds from the ice cap funnel down the fjord and can reach 185 miles an hour.

Well into the mouth of the fjord, on the first relatively flat piece of land we'd run across since leaving Constable Point, were several old Inuit dwellings and tent rings. It was the first and only sign of human habitation we'd seen since Scoresbysund. Just outside one house was a flat rock, which was apparently used as a place to scout for whales and seals. At the foot of the rock were pieces of clear quartz used as blades for knives and harpoons. It was as if a hunter had sat there the day before. A family of ptarmigan scratched for food in the thin grass around the dwellings.

We explored 2 miles farther down the fjord by kayak and came upon deserted huts, a hunting outpost for hardy souls from the Ammassalik district. Families periodically traveled here for weeks at a time to hunt for narwhal and seal. The small camp was the dirtiest conglomeration of makeshift shacks and garbage I had seen yet. Cans, plastic, old generator motors and fuel drums were glued to the earth by a thick layer of orange, putrified animal grease. We set up our tent for the night on the only clean piece of flat rock we could find.

With hard paddling, we were only two weeks from completing our rounding. The morning of August 18, weary but optimistic, we slid our kayak into the water. The 9-mile crossing of Kangerdlussuaq seemed daunting. By 9 am, the wind and waves were too much for us to go on, and we turned back to the old Inuit site. We had to time our crossing perfectly, with slack tide, for the safest crossing, which would take three hours of constant paddling. At 4:15 pm we set off again. Storm clouds were brewing in the southeast and the waves were too big for comfort. South of the fjord, our plastic kayak kept bouncing off heavy ice.

Relieved, we arrived at Aputiteq Island. We found a bite in the shore on the southeast side of the island, which allowed us to land protected from the surf. In the dim light, I spotted a polar bear track in the snow next to the beach. Bumping into a bear in visibility of 3 yards was a frightening thought. We'd ditched our headlamps months earlier when we had 24-hour daylight. Nervously, we grabbed our flare gun and looked for our back-up resupply depot.

We stumbled uphill and found a half-dozen, run-down, wooden storage buildings that looked vintage 1950s. Broken cables, empty fuel drums, rusted generators and antennae were scattered around. Before technology advanced and hermit meteorologists retired, Greenland was used as a reliable conduit for telegraph and weather information between Europe and North America.

We made out a lone, dark object about 150 yards to the southeast. This was what we were after—an orange 6-foot by 15-foot fiberglass travel trailer minus wheels. Huts such as these are sling-loaded by helicopter from a freighter and carried to remote locations, where they become instant weather stations. The trailers are outfitted with batteries that are charged by solar panels so that unattended equipment can send out wind and temperature readings. For us, this hut was a place to get out of the weather. We relished having a table that folded down into a bed.

Next to the trailer was a 7-foot-square metal shipping container, held in place against the gale-force winds by half-inch cable bolted to bedrock. Inside was a 14-day supply of dehydrated food, pairs of thermal socks to replace our tattered ones, and an ample supply of white gas for heating water. We'd get a desperately needed bath.

By midday, the wind gusted to 50 miles an hour and it started to rain. As the storm blew itself out, we rested our sore muscles, and filled ourselves with hot food and, best of all, coffee. As we left Aputiteq Island, we worried that the storm that held us captive for three days had also piled ice along the coast ahead. Softball-sized ice chunks bobbed alongside our kayak as we threaded our way south. House-sized slabs frequently blocked our path. Just as I'd done on countless other occasions, I scrambled to the top of one of these small bergs to search for a route that would pose the least resistance for our tandem kayak and its two exhausted occupants.

The way ahead was a solid mass of white ice cut by narrow ribbons of black water, with a few dozen large icebergs thrown in for good measure. I knew that 5 miles off to the southwest lay our overnight destination. We were trying to reach the narrow, 5-mile band of rock and snow called Deception Island. It seemed an oddly American name, and we wondered who'd named the island and how it had deceived them. Half crawling, half sliding, I returned to our kayak and slithered into the forward cockpit.

"It doesn't look good," I told John. "The storm pushed everything right up against the coast."

"Big surprise, ay, mate?" John said, with his delightful, dry Australian humor.

We dug our paddles in and continued to wedge our way through the increasingly condensed ice. After paddling into a number of dead ends, we resorted to man hauling our supply-heavy kayak over the floes that blocked us. By late afternoon we approached Deception Island from the north. The steep, black and gray rocks, wet from spray, were uninviting in the failing light. Tired as we were, we opted to pass up a marginal campsite formed by boulders.

Ahead of us, the shoreline bulged out towards the sea with a narrow spur of rock rising gradually out of the water to almost 8 feet high. The opening between rock and ice was narrow, with a bit of surge adding to the running swell. If the ice didn't shift, we'd be able to squeeze through. Halfway through the slender opening, a large, unexpected swell pushed our kayak onto the rocks. The bow caught on a small outcropping, tilting us precariously when the wave receded. "Pry the bow free with your paddle," I yelled to John.

It was too late. The next wave carried the kayak higher on the rock face. Then the wave quickly receded, carrying us with it and slamming the left side of the kayak against the flanking ice pan. The kayak instantly began to turn over. Using our paddles, we tried to brace against the roll, but the effort was fruitless. We were going over. "So this is how it feels to capsize," I thought. Then the reality of the situation pushed aside all other thoughts. Still in the kayak, we were upside down and completely submerged. I struggled free and felt the undertow pull at my body. I opened my eyes in the water and realized the bottom was moving, or rather I was moving over it. Instinctively I swam in the other direction. My head hit something solid, the underside of the ice pan.

Most drowning victims don't yell or wave their arms. They're in shock, struggling to breathe. I was no different. Out of the corner of my eye, I spotted the red hull of the kayak floating on the edge of the pan and, in clumsy boots and bulky dry suit, swam towards it like a lame seal. I popped up on the other side of the boat gasping for air. In a frenzy, I looked around for John and yelled his name. Seconds later, he surfaced next to the rocks. I felt a flood of relief. "John," I shouted, "are you all right?" No answer. "John!"

"Yeah," he replied. "How about you? You gave me a bit of a scare. How did you get back in the boat?"

There I was, sitting in 10 inches of ice water with the bilge pump in my hand. I had no memory of climbing back in. I stopped pumping and grabbed my paddle. With wet, matted hair, John left the safety of the rocks, swam among the ice chunks and gathered up valuable equipment. Our dry suits saved us from getting completely soaked, but the fragile latex neck gussets, worn and torn from pulling the suits on and off, had leaked, and the butts of the suits had deteriorated after weeks of sitting and twisting in the kayak. Our chests and arms were wet and cold. What wasn't wet was just plain cold.

I called for John, who had already recovered most of the gear. "Get out of the water. Let's go back to that boulder beach camp."

I dragged the kayak up the beach with a certain foreboding. Before opening the hatches, I wondered if water had leaked in, damaging our food, clothing and the equipment stored there. I was pleasantly surprised. The front hatch was dry, and the back hatch had leaked only a little water. By now, I was getting dangerously cold. I quickly stripped off my wet clothes. I was wearing most of what I had, so the only dry stuff available to change into were a pair of socks, underwear briefs, fleece hat and vest. I stood on the rocks, half-naked and shivering. Wet gear and clothing were flung on rocks in every direction. I was grateful to have at least some dry clothing next to my skin when I had to put the wrung-out wet stuff back on. Carrying a handful of soggy items, John was making his way toward me. I asked if he was cold.

"Not too bad yet, but I'd better get out of this wet stuff," he said and began to strip.

"Did we lose anything?" I asked.

"Nope," he said, "just a pogie off one of my paddles."

"Three thousand miles of paddling, and we get dumped in a spot that looked safe," I said.

We took the chill out of our bones with an extra-big dinner and let the stove run for an extra hour that night. Soon our curled-up, sleeping forms were as still as the surrounding boulders.

Still feeling damp and chilled when we left the next morning, we paddled swiftly past the scene of our dunking. It was a beautiful, sunny day with high, horsetail clouds and visibility at 40 miles. Our map showed that we might encounter a high concentration of large icebergs ahead. Our next destination was 21 miles away—Aggus Island, a sharp wedge of land rocketing out of the water above massive icebergs like a black lamb in a herd of sheep. In the washed-out light, mountains and icebergs were nearly indistinguishable. Here the ice varied from 125-foot icebergs to fist-sized chunks of brash ice in every imaginable shade of blue. Brash ice is an accumulation of ice boulders and blocks left floating in leads, which are lanes of open water.

We did the best we could to negotiate the ice, but a mile from Aggus, we only made progress when we squatted half in and half out of the boat, with one leg kneeling in the cockpit and the other pushing off ice chunks. After 14 hours in the kayak, we were as exhausted as we'd ever been. We conceded defeat and camped on a 12-square-foot ice pan a half-mile from Aggus Island. We felt extremely vulnerable and prayed that no storms developed overnight.

We slept until 8:45 the next morning, late for us. It was August 25, autumn in the Arctic. When we awoke, a little warmth from the sun was coming through the walls of our yellow tent. We threw down our coffee and oatmeal, and got ready to log that day's miles. Each night, as the temperature dropped well below freezing, a half-inch layer of ice formed on protected bays and fjords. We started out, jamming the tips of our graphite paddles into the ice. The kayak's bow rose up onto the thin ice, then broke through. After a couple of hard hours of what felt like going nowhere, we reached Aggus Island.

From our new vantage point, we could see compacted ice ahead of us. Fortunately, the area included larger pans of ice that were close together so we could haul our kayaks over them. For almost 10 hours, we slogged and made 6 miles before fatigue forced us to camp. Down the coast, shadow-darkened capes, steep and black, seemed to stretch into infinity.

This was the hardest stretch of the coastline for me, not so much physically, but psychologically. I could hardly summon the mental strength to keep going. I was fed up with being bone tired. I was sick of worrying about whether or not we'd end up in the frigid water. I missed the feel of toes on warm grass, the smell of trees after a spring rain and the sound of leaves rustling on an autumn day. I also missed exchanging gossip in the local sauna. My love for the Arctic hadn't waned. I just yearned for a change of routine.

At this point, we were facing a 15-foot rolling carpet of icy sea water. To complicate matters, John and I were both seasick. John was unusually quiet in the back, so between strokes I turned and yelled: "How ya doing?"

"I've been better," he murmured back. Clearly, I wasn't alone in my feelings.

At midday we turned the kayak toward the southwest side of a small bay. Before the keel even hit solid ground, I jumped off the bow and dragged the kayak up the beach. John jumped out two seconds after me. We secured the kayak's bow line to a large boulder and climbed a nearby hill to lay down on a patch of sun-splashed tundra grass. We let the warm vegetation comfort our chilled backs for the next two hours. It was a wonderful rest for every single part of us. We were so damned comfortable we could hardly bear to move.

The season for safe kayaking had passed a week earlier. Time and weather were now against us as we carried on south. Still, we had moments of joy. Seeing bears frolic in the snow and mammoth icebergs roll over to expose blue, water-sculpted underbellies kept us going. We passed the invisible line of the Arctic Circle and found a camping spot just south of two glaciers in a narrow, bowl-shaped bay. I could see two good campsites. John preferred another one a mule-pack away. We got on each other's nerves during these last days of the expedition. Whatever one of us said, the other contradicted. We were tired and stressed, aching to complete the journey.

The bay was like a huge coliseum. Black basalt veins ran from base to summit on 2,400-foot walls. The cupped bay faced southeast, so the mountains absorbed precious heat from the low sun, creating its own ecosystem. An esker, a ridge of stratified gravel, sat where a glacier once stood. The melted glacier was another sign of climate change. The esker was covered with a low layer of moss, manicured like a putting green and decorated with miniature white flowers and red patches of saxifrages. This was the most enjoyable camp of the 32 we'd had since leaving Constable Point. The moss created an almost perfectly level mattress on which to sleep.

An approaching storm haloed the sun at the opening of Nordre Ikerasaq, an inland waterway to the small village of Sermiligaq and the fjord that bears its name. An hour after we entered the fjord, Sermiligaq's colorful houses—bright spots of blue, red, yellow and green—replaced the starkness of the gray, brown and blue-white world we'd been living in. We entered Sermiligaq unnoticed in the early morning rain and pulled into a cleft in the rocks near the center of town. Chilled, we walked along muddy paths to the store's steps, where children giggled at us as we tried to communicate with them.

We bought Danish chocolate, coffee and oats from the rotund, smiling storekeeper. We inquired about lodging for the night and were put up in the community wash house. We were even more grateful for a bath than we were for a night under a solid roof.

The next day, in a small bay just south of the tiny village of Kungmit, a fin whale, second only to the blue whale in size, surfaced 75 feet from the kayak. This shiny, black submarine mammal rose up silently before breaking the stillness with a huge exhalation of spray and mist. Ignoring any thought that closing in on the whale might be dangerous, we eagerly paddled in for a good look. Gracefully, skin reflecting the sun and sky, the behemoth surfaced just in front of us and arched its back for a deep dive. Its dorsal fin followed like the keel on an overturned sailboat.

We were 17 miles from Ammassalik. We could finally relax and absorb the surroundings instead of having to concentrate on staying out of the cold water. We no longer had to race against the coming winter. We pitched the tent for the last time, and amidst dwarf willow and low Arctic plants bearing wrinkled overripe berries, the air smelled sweet and fresh. In the distance, we could see Ammassalik's landmark mountains in Kong Oscar's Havn Fjord.

Our last camp turned bittersweet when we saw 16 fiberglass power boats aggressively circling a whale. They opened fire with rifles and the whale dove to escape. This was no respectful subsistence hunt with harpoon and float to quickly and cleanly kill a whale. These people were making sport of the kill. I watched through binoculars as the boats raced ahead, anticipating the crippled whale's direction and the area where it would resurface.

"Those sons of bitches!" shouted John. "They know better than that. The whale must be suffering like hell."

Helpless to intervene, we watched for three more hours as the shooters ran their boats back and forth, aiming at the whale each time it surfaced. Ultimately, they seemed to lose the whale, which was sure to die now, and returned to their village. Why had these Greenlanders lost respect for the very animal that had kept them alive for centuries? Where had their cultural wisdom gone?

The incident quickly faded the next morning when we woke to clear skies and calm water. It was September 5, truly the last day of this extraordinary adventure. And in this spectacular setting, feeling as if I were in another world, I had the most ordinary breakfast imaginable—a cup of Nescafe, oatmeal with brown sugar and a multivitamin. Oh yes, and two ibuprofen.

CHAPTER 22

REALIZING A DREAM

Two miles short of the town of Ammassalik, we pulled up on a calm, rocky beach much like hundreds we had seen in the past four and a half years. I left John at the kayak and took a short walk on my own to reflect on the years we had spent entranced by this land. We were about to complete an amazing physical, cultural and spiritual journey around Greenland. I knew that in some small way we had a place with the long line of explorers who'd preceded us.

I was humbled by the realization that we had succeeded unscathed where others had died. I asked myself why. Was it because we had prepared well? Or was it because we had relaxed into the environment and followed rather than fought the elements? Perhaps it was both. Although we had made painstaking plans that sought to fit our mode of travel to anticipated conditions, we had to change travel strategies several times. If we'd simply tried to fight our way through adverse weather, we would surely have died in the first stage of the expedition. In some ways, the most difficult mental part of the trip had been accepting the need to stop and wait out bad weather. That's how a trip we thought would take 15 months turned into four and a half years.

I was overwhelmed by a feeling of gratitude, especially for my teammate John, who stayed true to our mission through miles of danger and years of logistical nightmares. Good teamwork was certainly one key to our success. I thought of the gift of the raven, which had brought me hope in the midst of doubt. Walking the shore, I also felt deep gratitude for the small population of Inuit in Greenland's far north. Even though John could speak a bit of Danish and I knew a few Inuit words, together we could barely form a complete sentence. Pantomime was how we'd made our meaning clear. Yet we had formed a deep bond with the Inuit, and I would greatly miss sharing meals and celebrations with them, learning string games from their elders, and hearing their serious concerns about what climate changes mean for them. In this remote region, sometimes in total darkness, we had always put total faith in our Inuit companions. We'd learned to laugh and take life on its terms, as they do. We had embraced their culture, which centered on the kayak and dog teams. And in doing so, I felt at one with the Danish explorer Knud Rasmussen.

I was also filled with sadness. As we traveled around the island, we had seen many Inuit who had lost their dignity and direction to alcohol. For centuries, the Inuit lived their own way, with little intrusion. Going from complete isolation to total immersion in modern life within a single generation was bound to have tragic results. And then there was the climate. Since 1992 the summer Arctic sea ice had lost an area as large as Alaska, California and Texas combined. The hottest years on record were occurring. Scientists were predicting that in a few years Arctic waters would be ice-free. This was decades earlier than the date they had estimated a few years earlier.

I knew that time was running out for the Inuit. Along the western shores of Greenland, where safe sea ice no longer forms in the bays and fjords, hunters were culling thousands of their sled dogs. Without sea ice for fishing and hunting, they had no means of securing food for their dogs. As the sea ice disappeared, violent, abrupt storms were becoming more common. Climate changes made it more difficult for villagers to hunt and survive in the traditional fashion. For centuries, winter travel had been by dog sled, but thin ice was making that increasingly dangerous. I saw elders sob at no longer being able to predict the weather and give their children the guidance they needed to survive—literally survive.

The condition of the land was no better. The permafrost lying just under the cushy tundra was melting, causing many Arctic buildings to sink into the mud. The melting permafrost also was releasing large quantities of previously frozen methane gas, which has an even greater warmth-trapping greenhouse effect than carbon dioxide. Animals that the Inuit rely on were also being affected by climate change. Warmer temperatures were creating freezing rains in late winter and early spring, normally the coldest time of year. As an Inuit friend, Jens Danielson, said, "If we have no more snow and ice, we will no longer be Eskimos."

Back in the kayak, we had only 40 minutes of paddling before we reached the end of our Greenland journey. Finally, as we rounded the last spur of rock, Ammassalik sprawled before us. The familiar red Kista Artica ship and sheet-metal warehouse of the Royal Arctic Line were the first landmarks we saw. Houses, shops and municipal buildings, all brightly painted red, green, blue and yellow, nestled on the shore of the fjord.

A small flotilla of boats gathered to meet us. Our friends Bendt and Rose Josovisen welcomed us with glasses of champagne. Their children squealed "Uncle Oomingmak," Uncle Musk Ox, because of the shaggy beard I sported. The Vagabond, a French research vessel with a team of kayakers, pulled alongside and shouted congratulations. They had attempted to get through the ice from Kangerlussuaq Fjord in kayaks but had been thwarted.

"How'd you get through the ice?" shouted Eric Brossier, owner of the Vagabond.

"We dragged the kayak over the ice!" John shouted back.

We chatted from our bobbing kayak and waved goodbye as the other kayakers left the harbor and headed for home.

We aimed our kayak at a dock at the end of the harbor. Floating among the steel ships and old, double-ended fishing boats, I felt tiny. I looked at John. He was in control of the rudder and had a big smile on his face. He swung the kayak around and headed for the bakery at the end of the pier. His smile read: "Danish pastries!" It was 5 pm on September 5 when we jumped ashore and peeled off our dry suits for the last time. A bath was at the top of my list, along with fresh fruit if I could find any.

We had traveled 6,517 miles around Greenland, 3,442 miles by dog team and 3,075 miles by kayak. We set out to circumnavigate Greenland, and we did it. Traveling on and around this island's savage ice against a curtain of naked mountains is like journeying through the Ice Age. As arduous and life-threatening as it had been, the sculpted beauty of Greenland's drifting, calving, rolling ice will always remain one of my most vivid memories. After being consumed by an objective for years, working single-mindedly to achieve it, I had fulfilled my dream and was returning to my Minnesota life.

In that moment, I understood the struggle of the modern Inuit youth, tugged by two cultures—hunting and traveling by dog team in the traditional way or leaving home and learning to survive in another world. For me, the choice was between living a peaceful family life in northern Minnesota and exploring the wildness of the Arctic.

As we left Greenland a few days later on our chartered flight, I peered out of the windows. Below us, rolling waves beat against the coastline. The only ice left after the summer melt was a handful of solitary icebergs, white and lonely in a sea of blue. After a moment, Greenland faded into the clouds.

NAVIGATING THE MELTING ICE, 2002–2009

"The lure of the Arctic is tugging at my heart.

To me the trail is calling!

The old trail—the trail that is always new."

—Matthew Henson,
African-American polar explorer

CHAPTER 23

PLANNING FOR THE SUMMER POLE

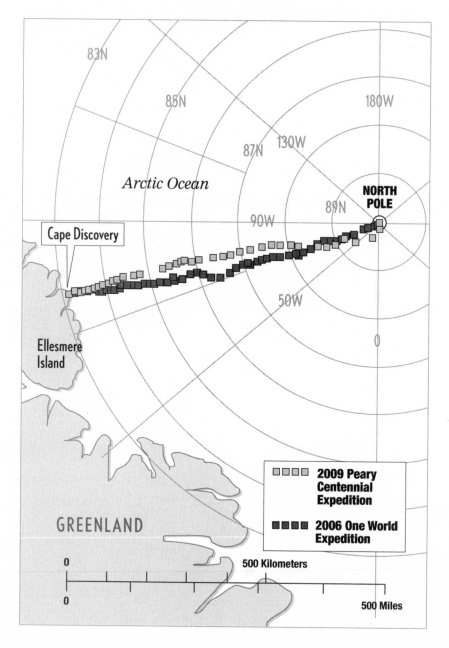

I began preparing for my next expedition in October 2002. My plan was to cross the Arctic Ocean via the North Pole. At the North Pole, all lines of longitude begin and extend until they touch every place on the globe. The Arctic is the place that connects us all. We named the expedition the One World Expedition.

The Arctic Ocean is one and a half times larger than the United States and covers 8.5 million square miles. It plunges to a depth of 14,000 feet. Until recently, it has remained mostly frozen throughout the year. Despite the climate's chilly hold, the ice is influenced by tides, currents and winds, and is in constant motion. Huge ice pans break apart and collide, creating gigantic ice pressure ridges and wide leads of open water. Seen from above, the Arctic ice looks like a maze of frozen puzzle pieces, a white sheet split by thousands of dark, watery lines. Polar bears roam this drifting pack in search of seals. Winter temperatures plummet to unimaginable lows and summertime readings hover close to freezing.

Although the Arctic Ocean seems to be permanently locked in cold and ice, scientific data and methodically recorded observations suggest otherwise. Arctic sea ice is only about half as thick, on average, as it was in the 1960s. Ice surface coverage has steadily decreased as well. Satellite images suggest that this will continue, with high Arctic summers being almost ice-free before 2020. Not long ago, that estimate was for 2050.

These days, planning an Arctic expedition based on past weather is a crap shoot. Even the most sophisticated technology isn't a match for the devastating effects of climate change. In places like Minnesota, where winters are milder and shorter by at least a month, it's tempting to simply enjoy late autumns and early springs. However, such pleasure comes with a price: torrential rains, frequent droughts and straight-line winds that wipe out thousands of acres of boreal forest.

I wanted my next expedition to expose how climate change

185

threatens the very survival of the Inuit people, and the animal and marine life they rely on. I hoped that this awareness could help protect the Arctic and its indigenous culture. To be successful, I knew my venture had to balance three elements: cutting-edge exploration, scientific contribution and public appeal.

My friend Eric Larsen decided to join me. Ten years my junior—a generation really—Eric was raised in rural Wisconsin near an outdoor environmental education center. His dad was the center director, and while other kids played, Eric banded birds, harvested maple syrup, collected insects, hiked the woods and canoed nearby waters. After studying biology in college, Eric had a variety of jobs and avocations. He had been a whitewater canoe guide, back-country ranger, competitive cyclist, bartender and chimney cleaner. He had also trained and raced sled dogs, and participated in a dog-sled expedition in the Sub-Arctic. In addition, Eric helped develop a comprehensive Web site and educational curricula for an expedition.

Eric and I wanted to show first-hand how the human lifestyle is destroying the Arctic. Americans are the biggest contributors to greenhouse gas emissions in the world. Although we are only 7 percent of the population, we produce 25 percent of worldwide carbon emissions and use 36 percent of the world's resources. To communicate the seriousness of the situation, we couldn't imagine a more powerful image than two Americans floating in a sea that most people think is permanently frozen.

Eric's main responsibilities were to develop a Web site and e-newsletter, and keep them updated during the expedition. He was also to research a science program focusing on climate change and implement it on the trail. Part of our research was for the National Snow and Ice Data Center (NSIDC). We were to measure the freeboard of the ice (the height above the water line) on at least one lead each day. This information would be used to better determine how much the Arctic sea ice was thinning. The process would be easy: our tool was a ski pole with a thin meter tape stuck to it. We planned to send out both digital pictures and journal entries via e-mail to our Web site, which would feature an electronic map plotting our progress. We would send updates to the site every day, audio updates every other day and e-newsletters every three to four weeks.

Leaving in the winter or early spring when the sea ice is frozen and stable wouldn't convey our climate change message very well. Besides, Robert E. Peary and Will Steger had already been to the pole by dog team in winter months. We needed to attempt a journey to the pole in the summer to accurately document climate change and its hold on the Arctic. Our summer trip would be a first.

When planning an expedition to the North Pole, there are only two logical starting points. One is Ellesmere Island, the northernmost point of land in Arctic Canada. The other is Cape Arkticheskiy in Siberia. Located nearly opposite each other across the Arctic Ocean, they are separated by 1,000-plus nautical miles of shifting ice. The North Pole is 524 miles from Siberia and 479 miles from Canada. On the Canadian side of the pole, sea ice tends to be thicker, with less open water. The ice drifts toward Canada and pressures up against land, resulting in massive ridges of ice, which create seemingly insurmountable obstacles. The Russian side has more open water to contend with and a bit of a longer route, but the ice tends to drift more northerly toward the pole and is far less pressured. Expeditions ending at the North Pole are split equally between Canadian and Siberian departures. Ocean crossings almost always start from Siberia. We decided to start in Russia.

In order to determine the best time to start the expedition, I needed to figure out how many days it would take to get to the pole. Using estimates from past experiences, I figured we would average 11 nautical miles a day, except on rest days. This average mileage, divided by our total distance, gave me a total of 98 days. I added a cushion of six days. In a pinch, we could reduce rations and extend our food supply for an additional seven days or so.

The 104 days needed to be strategically placed in the year to guarantee the best chance of success. Since the crossing would take place during the Arctic summer, we needed to consider details such as beginning and ending points, temperatures, the amount of sunlight each day, and ice and weather conditions.

At Cape Arkticheskiy, for instance, there are 24 hours of sunlight beginning April 11. At Ward Hunt Island, Canada, our ending point, the 24-hour light ends September 6. After that, the weather changes significantly for the worse, with snowstorms and significant drops in temperature. Leads begin to freeze over with thin layers of ice, which makes them extremely difficult to paddle across but too thin to ski across. Between April 11 and September 6, 2005, we would have 148 days in which to drop our 98-day journey. We chose May 10 to August 10. After the beginning of May, the Arctic Ocean turns into a deadly concoction of slush pools, grinding ice floes and chilling fog that makes navigation painstaking at best. Hypothermia is a daily threat. Our plan was to haul all the food, fuel and gear we needed for the entire journey.

When news of our expedition spread, several global explorers hinted that it was basically impossible, if not suicidal, to attempt such a trip. A handful thought it might be done, but not without serious hardship and some form of resupply along the way. In *Outside* magazine, polar explorer Ben Saunders spoke out: "I wouldn't say they're nuts, but it's a long way out there...a big step into the unknown."

We were not discouraged from our goal. Eric and I began training in March 2004, easing up during the heat of the summer and starting more intense workouts in late August when temperatures cooled. We decided to adopt a training method used by Olympic cross-country ski teams during the off-season, and spent five or six days a week dragging 16-inch steel-belted truck tires hooked to our waists. On back roads and trails, our workout with hiking boots and ski poles proved to be superb mental training as well. Again, northern Minnesota's Sawtooth Mountains and Boundary Waters Canoe Area provided ideal training for our expedition. With lakes that freeze as early as November and remain frozen until May, Grand Marais' climate was perfect for testing our equipment.

In August of 2004, Eric and I attended the Outdoor Retailer Convention in Salt Lake City to meet with potential sponsors and to gather necessary gear for our expedition. From there, we went on to Washington, DC, for meetings with National Geographic and Greenpeace. Though training, fundraising and organizing took nearly every waking moment, we still had a lot of research to do on the current environment of the Arctic Ocean. There was still so much we didn't know. What kind of ice conditions could we expect at any given time? How much rain, fog and snow would we encounter? What would the temperatures be? When could we expect to see meltwater pools forming on the ice from which to take drinking water? When would the sea ice begin freezing again in the fall? Would the ozone-depleted skies and 24-hour sunlight fry our faces?

More technical questions also needed answers. Would our solar panels work to power our communications and video equipment in the ambient light of whiteout and fog? Would our leather boots hold up to constant submersion in saltwater? Since no one had attempted to cross the ocean or go to the North Pole in the summer, little research existed. A few earlier explorers had taken advantage of the ice drift and ridden the ice during the summer melt when traditional winter travel by foot, ski or dogs was impossible. Wally Herbert's British Trans-Arctic Expedition and Ranulph Fiennes' Transglobe Expedition are examples of this.

The first explorers to travel any great distance over summer's soggy ice and open water were Norway's Fridtjof Nansen and Fredrik Hjalmar Johansen during the Fram Expedition of 1893–1896. In an attempt to reach the North Pole from their drifting, ice-locked ship, the Fram, they came up short and were forced to retreat to the closest land, the Franz Joseph Islands, hundreds of miles to the south. Their journey is one of the greatest tales of survival and hardship in the annals of polar exploration. Wet, cold and always on the brink of starvation, they owed their lives to two small fabric kayaks. With their remaining sled dogs too few and emaciated to pull through energy-sapping slush and freezing water, the two men lashed 12-foot-long canvas kayaks together and were able to finish their journey.

Our expedition required either floating sleds or sliding boats. I designed canoe-sleds based upon that need, expanding on the design of the Fram kayaks in hopes of making an even longer journey more comfortable. When we weren't paddling, we needed crampon-based snowshoes for rough terrain and skis for flatter pans. We needed clothing for both skiing on ice and swimming across leads.

After testing many small kayaks and canoes, we determined we needed a craft about 9 feet long, 26 inches wide and 14 inches deep. It needed to hold 300 liters. In the end, we concluded that a whitewater canoe worked best, and decided on an Esquif "Zoom" canoe, which also fit our specs for a sled.

These boats, manufactured in Quebec, Canada, and constructed of high-quality Royalex, are easy to load and unload, and have an ample rocker for maneuvering through pressured ice and deep snow. We needed to modify the canoes by adding a sheet of high-density plastic to the hull bottom, plastic runners, and waterproof covers with access zippers at the bow and stern. Straps sewn on deck would hold down gear and serve as handles. Special Voilé quick-fasten straps attached to the gunwales would secure our skis across the decks and create a catamaran configuration for safely crossing leads. A carbon-fiber paddle would double as a snow shovel.

Planning an expedition's start in Russia is nerve-wracking at best. Wiring large sums of cash ($75,000 to $95,000 a pop) made me nervous, and this anxiety was compounded by the fact that three separate North Pole expeditions had to be aborted a few months before our planned departure. Though official statements said otherwise, I believed Russian politics and bureaucracy were to blame.

I opted to organize our Russian support directly through my long-time friend and polar explorer Victor Boyarsky, the director of the Russian State Museum of Arctic and Antarctic in Saint Petersburg, and head of the Polar Commission of the Russian Geographical Society. He was one of the leaders of the Trans-Antarctica Expedition that crossed the icy continent by dog team in 1990 with Will Steger. Besides crisscrossing the Arctic, he led and participated in two expeditions to the North Pole. We were confident in Victor's abilities to make things work.

I arrived in Moscow on September 5, 2004, and flew on to Murmansk to board the Yamal, a Russian nuclear icebreaker. I was there for a two-week reconnaissance of the Arctic Ocean sea ice. The other passengers were there for the caviar. For $30,000, you can buy a trip to the North Pole complete with gourmet meals, an open bar, a sauna and a cozy cabin. I had free passage courtesy of Victor's arrangements. All I had to do while on board was give a few lectures about my Greenland and Northwest Passage expeditions. The trip gave me an inkling of how the ice would look after a complete summer's melt. It also allowed me to get to know the ship's captain and crew. This ship could be our safety net.

Fall colors painted both sides of the fjord on our way to the Arctic Sea. Even a bad case of sea sickness didn't spoil the sight of Fulmar and kittiwake sea birds hovering on thermals outside the windows, fresh polar bear tracks and lavender skies. The ship's hull sliced a clean path through the ice floe. Three 16-foot propellers moved the 450-foot ship along. Constructed of two layers of 48-millimeter-thick stainless steel, it moved through 12 feet of sea ice at 6 knots.

One night I was wakened by a severe shimmy that felt like beavers chewing the legs off my bed. We had hit the thick polar pack ice. I looked out the window and saw nothing but white and ice. The ship itself sounded like a freight train as it separated the ice. Thick, blue blocks of ice rolled over next to the bow. Two-inch codfish got caught on top of the ice in the turmoil and washed free again as water drained off the top of the ice. I wondered if these fish could provide supplemental food for an expedition. I moved to the stern, where the hull-separated ice left meandering black lines of water like ink spills on white paper.

I spent hours talking logistics with Victor and the pilots of the two on-board helicopters, which were capable of flying 2 degrees (120 miles) from the ship. Any deviation requiring the ship to veer from its scheduled route would be expensive—very expensive. Renting a nuclear icebreaker costs $33,000 a day. Any other emergency support had to be airdropped. The range limit of the helicopters made evacuation south of 88 degrees impossible. This trip met my expectations. It gave me valuable insights into weather, ice conditions and possible lifesaving support.

A week after returning home from Russia, Kelly and I were on a first-class flight to Paris, compliments of Rolex. Five months earlier, I had been named one of five "Rolex Award for Enterprise" laureates for 2004. It is an honor of the highest degree to be chosen for this coveted award given in five areas—exploration and discovery, science and medicine, technology and innovation, the environment, and cultural heritage. This biennial award provides "visionary men and women" worldwide with the financial support and recognition needed to carry out innovative projects that "expand human knowledge or improve the lot of mankind." I felt truly honored.

For nine days, Kelly and I were treated to the best Parisian sights and restaurants. Gifts from Rolex were placed in our room each day. I couldn't have been in a world more removed from my life on expedition—or from my life at home for that matter. At the awards ceremony in Paris, which was emceed by actress Charlotte Rampling, were Patrick Heiniger, CEO of Rolex SA; Francois Mitterrand, the former president of France; and Gilbert Grosvenor, chairman of the National Geographic Society.

I accepted the award by saying: "Generations of explorers have ensured that we know a great deal about our planet. Today, we know that it is changing. As an explorer of the 21st century, I believe our purpose is no longer to conquer places, but, instead, to protect them." I received a $100,000 honorarium and a gold Rolex chronometer. The award gave One World Expedition a huge media jumpstart and provided a third of our budget.

Back home in October, we started our grassroots fundraising campaign, which was spearheaded by Ann Possis, our expedition manager. With a background in fundraising for Planned Parenthood and various political campaigns, Ann was determined to put the "fun" in our fundraising. She developed our "One World Evenings." We supplied presentations by Eric and me (complete with Arctic "props"), custom invitations and postage. The hosts supplied the people, places and food. The more than 40 parties funded about one fourth of our budget. Ann and a team of volunteers also packed food for our journey, including 15 days worth of food stored in plastic drums that could be airdropped to us on the ice in an emergency. Milder temperatures meant fewer calories than winter expeditions, but we still needed lots of food—nearly 20 gallons of powdered energy drink, four gallons of olive oil, 20 pounds of dried salami, 25 pounds of dried caribou, a mountain of powdered goat's milk (easier to digest than cow's milk), 300 dried rye bread rounds, and pounds and pounds of oatmeal, egg noodles, dried potatoes and chocolate bars. And to that we added 800 Clif Bars, our primary midday energy source. Volunteers vacuum-packed the food by meal, then packed a bag for each day.

In February 2005, Greenpeace partnered with us, both as a funder and as a communications partner. I knew early on that if we wanted to spread the word about the climate change crisis, we needed to hook up with the experts. Since 1971, Greenpeace has been a leading voice of the environmental movement. They work throughout the world to protect oceans and ancient forests, and to fight toxic pollution, whaling, genetic engineering, climate change and nuclear threats. The thing I've always liked about Greenpeace is that they're not just talkers, they're doers. The downside of having Greenpeace on board was that the organization is controversial in the United States. Allying with them meant no further corporate funding. To counter that, we held more "One World Evenings" and had a going-away party that brought in another $7,000.

John Hoelscher, my former Greenland Expedition partner, arrived and became our One World Expedition field logistics manager. He modified all our electronic gear and made sure that it could withstand the rigors of a three-and-a-half-month Arctic Ocean crossing. He also tested and modified our solar panel so equipment could charge inside the tent while the panel rested outside in the sun. John would also have full authority over search and rescue, emergency resupplies, and communications.

Eric and I flew to New York for the launch of the Greenpeace/One World Expedition partnership at The Explorers Club. Our project was awarded a Scott Pearlman Field Award for Science and Exploration, a grant created by The Explorers Club to fund professional documentation of exploration and field research on expeditions led by members.

We were also awarded Flag #49 by the board of directors, an honor steeped in tradition and history. The Arctic explorer and navigator, Captain Robert A. Bartlett, flew this flag on the Roosevelt, the ship that accompanied Robert Peary to the North Pole.

Towards the end of April 2005, we got a call from ACR Electronics, which was providing us with personal locating beacons (PLBs), announcing that they would like to come on board as a major sponsor. This was a godsend, as the expedition was still strapped for cash.

Before we left, we had a necessary protocol to complete. In case of a fatality on the expedition between N 88 and the pole, we agreed to have our bodies evacuated by Yamal's helicopters. Outside of this area, we would be left on the ice. If no contact had been made from the expedition in four days, all attempts would be made for rescue until there was no remaining chance of survival. If I hadn't stopped to consider the dangers of our expedition before, I did now.

The plan was for John to travel with us to Siberia, where he would stay on for a few weeks to coordinate logistics. He'd then head back to Grand Marais for a month before boarding Greenpeace's ship Arctic Sunrise, where he'd lend his knowledge to their tour around Greenland. Josh Raisler Cohn, a committed Greenpeace activist, joined us in Minnesota for our final days of work. John and Josh left Grand Marais on May 1 to drive the truck with 800 pounds of gear and food to New York, where Eric and I would meet them. With our canoe-sleds tied to the roof of the topper, the truck swayed down the driveway as it left.

By May 2, news of our expedition had spread throughout the Midwest. We received front-page stories in the *Chicago Tribune*, *Minneapolis StarTribune* and *Milwaukee Journal Sentinel*. We'd also been interviewed by Minnesota Public Radio. An Associated Press story ran nationally, and *Mother Jones* posted an in-depth article on its Web site. Our climate change message was getting noticed.

At 4 am on May 3, 2005, Eric and I left Grand Marais for Minneapolis to tackle last-minute details and interviews prior to our flight to New York and our connection to Moscow. We stopped in Duluth to pick up a care package of homemade ribs and coleslaw from my mom, Kate Cartier. It was a tradition: trying to fatten me up one last time before an expedition.

When we arrived at the Moscow airport, Victor Boyarsky's right-hand man, Alexander Sheremetyev of Victory in Arctic and Antarctic Agency (VICAAR), met us. After our passports and visas were checked, Alex helped us clear customs, no small task in even the most normal traveling situation. We began to fill out customs forms, but Alex instructed us to follow him instead. We nervously looked back at all of our gear neatly stacked on carts and walked right past the serious-looking custom officials, the metal detectors and other travelers having their bags searched. It pays to have a good contact in Russia. A bit of "tip" money helps, too.

As we landed in Sredny, the wreckage of two crashed planes poked out of the snow alongside the runway. We made our way to our accommodations at a weather station 6 miles away called Golomiannyi. On a long dining table, Alex rolled out satellite images showing sea ice 2 miles off the coast at Cape Arkticheskiy. My greatest concern was capsizing our canoe-sleds in the early stages of the expedition, when we were most loaded down and vulnerable.

At 10:30 the next morning we loaded the helicopter and made goodbye calls to our loved ones. An hour and a half later, we were flying directly over the Cape with the icescape of the Arctic Ocean in front of us. The ice had drifted south since the last satellite image and was now too tight to land. Our first major obstacle was obvious. We'd need to haul our heavy canoe-sleds across 2.5 miles of extremely pressured sea ice near the coast. Eric was quiet. He said he'd never felt so scared and overwhelmed.

CHAPTER 24

FACING THE COMPLEXITY OF LIFE ON THE EDGE

We felt like two ants crossing a plowed field when we started out. Using snowshoes, we relayed our canoe-sleds one at a time, working together to heave them over the high ice for a half-mile, then returning for the second. For each mile of forward gain we traveled 3 miles. All we had to show for the first day was a mile and a half of travel.

Our Hilleberg tent was a welcome refuge after the day of struggle. It weighed only 3.5 pounds and set up in less than five minutes, even in the worst of conditions. It would be exaggerating to say we could adequately stretch out in the meager space, but there was enough room for eating and for writing in our journals. We were warm and comfortable. During the evenings, we also filled out psychological evaluation sheets provided to us by Gloria Leon, a psychology professor at the University of Minnesota. Her research focused on our specific stress and coping patterns during the crossing, as well as our decision-making processes and strategies for dealing with the dangers we encountered. The findings would be used by NASA as an analog for the types of situations that might occur in two-person teams traveling to Mars.

One day, we worked together towing one 370-pound canoe-sled a half-mile over what seemed like mountains of ice only to have to return for the second boat. With that accomplished and with snow falling, we aimed for a visible lead, an area of open water. We looked forward to paddling as a short reprieve from hauling. Hours later, we arrived at the edge of the lead exhausted and sweating. To our great disappointment, it was coated in a thin coat of black ice, too thick to paddle through and too thin to walk over.

Ducks and auks flew over our heads, signaling open water some-where, just not here. We were looking for narrow and calm bodies of water heading north that our modest 9-foot canoe-sleds could handle. Finally, we resigned ourselves to the labor of inching our way north through what seemed like an impenetrable roadblock of ice, laughing at the total drudgery and absurdity of it all. Here we were, heading towards a "place" called the North Pole, and once we arrived, it would look exactly like the ice we were standing on.

Eric, puffy-eyed and hacking, was sick with the flu, which had started in Siberia and was now full-blown. I marveled at his ability to still drag his heavy boat, and tried to ease his burden by breaking trail ahead of him and by scouting for easier routes through the maze of pressured ice. Once in camp that night, Eric took antibiotics and hit his sleeping bag.

The next day, we saw ivory gulls and bearded seals. They were a welcome sight in an otherwise sterile environment. The seals ele-vated themselves out of the water as high as their fast-moving flippers allowed and stretched to get a better look at us. It was a mixed experi-ence. Seeing the water-dependent creatures made me nervous. Their presence reminded me that each day we were delayed, the closer we were to summer. If we didn't start gaining ground soon, vast areas of open water would develop near the coast, too dangerous for our small vessels to handle.

One day, trying to negotiate thin ice, Eric fell into the water up to his crotch. We decided to catamaran the boats. He donned his dry suit, tied a line from the canoe-sled to his foot, jumped in the lead and swam a type of butterfly-backstroke to break the thin ice ahead. Once on the other side, kneeling on the two boats, he pulled me across the lead. We spent the rest of the day paddling large leads up to a half-mile wide. For a while, we closed our eyes and pretended we were crossing lakes in Minnesota's Boundary Waters Canoe Area. At the end of an exhausting eight-hour day, we checked our GPS coordinates and were devastated to find that despite our efforts, we had drifted backwards. We now sat a quarter of a mile south of the previous night's camp.

This was a perfect example of how ice on the Arctic Ocean is "alive," tugged by the moon, wind and currents. Contours and mountains on the ocean floor create vast eddies and spirals in the ice. Wind pressures the ice floes against one another, creating a sea of chaotic blocks and 30-foot-high ridge lines that run for miles. The very surface we stood on was working against us. I began to wonder if our journey was even possible, given the leads, the deep snow and the backward drift of the sea ice. We needed either more stable ice or long passages of open water, not a mix of the two. Despite our attempts forward, we continued to drift south and east at an alarming rate. Huge frozen leads barely supported our weight. After another difficult day, we had drifted a mile south and a full degree east of our last camp. If only we could break free of the unstable coastal ice to more secure ice 100 miles north.

Although we were at the mercy of the ice, we remained optimistic, believing things could only get better. After a long day of dragging our canoe-sleds through horrendous obstacles of brash ice, leads and pressure ridges, I glanced down at the bent shafts of my aluminum poles. I looked back at Eric's boat, which had deep, elongated dents and gouges running down both sides. We stepped out of our snowshoes and began unpacking. Eric set up the tent while I grabbed the cook kit and food out of my sled.

As I looked up from my rummaging, I froze. Sixty feet behind Eric was a polar bear. Eric saw the fear in my eyes and uncontrollably produced a sort of prehistoric grunt-scream, which momentarily stopped the enormous young bear in his tracks. We nervously dug through our pockets for pencil flares. In the stress of the situation, we both had trouble getting into our "easy-access" pockets. An observer would have been amused by the classic comic scene.

Realizing he had been spotted, the magnificent bear rose up. I knew he was young by his white unscarred face, and by the color and texture of his coat. Then, back down on the ice again, with his neck in the snow, front legs stretched along his side, belly low, he propelled himself across the ice with massive back paws. It's how polar bears stalk seals. When ice is not quite thick enough for bears to stand on, they get down on their bellies, spread out their legs to distribute their weight and crawl like a salamander across the ice.

When Eric moved, the bear stopped to avoid being detected. Then, just to make sure, he resumed his crawl toward us and rose again, swinging his head back and forth, before continuing our way. Eric fired the first rocket over the bear's head. The startled bear spun around on its hind legs and kicked into high gear. As he began to slow, about 100 yards away, he looked back at us. I launched another flare. The bear retreated in big strides, beautifully blending with the snowy ice until he eventually disappeared into the pack ice.

In our tent, the GPS told us that after five days of travel we had gained no ground and had drifted east, parallel to Cape Arkticheskiy. Despite the earlier visit by our big furry friend, we snored like freight trains almost before our heads hit the sleeping bags. That night, I had a "working dream." I was trying to figure out how to work around the inevitable ice drift and still gain ground. Awakened by a muffled crash and clang, I opened my eyes to find the tent ceiling pressed against my face. In a panic, I pulled at my sleeping bag zipper and tried to sit up. I couldn't, then realized there was a bear on top of the tent. A second later, the tent sprang back to its original form. Eric and I locked eyes and simultaneously projected a growling scream, much like a panicky bayonet-charge command, followed by, "BEAR!"

I grabbed the handgun, Eric the flares, and without even looking, Eric unzipped the tent door, stuck his arm out, and let a rocket fly. After the bang, he reloaded, and we poked our heads outside. The bear stood 50 yards away, looking very familiar in size and color to the 700-to-800-pound young white male we'd seen earlier. Eric fired another flare, which sent the polar bear running over the hummock ice and out of sight. We were lucky. The bear had pounced on the only body-free area of our tiny tent. Punctures in the nylon just inches from Eric's head made it clear exactly where he'd come down with his entire body weight, just as he would on unsuspecting seals lying in a small cave underneath the snow. We constructed a fence around the tent from various pieces of equipment and gear, and hoped that if the bear knocked it over we'd wake up. Neither of us slept much more the rest of the night.

Expeditions like this one offer ample time for revelation. I began to wonder if I carried more of life's baggage in my canoe-sled than actual expedition equipment. The more baggage one has, the harder the pull. Though I believe I have no more baggage than most, I wondered why I was out here. Was I running from something? What was I trying to prove? When I was young and expressed my far-reaching dreams, I was met with, "You can't do that." Was this trip simply another attempt to counter childhood rejection?

Some of my expeditions, though successful, hadn't run according to plan. Expeditions of this magnitude rarely do. It appeared this one was heading in that direction. Although I deeply believe that it's necessary and healthy to fill life with meaningful experiences and to share these experiences with others, I couldn't help but feel the extreme weight of my responsibilities: Eric's life, commitments to sponsors, finances, logistics. We had left the expedition office's ringing phone and pile of bills weeks ago, but my obligations continued.

I thought of something the poet Rainer Maria Rilke wrote: "And the point is to live everything. Live the questions now. Perhaps then, some day far into the future, you will gradually, without even noticing it, live your way into the answer." I reminded myself that I needed to hold on to the questions but be patient with the answers. Then I shifted my focus to the only place that mattered in this moment: the here and now. Our GPS showed that the ice we were on was drifting southeast at 8 nautical miles a day. We needed to make a drastic change to have any chance of making forward progress. In order to achieve 2 miles of progress north, we needed to travel at least 10 miles a day. We also needed to sustain this pace for 15 straight days to pull away from the unstable coastline.

Achieving those distances over such fractured ice and leads, with even the lightest load, required a Herculean effort. To have any hope of continuing, we needed to lighten our loads, so we decided to drop 80 pounds of food from each boat, leaving us with only enough food to reach the North Pole. At the pole, we would have the option of being resupplied via airdrop or icebreaker for the remaining 500 miles to Canada.

I contacted John Hoelscher, now in Moscow serving as our logistics manager, about our new plan. John began to put the logistics in place for our resupply at the pole. Over the satellite phone he gave us what we needed most, a good old-fashioned pep talk on the necessary paradox of an expedition: "Just take it one day at a time and try not to look too far ahead. And focus on the big picture." He told us the National Snow and Ice Data Center reported that the sea ice along the Siberian coastline was breaking up three weeks earlier then normal due to an abnormally warm winter. John's review of satellite images of the surrounding ice led him to advise us to get out of the mess by traveling about 10 miles east-northeast to the 105th meridian before traveling north again.

By the next morning, we had drifted farther to the southeast, and our position was more than 7 miles south of our starting point at

Cape Arkticheskiy. Determined not to be beaten, and with Eric now fully recovered from the flu, we headed northeast with a new plan and a lightened load. We pushed hard for 8 hours and made 1.5 miles north. Overcast skies blocked out the sun and created a whiteout. There was no detail or contrast to the landscape around us—no sky, no ground, no horizon.

We used up a lot of time negotiating lead after lead, and I found myself going half-mad from vertigo caused by whiteout conditions. Pressure ridges were magnified in the haze and looked like giant mountains. Between them, deep, endless valleys with lanes of open water in the ice imitated calm meandering rivers. By the day's end, we were so tired, we tripped and fell over every snowdrift and every ice chunk we encountered.

We were in desperate need of some good luck. Our only hope of breaking away from this southern drift was a shift in wind direction from the north to the south, which would push the ice pans north. We were 30 nautical miles east-southeast of Cape Arkticheskiy. Back in Moscow, John sent an email to Greenpeace, our environmental and communications sponsor, warning them that we may have to end the expedition if conditions didn't change. Simultaneously, Ann Possis, our expedition manager, received an email from Gordian Raacke, the director of Renewable Energy Long Island (RELI), the expedition's renewable energy partner: "Lonnie and Eric's courageous expedition and fascinating dispatches from the top of the world are a "Mayday!" call to the whole world. My hope is that the One World Expedition will serve as a wakeup call to alert the American public to the fact that polar ice caps and ancient glaciers are melting at a rapid rate as a result of our ever-increasing consumption of fossil energy sources...."

We received another email from John saying a helicopter would be at Seredny Island in the next few days to service another expedition. That same helicopter could lift us over the worst ice and deliver us 50 miles to more stable floes. Taking this helicopter flight seemed like cheating to me. If we took the flight, we would never know for certain if the trip could have been done entirely by sea and ice. I called John to tell him that we were going to try to continue on our own. It was not an easy decision. Flying ahead to better ice would cost at most $3,000, while being rescued later would run $102,000.

The sound of several sea mammals exhaling in a distant lead diverted our attention from the gravity of our situation. We left our boats to investigate. At the lead's edge, busting through the thin ice was a smooth, dark, spotted back. It dove as quickly as it surfaced, but it appeared to be a narwhal.

The distraction was brief. Although we had snowshoed for eight hours through snow and overcast skies, we were still 3 miles south of the Cape. Progress was painfully slow. Deep snow placed an additional drag on the boats, which created a deep trench, making it difficult to maneuver them. Resting on my poles, I thought of how the advancing summer's warmth would soon be turning this snow into wet mush that wouldn't support us. I also thought of the words of a fellow explorer, Sir Edmund Hillary: "It is not the mountain we conquer but ourselves." With wet eyes—and not from wind or cold—I moved forward, uncertain of our future.

Summer's melt progressed quickly. On May 25, the temperature reached 39°F, a temperature usually reached in late June. The south-facing sides of pressured ice blocks were melting, and their undersides formed long, dripping icicles. By midday the surface of the snow was sticky, and many of the leads were free of slush and ice. My mind drifted back to a recent conversation I'd had with my good friend Paul Schurke, who guides Arctic trips out of Spitsbergen Islands in Norway. The Longyearbyen Fjord, he said, was ice-free in April for the first time ever.

The little ice pan we were on, mostly surrounded by water, was visited by sea birds—ivory gulls, yeagers and white skuas with black, thick bills and feet. Instead of being glad of the company, they added to my anxiety. This too-early thawing was another sign of the Arctic Ocean melting. Fortunately, we didn't truly understand how precarious our situation was. According to a satellite image of the area, the ice we were traveling on looked like a white plate floating just off the edge of an Olympic-sized swimming pool of cold ocean. Open water with little-to-no ice stretched for 70 miles to the west, 30 miles to the south and 45 miles to the east. To the north was a group of floating pans, some touching, some separated by leads of various sizes. Even without this image I could tell enough. We were probably in the middle of the ocean's last cold summer.

One overcast morning, as I left the tent for the morning's toilet, I saw open water and brash ice in all directions surrounding our small ice pan. When I headed back to the tent, I had no more than got in and zipped the door shut before I heard massive steps breaking through the crusted snow just on the other side of the nylon. A polar bear had followed me to the tent. I heard him swatting the camera bag off my canoe-sled cover. He was too close for us to stick our heads out, so Eric unzipped the door just far enough to reach out and fire a rocket. I frantically removed the revolver from the gun case, checked that it was loaded and laid it on my lap.

Eric and I carefully peered out at a very large male bear, dripping wet from swimming across the adjacent quarter-mile-wide lead. Yellow fur draped his thin, hungry frame. His face was dark near the muzzle and heavily scarred. This is typical of older bears. Fights are the cannibalistic last efforts of starving bears that are no longer agile enough to hunt seals. Polar bears need ice from which to hunt seals, and ice forming later in the autumn and melting earlier in the spring was shortening their number of hunting days. This bear, 30 feet away from us, was starving.

I shot my pencil flare, and it exploded 15 feet above and just behind the bear. The bear moved slightly. Eric shot another flare as I reloaded. The bear moved a bit faster, 50 feet downwind. I sent another flare, which exploded in the snow just behind him. This time, he sat back on his huge haunches, looking around as if to take in what was happening. He aimed his cold, black eyes at us as we huddled inside the entrance of the tent. I was terrified. For the first time in my life, I truly understood what it was to be prey. Our rockets had been completely ineffective. I gave a warning shot with the .44 Magnum revolver. The bullet opened a hole in the ice between his two front paws. I was certain the deafening blast would frighten the bear away. Instead, he started moving towards us.

Shaking, I muttered, "Go away. I don't want to shoot you." At 40 feet, he charged us. I hesitated, then took careful aim. At 20 feet, the bullet hit his chest, just left of center. He kept coming, dipping his head to bite at the burning red spot on his chest. We cowered in our tent, as if the opaque nylon fabric could offer security against 1,200 pounds of charging carnivore. When he was 15 feet from us, I shot him again. Another red stain appeared on his fur, inches from the first. His left shoulder slumped, but he kept coming, pawing with his right leg through the deep snow. With the last round in the gun, I aimed for his neck and shot. The bear slowed and then slumped into the entrance of our tent. In complete shock and pushed against the back of the tent, we watched, only feet away, as he raised himself one last time. He twisted slightly, and then was still. Shaking, we silently watched him for several seconds. When we were sure he was dead, I lowered the gun and wept. I had just killed the very animal we were trying to protect.

The horror of this, along with the stress and fatigue of drifting around in circles, put us in a slightly confused and unfocused stupor. We broke camp and set out, shuffling ahead like zombies. I hit the wall both physically and mentally, realizing that we were not going to make it to the pole. We could not outrun the southern drift. There were too many open leads, and the snow was too deep. We were already a month behind schedule, and the snow ahead of us would only become softer and slushier.

Since leaving Cape Artichetskiy on May 10, we had traveled about 120 miles, but we had progressed just 32 miles toward the pole. We were unable to maintain the pace required to complete the expedition. Twelve of our first 16 days were blanketed by snow, and the drift continued to drag us backwards. Although my first priority was to keep us safe, I also felt the weight of our supporters' expectations. Yet I knew there was only one sane and safe response to our dilemma. We had to quit.

Eric and I hadn't had one single break on this project, and this had probably been the toughest 16 days of my life. I didn't think Eric realized the conditions we were facing. Everywhere I looked were water clouds, indicating breaks in the ice and open water ahead. We had just crossed ice barely thick enough to hold our weight. Had one of us fallen through, it would have been impossible for the other to rescue him. I was partially consoled by the irony of it all. Our failure was evidence of the very fact we were trying to illustrate.

Eric was not happy with my decision. "I've just wasted two and a half years of my life," he said. I told him we should be proud of our attempt and what we had learned. I reminded him that expedition work always involves ups and downs. "It's not all success and fame. Explorers and mountaineers greater than we are have had to return to the planning table after less-than-successful expeditions, some— like Will Steger, Ranulph Fiennes and Reinhold Messner—just a few days or weeks after starting out."

After a long talk in the tent, we left separately on short walks to clear our heads. I called Victor only to learn that the pilots had used our gas supply for other purposes. Victor assured me that he'd get someone to us, one way or another. I explained we would soon be floating in a sea with no ice if he didn't hurry, and reminded him that we'd paid good money to have ample fuel ready and waiting. Our small ice pan was drifting like a life raft at the mercy of the wind and ocean currents. The next day we needed to comb the area for an ice pan big enough for a camp in the event of a storm and thick enough to support a large helicopter.

We awoke to a Memorial Day of rain and temperatures near 40°F. We decided to stay put in our tent. On the Arctic Ocean, rain is common during July and August, not May. At midday, we met the fourth polar bear of our short-lived expedition. A young female came within 30 feet of us. She'd followed our ski tracks toward the door of our tent. We shot five flares to detour her, and Eric managed to chase her away, much like he'd have shooed away a stray dog caught eating out of a trash can. We were left with four bullets, a handful of flares and one can of mace.

As frightening as the bear encounters had been, it was still incredible to be able to see these amazing and majestic animals up close. They're so well adapted to the snow, ice and sea, they are able to survive in a place where we'd been struggling every minute just to inch forward. Eric checked out the tracks of one bear, which led to a nearby lead that would have been extremely difficult for us to cross. The ice was too thick to swim through and too thin to walk on. The bear, rather than using valuable energy to break the ice with its chest and paws, dove through the thin ice and swam under it to get to the other side. Although we were nervous about being in their habitat, it was also an honor. Yet, I was overwhelmed with sadness. If warming continued at its current accelerated rate and the Arctic had ice-free summers, the polar bear would most likely become extinct.

Our sudden inactivity was hard to endure while we waited. This two weeks was made worse for me because Eric stopped talking to me once I had made the decision to quit. For nine days, I got no response, no matter what I tried. In all that time, Eric uttered six words: "All our work was for nothing." Playing solitaire on Palm pilots and listening to MP3 players didn't replace the comfort of conversation. We were down to staring at the rip-stop nylon tent ceiling, all 2,304 squares per square foot of it. I was now on two expeditions—one to get us home safely, the other to keep from strangling Eric.

I knew I'd made the only decision that would keep us alive, but I wondered about my leadership skills. It was tempting to focus on Eric's youth and what I saw as stubborn selfishness. Yet, when I was not stuck in my own frustration, I admitted to myself that I needed to better understand how to deal with people of different personalities and experiences. In my heart, I knew that finding a way to get a person to feel heard and respected could mean life rather than death on an expedition. I just couldn't think of a way to change our dynamic. All I knew for sure was that unless I planned on taking nothing but solo expeditions in the future, this was still something I needed to learn. It wasn't as simple as thinking, "If I pick the right people, things will be fine...."

On June 3, to keep my mind busy, I began journaling new plans for another attempt to the North Pole the following summer. What could we have done differently to make this expedition succeed? Should we have left earlier? Should we have left from another location? Perhaps a summer expedition to the North Pole beginning in Russia was impossible now. While I was discouraged, I did not regret our attempt. I balanced my questions with the words of one of my favorite Nordic sayings: "Fear regret, not failure."

We had marked a landing spot for the chopper with red powdered fruit drink over what we believed to be the thickest parts of the pan. It finally arrived late that same day. Out of the small, round helicopter windows, I watched with bittersweetness as we left behind the ice pan. Our camp was on a thin, lone piece of ice surrounded by a vast sea of open water to the east, west and south. To the north was nothing but a narrow band of consolidated brash ice separated by leads resembling mismatched puzzle pieces. I wondered if even winter attempts on the North Pole would be possible in the future because of the vast amount of water off the coastline.

Even though I could so clearly see how precarious our situation had been, I knew, just as certainly as I had known many times before, that I would come back.

CHAPTER 25

WAITING DOESN'T MEAN QUITTING

By June 8, 2005, we had traveled from one extreme to the other. Eric and I found ourselves in New York City, running from one media interview to the next. In melting 91°F heat, we both wished for a bit of Arctic weather. A couple of weeks later, NSIDC, using remote sensing imagery to survey ice cover at both poles, reported that June readings indicated the sea ice was at its lowest level ever for that time of year. According to Walt Meier: "The ice actually melted back farther than normal pretty much everywhere around the Arctic. Where it's been retreating the most has been north of Alaska and north of eastern Siberia."

In other words, the Arctic Ocean was breaking up a month early this year, the NSIDC reported. Weather stations around the perimeter of the Arctic Ocean all recorded very warm winter conditions for extended periods. That made the sea ice thin, breaking it up earlier than anticipated. Many leads were only partially frozen and had much brash ice. This explained why we couldn't ski or paddle across them.

My mind reeled with all the tasks that required attention when we arrived home. We needed time to assess what had happened, what we'd seen and learned. We also needed to do more research on the ocean's rim before we could initiate another attempt. Meanwhile, through our Web site and presentations to schools, corporations and nonprofits, we voiced our concerns about climate change and reported our findings on its effects.

The One World Expedition had garnered tens of millions of media impressions worldwide. Though we had not yet reached the North Pole, the expedition had helped to solidify the fact that climate change is devastating the Arctic. I flew to Long Beach on behalf of Greenpeace to convince California State University and its trustees to pass a resolution for the university to get 20 percent of its electricity from solar technologies, which they did.

Eric toured the Midwest on a similar mission. He also visited Amsterdam on his way to Greenland and the Greenpeace ship, Arctic Sunrise. He would fill in as a deck hand and relieve John Hoelscher, who had been there since the beginning of June. Arctic Sunrise's crew had discovered that Greenland's Kangerdlugssuaq Glacier melt had accelerated in the past nine years and become one of the fastest-moving glaciers in the world. This glacier alone transports or "drains" four percent of the ice from the Greenland ice sheet. Such change in glaciers causes a significant rise in our planet's sea levels.

In November, Ted Scambos of the NSIDC emailed us: "It seemed to us that the main thing that you both observed in your trek was that the sea ice pack was rougher than you expected— rougher than earlier explorers described. We latch onto this as a possible indicator that the ice is actually getting thinner; because the plates are thinner, they are more easily buckled and crushed by winds and ocean currents.

"What we're now doing is going through satellite data in a new way, looking at signals of ice surface roughness....Your data on free-board and snow thickness will be important to us—even more important are the photos of the ice surface that you crossed, which can be compared to past photos of the Arctic ice in the same regions. It is a lot easier to measure sea ice roughness from space than sea ice thickness."

I was especially heartened by his last words: "Science is slow, slower even than a polar traverse. But we'll get there." Although we had not yet met our ultimate goal, our expedition was making a difference. I spent late 2005 and early 2006 preparing for another summer attempt to reach the North Pole. By now, the drill was familiar—fundraising events, planning sessions, physical conditioning. I struggled with whether to replace Eric as my teammate.

I'm pretty easygoing, but I'm also strong willed. I tend to go inward when things aren't going well, and I do best with mature, seasoned teammates who are as stoic about problems as I am. With them, I enjoy the deep rapport that eases the isolation and hardships of a long exploration. Patience doesn't come easily to me, and I'm especially impatient with teammates whom I consider long on raw nerve but short on the wisdom that comes from experience. I can deal with brash ice on an expedition. Not so easily a brash teammate. Yet, when I weighed all the pros and cons, it seemed better to stick with Eric. Optimistic by nature, I hoped we'd both learned something from our differences and could bring that to our second attempt to reach the pole in summer.

With nearly everything set for a May 1, 2006, departure, Victor Boyarsky informed us that we should expect a sharp increase in what we'd have to pay Russians for their help. In addition, because of anticipated fog, no helicopter would be available during emergencies. Although crisis management is what expedition groups often excel at, raising another $100,000 in two weeks seemed a bit unlikely.

We quickly realized the better option was to depart from Ward Hunt Island in northern Canada.

Our Russian route, with its unpredictable currents, had concerned my friend and fellow explorer, Will Steger, and he applauded our change of plans. "The ice off the coast of Ellesmere is thick and relativity stable," he wrote. "You are making the right decision, so relax with it and good luck on the ice—I wish I was with you." What had taken me nine months to organize for a Russian departure took two weeks for the Canadian launch. Although our route had changed, the expedition goals had not— highlighting the climate change crisis, and the consequent plight of the Inuit and the polar bear. We felt even more dedicated than before.

I greatly appreciated that Greenpeace had decided to support us again. Mike Johnson, a Greenpeace technology genius who attacks quantum physics problems for fun and considers Max Planck's *Eight Lectures on Theoretical Physics* a great read, arrived a week before our departure to check our computers, gadgets, cables, chargers and solar panels. He updated our equipment to make sure we could regularly update our Web site, send pod casts and travel safely. Mike also got us a rugged PalmPilot used by the military. This new, solid-state unit charged easily off of a new solar panel, and we could use it in conjunction with our satellite phone.

Scientists from the National Snow and Ice Data Center equipped us with the knowledge and tools to take samples and to document melt-water pools as well as measure ice thickness, snow depth and snow density. We could provide scientists with measurements never before taken. Scientists at NSIDC were calling the data that we would gather the "Holy Grail" of sea ice studies. We had one final media appearance on *The Tonight Show* with Jay Leno before our hometown send-off party. Then we were ready to travel to Resolute Bay, on Canada's northeastern coast.

CHAPTER 26

STARTING THE JOURNEY AGAIN

Whether or not a person actually wants to go to the top of the world, the North Pole's mystical, otherworldly force has a powerful draw for most people. Only about 200 people have ever reached the geographical North Pole. And of those who attempt it, few make it past the first two weeks of an expedition. Prior to 2005, no one had ever successfully traversed the summer's shifting ice. The difficulty of the task we had set for ourselves was aptly put by Reinhold Messner, the world's foremost alpinist, in his book, *To the Top of the World*: "Everest is very dangerous, but crossing the North Pole, which I attempted to do....is ten times more dangerous."

Making this journey in summer had been considered an impossibility. Many in the polar community were politely supportive of our plans. Others were more openly frank, such as one of the world's premier polar explorers, Canadian Richard Weber, who completed one of the toughest and most brilliantly executed expeditions from Ellesmere Island to the pole and back with no resupplies. Weber said flat-out in *Outside* magazine that "summer travel on the Arctic Ocean is not possible, due to high rates, sometimes up to one-half nautical mile an hour, of unpredictable and uncontrollable drift....You cannot travel against these forces of nature."

We were not deterred. Again, I was grateful to be as persevering as I am, especially in the face of difficulty. A departure on May 1 was crucial. Any delay could spell failure. The longer we stayed put, the greater the chance of the coastal sea ice breaking up. Our chances of survival in early breakup conditions were borderline at best. We were already receiving satellite reports from the NSIDC of a nearly 10 percent increase in the amount of open water compared to the same date the year before.

Traveling back to the Arctic, as I watched the landscape pass beneath us, I wondered how we would fare this time. Would the ice and drift be kinder to us? Would our health hold up? At 45 years old, I wondered about my own physical capabilities. I was confident about how arduously I had trained and prepared for the expedition, but I was aware of how physically vulnerable I felt during our first attempt. It's one thing to test your body by training in controlled environments and quite another to drag a 225-pound canoe-sled for 10 hours over a maze of up-heaved ice blocks.

Resolute, Canada's second most northerly community, lies in the Nunavit Territory and the Northwest Passage, and has a population of just over 200. Only the community of Grise Fjord on Ellesmere Island is farther north. Resolute is nestled in an archipelago of islands and channels that remain frozen most the year. Its air of expedition history is palpable. The English name comes from the HMS Resolute, one of the vessels that had searched for Sir John Franklin's lost British expedition. You only need to see this town on a map to understand the local saying: "Resolute is not the end of the world, but you can see it from here."

Four Greenpeace members were in Resolute with Eric and me. "Mikey-J" programmed our phones and e-mail, and presented lengthy overviews to us on each technical piece. Mark Warford, the point man behind our partnership, spent much of his time preparing the video cameras for our journey north. Mark had been with us from the beginning of our first attempt. Like most other Greenpeace employees, he was multitalented. From guitarist to award-winning photographer to pilot, Mark was the rare Jack of all trades and master of most. The third member of our small crew was Melanie Duchin, Greenpeace's chief spokesperson on climate change. A rare combination of idealism and dedication, Melanie had been at Greenpeace for years. Greenpeace had been involved with our expedition for almost two years, and although all efforts now were focused on getting two stubby explorers onto the sea ice, our combined efforts also served a larger agenda, the planet earth and her polar bear. We had made the decision to use the survival of the polar bear as the symbolic focus of our venture.

On April 29, 2006, we received final word from Kert Davies, research director at Greenpeace, on the NSIDC's analysis of the current satellite image of the Arctic Ocean ice. "Essentially, the story is: Ahead of you, completely fractured ice. Lots of leads in all directions. Drift is still to the west, at about 3 km per day. The region is now loosening and moving west, and is somewhat unusually open for so early in the season. Passive microwave data shows areas of only 90 percent and 85 percent [ice] coverage nearby. This is a bit unusual; the past two years show solid 100 percent [ice] between the coast and pole here at this time of year."

Eric and I had our work cut out for us. The next day, at 5:15 pm, we lifted off the runway. We flew over Ellesmere Island on one of the most beautiful Arctic days that either of us had ever seen. Startling blue sky stretched over an endless procession of frozen peaks, snowy valleys and glaciated fjords. We had prepared meticulously. We were not overly anxious, simply eager to get on the ice and start traveling. The trials of our first attempt meant we were more experienced. I looked down at the surface of Ward Hunt Ice Shelf. The snow looked rough and wavy. As I clutched the bottom of my seat, the plane's skis hit the firm, wind-swept snow with a shutter and bang. It took six attempts to make one very rough landing.

At 10 pm, our feet hit frozen earth. Within minutes, our backs were bent over our skis under the weight of the sleds. As the Twin Otter waved its wings goodbye, the realization that we were once again alone hit me like a glacial wall. My career as a polar explorer would take a serious dive if we didn't succeed on this second attempt. Would we reach our goal, or come home to sponsors and fellow explorers offering half-hearted condolences?

The clock ticked just past midnight. It was May 1. We pulled our sleds a short distance north from Cape Discovery in the -9°F air and stopped at the very edge of the stable Ward Hunt Ice Shelf. Our position was N 83 05.31, W 77 26.26. Directly in front of us was the "live" Arctic Ocean with busted sea ice 15 feet thick. We set up what would be our only really solid camp for months.

Waking up the next morning in the tent was so familiar it seemed as if no time had passed since our last attempt. Then we looked outside. The mountains of Ellesmere Island rested in the background of bright magnificent sunshine. Last year's attempt brought only two days of sun. We opted for skis for the first hour of travel in our 600-mile journey, but we quickly encountered blocks of ice rubble piled high for as far as we could see. We picked and crawled our way on all fours through the chaotic mess like sled dogs. Our sleds twisted and contorted behind us, through cracks and small valleys in the towering ice. By day's end, we'd inched 3.75 miles north. We were too tired to be scared or nervous about the future.

At the end of our third day on the ice, I thought wistfully about our training back home when we pulled tires 3 miles every morning up 1,200 feet of elevation. Here we had flat pans anywhere from 50 to 400 yards in diameter, and in between was jumbled ice 5 to 30 feet high. It was as we expected, and we just had to find the best way to get from pan to pan. It would be the same for the next 100 miles. I kept reminding myself to take it one step, one mile, one day at a time.

From a vantage point atop a mountain of blue ice blocks, we gazed ahead at sea ice pressured into a series of 30-foot-high hedgerows that were spaced 300 yards apart. Each ridge of pressured sea ice was made up of precarious blocks and slabs of car-to-cabin-sized, turquoise-colored ice. Between these backbreaking blockades lay a maze of willy-nilly ice boulders.

Good expeditions boil down to a schedule in tune with the environment, with each team member having a set routine. We attempted to travel eight to 10 hours each day, passing off the duty of breaking trail every 90 minutes. We had 10-minute breaks after every three hours of travel, and we stopped to set up the tent around 5 o'clock. At the end of each day, Eric collected snow blocks to melt into water and took measurements for our science program. I organized the inside of the tent, got the stove started, took our GPS position and filled out our daily log. Eric then wrote the bulk of the daily Web update and sent it off with a picture.

After nine hours of sleep, I woke at 6 o'clock each morning to make breakfast. I woke Eric at 7, and by 7:30 he was out of the tent finishing off any science measurements we needed. Meanwhile, I mucked out the tent. By 8 o'clock, we'd packed the canoe-sleds and were off. We scheduled a half-day rest after every seven days, and a full day off every 21 days. If we were forced to stay put during a storm for repairs or some other logistical reason, we planned to count this as a rest day and start the sequence over again.

Each day was a long day with only a few miles to show for it. And those were the good days. At one point, we found ourselves trying to ease our sleds down 10-foot drops, only to heave them up and over our heads a few minutes later. We weaved, wiggled and wedged our 9-foot sleds north, hoping not to dislodge ice that could squash us like a bug. With our heavy loads, even our snowshoes didn't provide enough traction. We resorted to crawling on all fours, and clawing our way up and over the chaotic clumps of snow and ice. At one point, Eric and I looked at each other between deep breaths and laughed almost hysterically at the absurdity of what we were attempting.

Cape Discovery to the North Pole is approximately 415 nautical miles. A general rule of thumb when traveling over this maze of ice in the winter is to add 25 percent for route deviation. In our case, since we were traveling during the summer with more obstacles, leads and fields of brash ice, our percent of deviation was about 27 percent, or 519 nautical miles, approximately 596 statute miles.

After only four days in an expedition that would last months, we knew it was best not to think past the next day. We tried to live in the moment and not focus on the future, but we couldn't help but be excited by the prospect of a newly frozen lead running north or a big smooth floe on the horizon.

On May 6, we camped on a small pan, about 100 feet by 200 feet, in the middle of some of the most severely pressured ice we'd seen. Our tent gave us a short respite. The thin red nylon of the tent door zippered away the toil of the day and shielded us from the next day's challenges. Above us was wet clothing hanging on a string. Under us, the ice undulated and groaned. At the edge of the ice floe, a new pressure ridge was being born with a sound like a jet going overhead.

In the morning, the sun sparkled through long crystals of frost that formed on our equipment overnight. We worked for 30 minutes stuffing our feet into frozen, stiff boots. After an hour of snowshoeing, the frigid leather finally conformed to our now-cold feet. Snowshoes were far superior to skis that day, offering more traction, dexterity and balance in the dense rubble. By midmorning we had stumbled onto a gloriously flat lead that headed due north. We switched to our skis, which cut through a garden of 3-inch frost flowers covering the thin gray ice. We knew a lead was safe if it was covered in ice flowers. The newly formed ice, bowing under our weight, allowed us passage as long as we kept moving and distributing our weight across the fragile ice. Sometimes the ice bent so severely under our weight the top of the pan was eye level.

Pulling canoe-sleds through, around and over the ice helped keep our blood pumping. Our inch-by-inch battle meant a day-long sweat, but we froze the moment we stopped to rest. During one break, between frozen bites on an energy bar, a plane flew above us—most likely an SAS flight and probably the start of cocktail service. Didn't we wish.

In the thick of pack ice, Eric fell and smashed his knee. The pain was so great he nearly vomited. That evening, we experienced our first equipment glitch. None of our three PalmPilots worked properly. One was able to send out text but no pictures, one wouldn't connect with our satellite phone, and the third wouldn't take a charge. We needed them to update our Web site with images and journal entries every day, and for basic communications with our support staffs back in Minnesota and Washington, DC.

I was irritated, primarily because we had the same silly image problem last year. In both cases, it had been Eric's responsibility to resolve the technology glitches months before the expedition's departure. I was not entirely sure my anger was justified, so I held my tongue. Eric worked long into the night to remedy the problem. By morning, after several expensive satellite calls to Mikey-J in Washington, Eric managed to get one of the PalmPilots to work. We could now send pictures, which provided a crucial visual record of the summer Arctic Ocean.

Morning brought treacherous skiing across fairly large cracks. Trying to cross the yawning gaps with slipping skis and sleds pulling us backwards—or worse, running us over—required a resolve stemming from one simple truth. The only way out was to keep moving forward. Even with a 24-hour sun at our backs, our faces were burnt and leathery. At 0°F, we fried on the outside and froze on the inside.

The same questions nagged me every day. Would we be stopped dead from fields of consolidated brash ice too thick to paddle through and too unstable to ski across? Would the fog become too dense to navigate? Would we make our goal? A wide swath of multiyear pressure ice made for difficult passage. Ice chunks and snowdrifts were everywhere—some hard-packed, others soft. If we hauled our sleds up one side, they crashed down the other unless we were very careful. After a full week on the trail, we were weary to our bones. We took a half-day of rest. We slept in, made equipment repairs, charged electronics, and hit the trail at 1 pm to put in four hours of travel.

A light snow, which had begun late the night before, continued through the morning of May 9. The warm temperatures and cloudy skies made for the worst traveling conditions imaginable. With no shadows on the snow, our depth perception completely vanished. It was impossible to look at the snowdrifts and determine if they were sloping up or down. We spent most of the day flailing over snowdrifts. Each time I looked ahead and saw Eric stumble on the ice, I cringed. I knew I was next.

Once again I felt on the edge of madness from vertigo created by whiteouts. When I switched my eyeglass lenses from red to yellow for even a little definition, a seal came into focus. It bobbed up and down to get a better look at us. To deal with the irritating whiteout conditions, we switched from daytime to nighttime travel. With the sun casting shadows, we had at least some contrast in this frozen sea of white. It made for easier navigation.

We both fought off negative thoughts of what the future held if these conditions continued. At one point, we became giddy, almost hysterical. Clearly the load was getting to us. Much of our stress came from knowing we couldn't be rescued for any reason. Fixed-wing aircraft couldn't land on the Arctic Ocean after May 1 due to soft snow, unreliable ice and overcast skies. It was too far and too foggy for land-based helicopters to fly. We knew we had to stay motivated and be careful. Our lives depended on it.

Thankfully, we finally emerged into a series of large pans and easily negotiated leads. A Twin Otter flew overhead through the clouds. Kenn Borek Air was on the way to supply Canadian Paul Landry's dog-sled crossing of the Arctic Ocean. They had run into continuous problems with difficult ice since leaving Russia and should have been off the ice at least two weeks ago. It felt good to know there were other expeditions on the ice besides us. It didn't matter that we were scattered across an area half again as big as the United States. Besides Landry's dog-sled expedition, two Danes were pulling sleds. Both teams were attempting to complete a winter crossing of the ocean from Russia to Canada. At the start of their journeys, both had to be flown over open water to more stable ice. A third expedition, led by Richard Weber's wife, Jose, was a Canadian team attempting to head south to Ellesmere Island from an ice island near the pole, where they were dropped off by plane. All were behind schedule, thanks to the same ice conditions and open water we were experiencing.

In the midst of another slogging day, my ankle locked up. I'd broken both ankles in a fall at home, and my ankles often get stiff and achy. The irony was not lost on me that I hurt myself more severely in my work as a carpenter than I ever did as an explorer. In a curious way, that accident is one of the most important things that has ever happened to me. I was working on a friend's house when I fell off the roof. I ended up in a wheelchair for two and a half months. My friend has a son, Dan, who is disabled and will spend his whole life in a wheelchair. While I was able to count the days before I was up and walking again, Dan will never walk again.

I've taken this lesson to heart, so I carry it with me on every expedition. It's one of the quickest ways for me to snap out of self-pity and rememeber how lucky I am. It gives me instant perspective. This time, after several attempts to move my ankle through pressure massage and stretching, I managed to get it working again. My relief was immense. Even the smallest injuries can turn deadly in the Arctic.

We passed the significant "two-week" point when many North Pole expeditions call it quits. Too tired to mark the moment, we just went to bed. We woke to clear blue skies and 10°F, perfect for traveling. By 8 am we were skiing, with me leading, navigating and breaking trail. We still switched lead every hour and a half, so six separate marches gave us nine hours of travel. We were beginning to get in tune with our surroundings. Our first march of the day was through a heavily drifted area of old pressure ice at N 84 15. We assumed a series of lake-sized leads were created by ocean currents. The ice and leads were fun to travel, and we zigzagged our way west while I played the game "connect the pans."

Our days were governed by three basic principles—ice time, tent time and food. We discussed the first two nearly every day. What we ate was directly related to a relatively regimented time schedule. Our 7 am breakfast was oatmeal or rice pudding, washed down with coffee or an energy drink. We were on the trail by 8 am, and at the first switch of lead skiers, we ate an after-breakfast snack, which was a Clif bar and energy drink. Our first sit-down snack, from 11 to 11:10 am, was a Clif bar, peanuts, a piece of candy plus an energy drink. At 12:40, we often had a piece of candy and energy drink. Our second sit-down break was from 2:10 to 2:20 pm, when we consumed our daily favorite, a stick of salami, with a Clif bar and a piece of candy, washed down with a cool gulp or two of energy drink. At 3:50 pm, we each ate three cubes of Shot Blocks—the energy-packed version of gummy bears. At 6:30 pm, our appetizer was crackers and more energy drink. Dinner at 7:30 pm was noodles or rice, and our 9:15 pm bedtime snack was a piece of candy and a Clif bar, followed by the occasional sleeping pill we took when we switched from day to nighttime travel, or when we were in a considerable amount of muscle pain.

Eric is definitely not a morning person. From 6 in the morning until about midday, he generally had almost nothing to say. This lack of communication frustrated me. Even though we had worked together for almost four years, I still couldn't figured him out. He seemed completely unconcerned about the team process, which is what I enjoy. We finally sat down and had a good talk about getting our feelings out. We even cried a bit. He explained that he was experiencing an emotional roller coaster. Whenever he thought about home, it made it worse for him, so he tried not to think about his family, especially his nephew. He only allowed himself to occasionally remember that he had people who care about him.

We discovered that we had a different way of being optimistic about this expedition. I tried to be totally optimistic on the outside, even when I was full of doubts on the inside. I still didn't really have much of a sense of humor, but I tried, thinking it would help ease some of the tension. "Going to be flatter," I said one day. "I see some flat up there. It's about 83 miles away." He rarely thought I was funny. For Eric, being too optimistic came with a price. "I feel like I'm pretty optimistic about the trip," he explained, "but I need to be realistic about the conditions, because if I think it is going to be good, and I see some bad ice, it just brings me down."

This was a breakthrough for us, and we agreed to try to stay positive, deal with our feelings as they arose and not let them stew. It made me feel better about traveling with Eric. I hoped it would keep improving, but I was nervous it wouldn't last. It turns out I'm not an optimist about everything.

Finally, we emerged onto a large expanse of relatively flat ice. For the first time, we could see quite far ahead, and we could no longer see Ellesmere Island behind us. We whooped and hollered at our luck. The nautical miles cruised by effortlessly for almost three hours. In the distance, we spotted two dark clouds, which formed above leads and which indicated lots of open water. We veered in between them to miss most of the mess. Sometimes this worked, sometimes it didn't. Although we missed the water, we entered an area of thick ice slabs pressured together. The ridge of blocks running parallel to our travel was like a stone fence in England only constructed of blue slabs of ice. It was truly incredible to snowshoe between the 5-foot-thick blocks perched at hundreds of different angles. In some places, the pile rose to almost 20 feet.

Earlier on, we'd resisted listening to our MP3 players while skiing so we could communicate more easily and stay alert as we became more familiar with the ocean. Now that the ice was a bit flatter, staring into the big, white nothingness had its limits. We reversed our decision. I zoned out to Bob Dylan's "Blood on the Tracks." Time seemed to pass more quickly.

When leading, we approached navigation differently. Eric, young and strong, took the shorter "straight on" approach through mountains of ice. Older and smaller, I took the longer route around. However we went, the highlight of each day was stopping in the evening. What we looked forward to most was reading our position on the GPS. We made bets on the distance and our location. We also checked our PalmPilots for messages, the closest thing to entertainment that we had in this vast, white landscape.

When we took our next half-day rest, we reveled in the luxury of our sleeping bags until almost 10 o'clock in the morning. I felt better, partly because I changed my underwear for the first time in 18 days.

Now and then the sun poked through the clouds and acted like a shot of adrenaline. However, as soon as the sun sank behind the clouds or fog, our spirits did, too. Shortly into one afternoon march, rain coated our glasses with a thin film of ice. The conditions left us singing, "Skiing in the rain, we're skiing in the rain, what a not-quite-so-glorious feeling...." Anything to keep going.

We headed more west than north both to avoid leads and to

compensate for the easterly drift. We found ourselves confronted by a series of wide leads covered with very thin ice. It took only two pokes with a ski pole to break through to water. It was so thin that waves formed on the ice in front of and behind our skis as we shuffled ahead, fast and wide-legged to distribute our weight. To stop mid-lead meant, at best, a cold swim.

I couldn't help but think of the explorers before us who'd died out here. Several years earlier, Japanese explorer Hyoichi Kono had frozen off the coast of Ward Hunt Island. His body was found with his legs entangled in the rope from his sled, evidently attempting to cross an opening in the ice. Dominick Arduin, a French-Finnish explorer, had paid the ultimate price for going solo. More than a year before our expedition, she'd left Cape Arkticheskiy. It is speculated that while attempting to cross a lead, she'd either drowned or died of hypothermia. Her body was never found.

We were in too much of a hurry to don our dry suits to cross a lead. If one of us fell through the ice in the middle of one of the wide leads, the other couldn't have helped. The leads were too wide to throw a line across, and the ice was too thick to allow a boat through. It would have been impossible for the one who fell in to crawl back into his tipsy canoe-sled. We managed to make it through unscathed, but we were wet to the knees.

One day, we were greeted by a huge, full-arching rainbow. The only natural colors we saw day to day were white, blue and gray. We had not experienced an entirely sunny day in a week and a half, much less this welcome array of colors. At N 85, we were also happily surprised by the visit of a snow bunting. We also came across a lone set of fox tracks. Although we had yet to see a bear on this trip, we knew they weren't far away. There are 23,000 polar bears in the Arctic, a relatively small number considering the vastness of their domain. The question is not whether they'll soon be extinct. The question is when.

We learned by radio that Paul Landry had gotten himself into a bind. The ice and snow had deteriorated to the point where his dogs couldn't travel efficiently. The skies were too overcast and the snow too soft to land a plane. His dogs were holding his team back from escaping the deteriorating ice. Their only hope was to receive an airdrop of pulk sleds and dry suits so they could try to make it to land. The ice already was pulling away from the coastline, and there was quite a distance for them to swim.

After 23 days without much of a break, we spent an entire day resting in our small tent. With the door zipped shut to the icy environment outside, we could have been camped anywhere in the lower 48 states. We imagined being surrounded by the trees, lakes and granite cliffs of northern Minnesota. I slept for 12 solid hours. Then I spent my free day repairing my ski pole baskets and applying epoxy to my ski tips, which had delaminated. Because it was too cold for the epoxy to set without a bit of help, I covered each ski tip with an empty black food bag and propped the ski upright in the sun. The solar radiation heated the air inside the bag, which cured the epoxy. The rest of the day I snacked on smoked beef sticks between naps. Later, we looked up meanings of words in the miniature travel dictionary we had. Wet gloves and stinky socks hung on a string from the ceiling. Wet ski boots with the insoles pulled out to dry were perched near our heads. Despite the clutter, the cozy tent felt like home.

One midday, we spotted a dark, cigar-shaped object on the ice about 100 yards ahead. It turned out to be a large seal sleeping next to a small lead. We tried to sneak up on it, but it saw our red coats, rolled over and dove under the ice. This interaction, although short, was the highlight of our day.

Through the clouds, we heard the distant sound of a Twin Otter overhead. It was no doubt Kenn Borek Air attempting to rescue Paul's dogs, perhaps dropping supplies. Eric and I discussed my concerns over ice reports from the Kenn Borek pilots and NSIDC. The sea ice had pulled away from the coastlines of Greenland and Ellesmere Island, basically cutting off any possibility of a return journey to land after we reached the pole. A large area of water had already opened in the Lincoln Sea between the two landmasses, and it was only the end of May. Climate change had reduced the sea ice so greatly there was no longer enough ice mass to keep the sea ice pressured against Greenland and Ellesmere Island as in previous years. I could only imagine what it would be like in August.

Our small canoe-sleds were no match for the windy, wide-open seas. I made the decision to follow our fall-back plan and take only enough provisions to get to the pole. From there, a Russian helicopter supported by an icebreaker would take us out. Eric didn't take my decision well. Our experiences so far told me that returning the way we came was out of the question. Eric was determined to attempt to return. However noble and courageous his position seemed, all I could see was the curse of the young, the naive feeling of immortality that comes with inexperience.

Despite our disagreement, we continued on, switching our position as lead skier each hour and a half as we'd agreed. We were soon met with more rubble and slab ice. At one lead, too frozen to paddle across, we found a spot where it narrowed to 4 feet and leaped across. At another, we lashed the canoe-sleds together, used a paddle to chisel the thin ice just in front of the bow and paddled our way across. At yet another, we hopscotched across slippery ice chunks that were semi-frozen into brash ice.

Suddenly, two sets of fox tracks crossed under my skis. This time of year, foxes pair up and mate. We were now traveling almost directly east of magnetic north and had set a W 85 declination to our compass. It felt odd to have the red north needle on our compass point to the west. The closer we were to the pole, the weaker the magnetic force was, which required additional time for the needle to settle. It fluctuated back and forth as we waited impatiently to shoot an accurate bearing toward true north and the top of the world.

May 24, 2006, started off nicely with a bit of sun and high wispy clouds, but a southwest wind soon turned the day. During our first sit-down break, we huddled behind a chunk of ice to protect us from the biting wind. We trudged on for about four and a half hours in the first snowstorm of this expedition and managed to cover about 6 miles. The conditions deteriorated to 40-mile-an-hour gusts. Visibility was zero. We were forced to cut our day short and hurriedly set up the tent. We sat in relative comfort while a storm raged outside. As we waited, we also knew that this strong wind was pushing the ice east. Our fate, for now, was largely out of our control. Happily, however, our GPS told us that we had just reached the 86th parallel.

While we slept, the storm moved our camp nearly a full degree of longitude east. Unzipping the vestibule of the tent, we were greeted by 32°F temperatures and a 2-foot wall of wet snow on the leeward side of the tent that also covered our canoe-sleds and snowshoes. The snow had slowed a bit, but the visibility was still only half a mile. The stiff southwest wind continued to push us to the east at a good clip. We skied northwest. If we didn't stay on top of the eastward drift we could miss the pole. We had to travel lightly and quickly, taking only what we needed to get to the pole. We also had to approach from the west and allow the current to drift us over the pole.

During breakfast, we started to argue again about what we'd do when we reached the pole. Eric wanted to keep going. He argued that if we made it to the pole, we could make it back. I again brought up the melting ocean and breaking ice behind us. We couldn't agree, perhaps never would, but I was leading the expedition and it was my responsibility to make the decision. I gave John Huston, our expedition manager back in Minnesota, instructions to begin the process of extracting us from the pole and getting Russian visas for us, two very difficult tasks. The Russians wouldn't welcome surprise visitors.

Freezing rain forced by a stiff breeze coated our glasses and the entire right sides of our bodies with ice. Despite the inclement weather, we were making great northerly progress. We started to encounter more open water and less brash ice, and we became quite proficient at crossing leads. We got the process of rigging our canoe-sleds, crossing the water and unrigging the canoe-sleds down to about 10 to 15 minutes for a medium-sized lead.

We were 244.2 statute miles north of Cape Discovery and 235.8 miles from the North Pole, a little over halfway. We celebrated the accomplishment—along with Eric's 35th birthday—with an extra Clif bar. We could spare them. We'd brought 800 with us.

The sun's radiation through the fabric tent walls heated our small tent to nearly room temperature. Sometimes, we could even lie outside our sleeping bags. We were now scrawny, unsightly men in long underwear who hadn't bathed in a very long time, so it felt better than it smelled. I looked up at our red tent ceiling and wondered where this expedition fit in the big picture. Man against nature? And why? The human body's ability to overcome adversity had already been well documented through much tougher ordeals. We were not discovering new territory, rather we were contributing to its survival. Many days this is what got me out of my sleeping bag.

Being able to relay images and words via satellite was the key to our contribution. Yet, even with all of our modern gadgetry and electronics, like polar explorers before us—Peary, Amundsen and Nansen—we had put ourselves out of the range of rescue. No plane or helicopter could reach us. Traveling over the shifting ice was our only way out. Every day, the climbing heat ate away more of the ice beneath our skis.

One morning, something seemed off as I got out of the tent. The

sun was in the wrong location. We checked our compasses and realized that currents had rotated our ice pan 180 degrees overnight. Our
incoming tracks from the south were now due north. We had reached
the very limit of where we could receive our airdrop resupply. A GPS
check revealed we were just a few hundred meters away from N 87 on
the south side of a large lead. While we were getting the sleds ready
to catamaran, a seal poked its head out of the water. We watched in
awe for a few minutes while it tilted its head back, took a breath and
slid beneath the surface. I'd never heard of seals this far north. After
a short paddle, we found ourselves camped safely on the high side of
N 87. We had catamaraned the boats 11 times in the past four days. It
appeared that we were in for less ice and more open water.

CHAPTER 27

NEARING THE END OF ANOTHER EXPEDITION

It was time for a full rest day, which we would use to our full
advantage. It was also time for an air drop of supplies. A Twin Otter
stationed eight flight-hours away and modified with an extra fuel
tank would fly from Resolute Bay to Eureka, a small research outpost
on Ellesmere Island, where they would refuel. We relayed our current position and the weather conditions to Kenn Borek's headquarters, which in turn relayed the information to the pilot. We stayed put
until our supplies arrived. Depending on the weather, that could take
a few days. Once we were settled in, we made a call to "Command and
Control" in Minnesota: "Houston we have 87." John Hoelscher con-
gratulated us on making it to this key location. We expected the ice to
improve from here to the pole. John told us that Al Gore's movie, *An
Inconvenient Truth*, had just opened that weekend to rave reviews.

On a bright sunny day, I "showered" and shaved. Eric just shaved. Once we'd finished, we barely recognized each other. Shed of whiskers and pounds, we looked like younger versions of ourselves. The rest of the day we consolidated and shifted our equipment around in preparation for the coming supplies. We also aired out our sleeping bags and shot a video survey of the sea ice, including underwater shots at leads. On the second day of waiting, Greenpeace asked us to deploy the banner "Save the Polar Bear—Stop Global Warming—Greenpeace." A NASA satellite would take a picture of our camp from outer space. Amazing!

We marked a drop zone with red food sacs just a little more than 200 meters from our tent. The pilots almost nailed the zone exactly. It was amazing to see how they skillfully maneuvered not only the plane but the supply drop. "I hope I didn't break the eggs," pilot Stephen Kaiser said over VHF as he flapped the Twin Otter wings to wave goodbye. We ran toward the supply drums whooping with excitement. The new rations offered us a smörgåsbord of new flavors. Although the amount of food per day—30 ounces per person—was the same, we had changed the menu slightly—aged Italian salami, aged Parmesan cheese, dried Finnish rye bread, and chocolate with hazelnuts and raisins.

After sorting through our newly acquired riches and packing the canoe-sleds, we rested in the tent for our final push to the pole. We had been up much of the night talking with Kenn Borek's headquarters about sea ice conditions reported by their pilots—very busted up. We'd been recharging on this comfortable piece of ice, drifting north, for three days. Our muscles and joints were ready to be on the move again. We still had 180 miles to reach the North Pole.

Before leaving, we waited to hear Greenpeace's opinion of our plan. We knew we might have to take a helicopter from the Yamal, a nuclear icebreaker, if other options fell apart. We imagined this might anger Greenpeace, as they spend a great deal of time boycotting nuclear energy. The satellite phone rang, and, as we suspected, Greenpeace was angry. They threatened to declare the rights to all expedition images and videos, and urged us to either return to land or get pulled out another way. Both of our offices were working diligently to find an alternative, but I knew there were few, if any. We'd made final adjustments and repairs to our equipment for our last push, but I still worried that if something went wrong between here and N 88, the next 60 miles, the helicopter couldn't reach us. We needed to be extra careful, especially with the added supply weight.

I was grateful for a few good omens. The sun appeared after five long, cloudy days, and a slight southeast breeze pushed the ice in a north-northwesterly direction. This was the course we needed in order to counter the easterly drift farther to the north. The next day brought a full monty of Arctic hardship—cracks, pressure, brash ice, leads and broken ice. We shouldn't have been surprised, but we'd slipped into thinking conditions would improve. It felt as if the ice was literally melting under our skis, and we were just able to stay ahead of a sea of open water. We traveled for nine and a half hours in fog to advance just a little more than 6 miles.

On June 5, 2006, we woke to a sunny and warm morning. It was 32°F when we hit the trail, a temperature almost too warm for traveling, as we easily overheated. We skied wearing only our long underwear tops and boxer briefs under wind pants. The southerly breeze was eating up the snow, leaving it wet and sticky. The bright day allowed us to navigate relatively easily. The sun is an amazing force, and it was easy to see how climate change affects the sea ice. Past research led us to expect that by N 87, conditions would flatten out, and small broken slab ice would diminish. Instead, conditions continued to get worse. Climate change was creating thinner and thinner ice, which is more easily fractured and pressured by currents and wind. White snow and ice reflect energy back into space, whereas darker water from melt pools and leads absorb heat 100 times more. The more water, the more heat that's absorbed, which melts more ice, which creates more water, and the cycle begins again. This causes havoc all over the world, with rising sea levels and severe weather.

I wanted to get to the pole as quickly as we could, but nine to 10 hours of travel each day was all we could muster. A cold, damp fog shadowed the ice. Soft, wet snow balled up under our skis, eliminating all glide and adding weight to our feet. The warmer temperatures made our ski poles stick after each planting. The wet snow soaked our ski boots, despite heavy oiling.

Only music got me through the arduous progress of each day. Suspecting that blues tracks and Prince rocking about sex would be bad choices, I stuck to Aretha Franklin, Bonnie Rait, Neil Young and Bob Dylan. One day Dylan's "Maggie's Farm" held special appeal. "Well, I try my best to be just like I am, but everybody wants you to be just like them...." That night in camp, we pulled out the pure grain alcohol brought for medicinal purposes. I added it to an energy drink and drank it conservatively to soothe my aching back. I knew that I needed to get up in the morning and do it all over again. I drafted an email to Greenpeace explaining our situation in greater detail.

On our next day of rest, we transcribed data we'd collected over the last month about snow depth, snow density and ice thickness. We also caught up on communications. Greenpeace gave us an encouraging polar bear update. The U.S. Senate had passed legislation to enforce the Polar Bear Treaty that Russia and the United States had reached six years earlier and the bill would now move to the House.

The Center for Biological Diversity and Greenpeace were working to require that the federal government list the polar bear in the Endangered Species Act. The goal was for the U.S. government to come up with a plan to protect the bears' sea ice habitat. The only way would be to cut back on pollution that causes climate change. The downside of the day was that Greenpeace was fuming about my decision to be evacuated from the pole. I still asked John to begin the visa process for us to enter and exit Russia. It would be difficult. The Russian Embassy had never granted a visa without first obtaining a physical passport. I gave John a list of contacts in both Russia and the United States, including Minnesota's two senators. In the meantime, we took photos of our passports, e-mailed them to our office and hoped the Russians would bend the rules a bit. We heard that Kenn Borek Air had rescued Landry and the two Danes. Had they kept on, they certainly would have died. Evidently, it was a dangerous landing and near-catastrophic take-off. "The Arctic Ocean was a rubble field," Paul wrote in an email to our office. "Gone was the pattern of pan followed by a pressure ridge....we found very few pans and the ones we did find were very small."

After disconnecting from the outside world, Eric and I played chess and watched two ivory gulls swooping above us. The next day, we crossed our first set of bear tracks since leaving Ellesmere. They ambled off to the west and because they were drifted over, we judged them to be old tracks. Nonetheless, we went on orange alert, stationed our canoe-sleds, skis and poles in strategic places around the tent, and kept the rifle and flares close by.

We soon received a report from Kenn Borek's pilots that there was a 50-mile-wide lane of open water off the coast of Ellesmere. Returning to land was out of the question. I decided we would take only what we needed to make it to the pole. From there, the only logical solution was to be lifted out to the Yamal. Greenpeace was still upset. While I understood and agreed with Greenpeace's non-nuclear policies, I had no interest in being a martyr. After brainstorming with Greenpeace representatives about how to protect them from unfavorable media backlash, we agreed to remove all Greenpeace insignia from expedition gear and clothing before the Yamal's chopper picked us up. We would also work with Greenpeace on an official statement ending our relationship at the pole. Between the Yamal pickup and our arrival home, we would talk to no press.

If anything, our last push got even harder. We stretched the limits of safety and had near misses with ice breaking beneath us. We bridged nearly 4-foot gaps with our Asnes skis, and were convinced that any other skis would have broken in two. Luck and last-minute lunges kept us dry. Our expedition manager, John Huston, emailed us good news. Our Russian friend Victor told him that the U.S. Consul General in St. Petersburg would issue us visas. The chief of security for the Yamal would be on board the chopper that picked us up. We needed to give him all firearms, flares and left-over fuel.

In mid-June, we came upon an area of flat, multiyear ice with few leads. The thick floes were marked by dirty, rounded tops from past summer seasons. We supposed the dark material was an accumulation of air-born coal soot and pollution trapped in snow and exposed now after years of melt. The particulates would be in the snow samples we'd been collecting for Tom Grenfell at the University of Washington. Scientific tests would determine their exact nature.

At exactly 12:01 am on June 21, we stopped to pay homage to the summer solstice, the longest day of the year. We wished we were more excited by the first day of summer, but it played out much like all our other days on the Arctic Ocean. We hadn't seen a sunrise or sunset since arriving in Resolute at the end of April. Deep snow as soft as sugar no longer supported our weight. Even though we sank in well above our shins, using skis was still better than walking. The weight of our bodies set off a settling of snow over a vast area. We heard this "woomff" over and over but it never failed to startle us. The conditions were so bizarre, all we could do was laugh, mostly at ourselves.

Staying upbeat wasn't easy for either of us. Trying to keep things light, Eric quipped: "What were we thinking when we decided to go to the North Pole in summer?" On our video journal, he recorded his true feelings: "I almost gave in today....I was this close to saying, 'Let's camp early.' Then I looked down at my skis...and it says, 'Begin with one step.' And that is all I thought, just one step. And then, and then worry about the next one."

We shortened our marches to six hours to conserve our strength, but still managed 7 to 8 miles a day. We traveled during the day. With the sun remaining at nearly the same azimuth above the horizon day and night, the fluctuation in temperature was minimal. We would gain no advantage from the night's cooler temperatures and firmer snow conditions. It was preferable to have the sun in front of us, throwing what shadows it could on the contours.

We could hardly believe what we saw next—seals at a latitude of N 89 10.00! We had never heard of seals this far north and wondered if the lack of ice in the south was driving them north. It was another stark reminder of the climate change crisis. We were two days short of the pole.

It rained most of that night, transforming the icescape into water pools and settling the snow into a layer of ice granules. The remaining snowbanks didn't support our weight at all. We sank in 12 to 16 inches with each step through the deep snow. "It's like skiing through mashed potatoes," Eric said. It took extra food, sometimes four Clif bars in the first part of the morning, just to keep going. Even our toboggan-bottomed canoe-sled sank 8 inches or more. Instead of 90-minute shifts of breaking trail, we switched to an hour at a time. With our weaker physical and mental states, the work was too hard to do more.

We had eaten breakfast, lunch and dinner together for 57 straight days. We went back and forth from light banter to disagreements, some trivial, some serious. Despite all this, we were still on speaking terms. We had some good laughs, at silly things, like how much I resembled a little kid in my long underwear shirt. I'd lost a significant amount of weight. Eric called me "tiny dancer." I hadn't been this skinny since I'd nearly starved to death in Alaska 20 years earlier.

The Arctic Ocean continued to break up underneath us. The fractured slabs of ice we traveled across made us reassess everything we knew—or thought we knew—about sea ice. The "good ice" we had been hoping to see for so long didn't exist. Instead of one big sheet of ice in front of us, there were literally hundreds of small pans, 10 to 100 meters in diameter, as far as we could see. We had set a goal of reaching the North Pole by July 1. While we were narrowing the gap daily, it was slow and required maximum effort. With 23.5 nautical miles to go, we didn't know if we'd make it on schedule, or make it at all for that matter.

At one point, when we entered a vast area of active sea ice, we stared, mouths hanging open, at the scene ahead. As far as we could see, small pans, 75 meters in diameter, were stacked up and grinding against each other. Soft brash ice and ice chunks choked the gaps between each pan. The whole mess was not only moving, it was moving fast due to the full moon and ocean currents created by an underwater mountain range called Lomonosov Ridge. Underfoot, pans undulated, forced into clockwise rotation by adjacent grinding floes.

The fragile pan we stood on pitched a few degrees, and a truck-sized piece of multiyear ice rocketed up just in front of us at the edge of another lead. We moved, and quickly. To our right, car-sized pieces of ice turned over, exposing blue underbellies. We snowshoed in earnest to the left and hopscotched over blocks of ice the size of hay bales.

There's nothing like imminent danger to stimulate action. It was obvious that we had to get out. Now! Leaving my canoe-sled sitting in the brash ice in a narrow lead, I went back to help Eric, who was struggling behind me, only to realize my canoe-sled was being crushed as the two pans came together. For a split second I thought, "Good, I hope it crushes." Then I remembered it contained our food. Laughing, I dragged it to safety. Meanwhile, Eric pulled at his canoe-sled to get it up and over an uncooperative 10-foot chunk of ice surrounded by brash ice. His canoe-sled stuck fast and when it suddenly came free Eric slipped and tumbled forward, almost falling into the open lead. His canoe-sled was stuck again, this time resting sideways and in danger of getting crushed by rafting slabs. We freed it but we weren't in the clear yet. In a minute, the lead I'd just crossed would be impassible for Eric as the moving ice pan released the pressure holding the brash ice together.

"Don't think, just go," Eric muttered to himself as he headed my way. It seemed to take hours to race through the turmoil, though in reality it only took 45 minutes. A short ski more and we were on some of the best ice we had skied on yet, with not a lead in sight. We breathed a sigh of relief. Then breathed another. I hit the wall by afternoon, and it was everything I could do—mentally and physically—to keep pushing my legs forward. It seemed like every time we took a little turn, the canoe-sled got hooked and I couldn't pull it free. Snow stuck to our skis. We plowed snow with our shins and hit slush pools on every pan. In fact, we were literally plowing trenches with our sleds through the water-laden snow. We had 15 miles to go. It might as well have been 1,500 for how near-impossible it felt.

"One more step," was our mantra. Only a few miles from the pole, we saw more open water than even our worst-case guesses. We stopped every hour to check our declination with the GPS. We were so close to the North Pole that if it had been possible to stand on top of our tent, we would have seen it. Not that it would look any different from the ice and water all around us.

Many times during this journey, we felt that the pole was just an arbitrary point. What makes it different from any other point around it? The importance, of course, was not the pole but the journey. Each day brought amazing insight and personal connection with a fragile environment. We could never have guessed how much the ice could change in character and personality. The Arctic ice was a moving, living eco-system of birds, seals, bears, snow and amazing forms of ice sculpted by Mother Nature.

Open water now surrounded our camp. At 4 o'clock the next morning, Eric heard a noise outside that sounded a lot like footsteps in the soft snow. On a completely calm night, even the thump of my heart beating sounded like the steady footfalls of a stalking predator. Many times we had both mistaken a random noise for something sinister, only to find nothing more formidable than a snow flap blowing in the wind. I opened my eyes and saw Eric staring at the tent wall. The guy is going crazy, I thought. He looked at me and said, "Bear!" I thought he was messing with me. We hadn't seen a bear on the entire trip, and now that we were basically at the pole, we see a bear? I heard nothing. We were on young ice, with seals and hundreds of leads all around. It seemed plausible that a polar bear could be here, but they rarely traveled so deep into the ocean. Food was too scarce.

Eric put his arm out the door, fired off a rocket and looked out the door. As he pulled his head back in and I saw his eyes, I knew he wasn't kidding. Walking 10 feet away, a young but very large and unusually white male polar bear was investigating our camp—exactly 1.5 miles from the North Pole. He wasn't in a big hurry to leave and stopped frequently to sniff the air. We sent up a second flare and shooed him away. He was not aggressive and didn't damage any equipment. He seemed more curious than anything else.

By this time, I had the video camera running and caught a few of the bear's farewell glances on tape. We hurriedly put our boots on to assess the scene. The bear had followed our ski tracks into camp. He came from downwind to disguise his scent and used several small drifts to hide behind as he stalked us. Then, he circled slowly around the tent, coming within 5 feet of us.

Our last day of the expedition was the first day I relaxed. I finally felt as if I didn't have to worry about injury, or about whether we'd make it to the pole and ever see our families and friends again. Despite the hardships, I had enjoyed the challenges and lessons of the past 61 days. Today I enjoyed them even more. For the first time in a very long while, I felt cheery.

After an hour ski, Eric and I approached the pole. For the last 100 meters we walked in circles together, shoulder-to-shoulder, in search of the exact spot. A half-hour later we pinpointed the earth's hinge-pin. I recorded the event: "We are about 200 meters from the pole and it is in front of us somewhere; we should get there shortly. I think we skied past the pole. We are going to go back and check. We are at N 89 59.57.2, so less than a couple hundred yards here, so we are going to check. YEEHAW! The North Pole."

We reached the North Pole at 12 noon on July 1, 2006, 62 days after leaving Ellesmere Island. It was 32.5°F, overcast, with freezing rain. We took a few pictures to document the moment, then watched the GPS coordinates scroll south on the screen due to the rapid drift of ice. In a few minutes, the pole was completely covered in water, a huge lake-sized lead. We stood quietly for a while, staring with exhaustion at the lake in front of us. It was a moment of complete anticlimax. We had used up all our emotions over the past four years trying to get here.

CHAPTER 28

WAITING FOR A RIDE HOME

We set up our tent and celebrated with the treat we'd reserved for this moment. A Clif Bar, of course. Above us flew a guillemot, orange feet stretched beneath its black and white body. It landed in a lead with an ungraceful splash in front of us. The sea bird reminded me of rounding Greenland. These chubby birds saved us from starving on that expedition, and I wondered if the 12 seals we had seen en route to the pole could have done the same for this expedition if we had run out of food. For the next week, we rationed our food while we waited for the helicopter to pick us up and take us to the ship. Our camp drifted approximately 4 miles each day away from the pole. The direction of the drift was contrary to all research and ice charts of the past. Instead of drifting from the pole toward the Greenland Sea (transpolar drift), the ice was drifting in the opposite direction, towards the New Siberian Islands. Normally, this change in oscillation didn't occur until late August. Even then, the traditional drift of 0.6 miles a day was nowhere near as strong as what we were experiencing. Perhaps it was just a short fluctuation in ice direction, or perhaps it was because there was less ice in the Arctic Ocean pushing to get out.

We greeted each morning in the eastern hemisphere singing the Beatles song, "Back in the USSR." Every day, all week long, we picked up camp and moved it back to the pole. We navigated by dead reckoning—keeping track of wind direction and sun position. Once close, we pinpointed the pole with our GPS. As Eric summed it up, "We have been to the North Pole—seven times."

With the ship headed directly to the pole, I wanted to be as close as possible to make it easy for the helicopter to reach us, especially in the event of fog. After seeing all the press our expedition was getting, the Murmansk shipping company, which owned the icebreaker Yamal, decided to turn the pickup into a patriotic rescue. Russian newspaper headlines billed it as a Russian rescue of American polar explorers. We were upset by the shipping company's media ploy. Having worked in Russia before, however, we weren't surprised. In the end, I was pleased that the Russian news release gained no ground in the international media.

July 6, 2006, began with a summer rain. Big drops soaked our jackets and fogged our glasses. We skied through numerous melt pools 3 to 6 inches deep as if our snow skis had turned into water skis. The ice was thin, about 3 feet or so. We needed to find something thicker than 6 feet for the helicopter to land. Eventually, we found an 8-foot-thick pan, set up the tent and called our ship liaison, Laurie Dexter, to confirm our position.

With rain drumming off the tent's fabric, Greenpeace's media department coordinated calls between us and the American media to discuss the melting ice we were camped on. We no longer had to melt snow for drinking and cooking. We simply camped next to a meltwater pool and filled our Nalgene bottles and cook pots with all the fresh water we wanted.

To be ready for our pick up, we packed the canoe-sleds with our nonessentials, including our skis, poles and snowshoes. We took a little extra time to sort and inventory gear. All of our equipment seemed to have survived the journey with little damage, most notably our sleds. Despite nearly 600 miles of severe conditions, they looked brand new. We were a bit superstitious about putting our skis away, fearing it might jinx us into having to spend more days shuffling ahead to relocate the pole if the weather went bad.

On the day the helicopter was due to arrive, the day passed with no sound of its arrival. We assumed it was because of the overcast skies and fog. I lay on my sleeping bag and resigned myself to a long wait. I jammed my MP3 ear buds in and put on "No Direction Home" by Bob Dylan. "Set my compass north, circumscribe the earth...."

Before long, Eric yelled, "Chopper!" We were completely caught off guard. Dressed in long underwear, I frantically started stuffing bags with whatever was in arms' reach. Without even putting on my pants, I put on my boots and crawled outside. I grabbed the launcher, sent up four red flares and waved the chopper to land. I ran back in to gather my gear, but the violent prop wash flattened the tent to the ground, making it impossible to do anything. I backed my way out under ripping tent fabric. Standing 30 feet above me in the cargo door opening of the chopper was a man holding a scoped AK-47 assault rifle. He motioned us to get down on top of the flapping tent. He was part of the nuclear icebreaker's security force, double-checking to ensure we were harmless explorers and not part of an elaborate terrorist scheme to take over the ship.

As the helicopter settled on the ice just inches from the tent, Eric and I lay on the flapping red nylon. Four very serious-looking armed men jumped out. One, with a deep scar running from the top left of his forehead across his face, yelled in a Russian accent, "Any guns?" Eric pointed to the rifle. The Russian motioned him to dump it in a lead 50 feet away. The three other men shouldered their weapons and loaded our canoe-sleds though the hatch. Unable to get the tent poles out of their nylon sleeves because of the pressure of the prop wash, I frantically broke each pole and rolled the whole works up like a big red burrito—sleeping bags, clothes, diaries, electronics, cameras and all—and shoved it through the door.

In less than eight minutes, we were off the ice. The pilot and security officers were a scary bunch of veteran military elite from the Afghanistan war, now rewarded with the cushy job of guarding a nuclear ship. As I sat on the drab fold-down seat in my long underwear and fleece top, "Scarface" looked at me and demanded, "Passports! Passports!" Our liaison on the ship, Laurie Dexter, who was in the chopper, was mad as hell. They ignored him. I understood their behavior. They were trained to take their jobs seriously. As we approached the ship, sitting in the ice 13 miles away, each of the security men lowered their guns and grinned at us. "Scarface" handed our passports back. "Welcome to Russia," he said.

Scores of passengers, scientists and crew greeted us on deck with congratulatory champagne and vodka. In my cabin was a package of gifts from home. I pulled out my favorite Greenpeace T-shirt and pair of worn Carhartt work pants. Holding the fabric up to my nose, I could still smell the forest fragrance of Grand Marais. The Carhartts hung slack around my waist. According to the scale in our cabin's bathroom, I weighed 143 pounds. From the bottom of the box, I retrieved my old pair of running shoes, with money Kelly placed there to help ensure a more comfortable passage through Russia. Life was almost back to normal.

Later that evening, Laurie, who had skied to the pole twice, said, "When I first heard of your summer expedition, I thought you guys were nuts and asking for trouble. Flying out, the ice looked like a massive jigsaw puzzle of broken pans with leads everywhere. I don't know how you did it, but I am proud of you."

I had to agree that going to the North Pole in the summer was the greatest, most successful act of stupidity I had ever dreamt up. But it was worth it. Eric and I had gathered first-hand information that could help make a difference. We estimated that we reached close to 68 million people with messages about climate change through our Web site and media contacts.

I was sad that Greenpeace hadn't benefited from the publicity the expedition received. I thought they were wrong in not trusting the public to come to the right conclusion about our decision to leave the pole on a nuclear ship.

Again, I was conscious of how bittersweet these expeditions were. My pleasure at accomplishing our goal was tainted by what I'd found. I was disheartened that governments and companies were blindly focused on new Arctic shipping lanes to extract from the ocean's floor the very thing that causes the rise in global temperatures—fossil fuels. It's true that the Arctic thaw allows access to valuable minerals and new untapped fishing stocks, but it also opens the door for the exploitation of billions of tons of gas and oil. Nothing will stop this exploitation and its implications unless a strategic mass of people realizes the dangers. The fate of the Inuit and polar bear should matter to us all, but if that isn't enough to raise the alarm, another reality should. The disappearing ice that regulates the temperature of our whole planet impacts every one of us.

As I left the Arctic again, I was plagued by a dual question: Will it matter to enough of us, and will it matter soon enough? I didn't have the answers. All I knew for sure was that every trip to the Arctic made me even more passionate about doing my part to make a difference in the world that had become my second home.

CHAPTER 29

HONORING PEARY AND HENSON

Returning home, I couldn't push aside my concern that so many governments—Canada, Denmark, Finland, Iceland, Norway, Russia, Sweden and the United States—were rushing to stake a claim in the Arctic Ocean. I knew that my next expedition needed to focus on the importance of these Arctic countries joining in a treaty and working together to protect this ocean, its marine mammals and the surrounding ecosystems. It may have been too late to keep the Arctic sea from melting, but it wasn't too late to halt the exploitation of this fragile environment. Even though I could hardly believe I was going back to the North Pole so soon, I knew we were running out of time. I had an idea for how to attract attention to this problem, and I knew I had to act quickly.

On April 6, 1909, explorers Robert E. Peary and Matthew A. Henson, along with an Inuit team, claimed they reached the North Pole. For Peary and his entourage of 23 men, 133 dogs and 19 sleds, it was the culmination of an expedition that had begun on a bitterly cold March day on Canada's Ellesmere Island. As the men and dogs traveled farther and farther north, they lightened their loads and reduced the size of their party. Ultimately, only six men—Peary, Henson and four Inuits by the name of Ootah, Egingwah, Seegloo and Ookeah—set foot on the pole.

Peary's success, where all other explorers had failed, was due largely to his wisdom in taking Polar Inuit dog drivers. They can handle dog teams and sleds with grace and style better than any Arctic adventurer. It was not uncommon for the Inuit to travel 40 to 70 miles in one continuous run with good loads, and even in marginal conditions. Peary carried light sled loads and had a great motivation to keep moving—avoiding death.

For 80 years, skeptics disputed Peary's claim. In 1989, the Navigation Foundation upheld the accomplishment of Peary's team. Despite that, controversy remains. I stand on Peary's side, firmly believing they were the first to reach the North Pole. My confidence in Peary's success comes from traveling thousands of polar miles by dog team, and living and traveling with the Inuit over many years.

On the other hand, I don't believe that Frederick Cook's claim to have reached the pole in 1908 holds up to close scrutiny. The math doesn't work out when you consider the amount of dog food, people, food and gas Cook needed to get to the pole and back without any support parties. He accomplished an amazing trip on his way to and from the shores of the Arctic Ocean from the Qaanaaq district, not to mention his wintering at Cape Sparbo on Devon Island. However, according to Inuit testimony to Danish explorer Knud Rasmussen, Cook never made it to the pole or out of sight of land. He used light-weight, stanchion-type dog sleds, which would have busted up completely on the pressure ridges off the Canadian coast.

In 2009, I worked with my long-time friends Rick Sweitzer and Annie Aggens, owners and operators of the Northwest Passage Outing Club in Chicago, to plan a commemorative ski expedition in the footsteps of Peary. The purpose of this expedition would be to encourage and engage governmental policy for the foundation of an International Arctic Treaty, an agreement for the preservation and protection of the marine life in the Arctic Ocean and the culture of the 4 million indigenous peoples within the Arctic Circle.

Joining me were Stuart Smith and Max Chaya, both Northwest Passage clients. Together, they funded the expedition, Stuart out of his own pocket and Max through sponsors. I had reservations about taking clients rather than teammates to the North Pole, but with the downturn in the economy, I hadn't been able to find another way to fund this trip. When you're all teammates, even when you're the team leader, the responsibility for staying safe and making wise decisions is a shared responsibility. Not so when you take paying clients. That responsibility lies solely with the experts, in this case one expert—me. In the end, I let my desire to commemorate Peary and Henson, and draw attention to the melting Arctic Ocean override my concerns. I hoped that once back home, Stuart and Max would help me spread the word about the melting sea ice.

I checked to make sure Stuart and Max, both athletes and adventurers, were physically fit and suited for the trip. Stuart, a 48-year-old civil trial lawyer in Waco, Texas, had competed in 14 marathons and four 50-mile ultra-marathons. He'd climbed five 8,000-meter peaks, and summited four. He'd also climbed the Seven Summits, the highest peaks of every continent: Africa's Kilimanjaro, Antarctica's Vinson, Asia's Everest, Australia/Oceania's Carstensz Pyramid, Europe's Elbrus, North America's Denali and South America's Aconcagua. In 2004 he skied 600 miles to the South Pole from Hercules Inlet. Stuart had trained with Børge Ousland, Norwegian polar explorer, on a Last Degree North Pole trip. His extremely calm demeanor, attention to detail and team-player attitude made him a great candidate for any polar expedition. Max is built like a quarterback. He was raised and schooled in Lebanon, France, Greece and Canada, and is fluent in English, French and Arabic. Besides holding an honors degree in economics from the London School of Economics, he is a triathlete. He'd also climbed the Seven Summits, plus a number of 8,000-meter peaks. His polar expedition experience consisted of a 2004 North Pole Last Degree trip with Børge Ousland and a 47-day unsupported trek to the South Pole in 2007.

On March 4, 2009, our three-person team launched our North Pole expedition from Cape Discovery on Ellesmere Island. The straight-line distance to the pole was 478 statute miles. We knew we would travel farther than that as we navigated our way around various obstacles. The launching point for Canadian polar trips is the tiny hamlet of Resolute Bay. We left Resolute Bay at 8:10 am. From the window of the old DC3 bound for Eureka, even the low-hanging sun looked cold. Max had pre-expedition jitters. Stuart remained calm and cool. As we came in for landing, the pilot gave the usual fasten-your-seatbelt warning and the temperature. It was -25° F.

At Eureka, a small research station at N 79, we transferred to a Twin Otter for the flight to Cape Discovery, a 90-minute flight. This was where Eric Hansen and I started in 2006 because of better ice conditions than the typical takeoff point of Ward Hunt Island 20 miles to our west. Stuart, Max and I readied ourselves for the deep freeze we faced by applying petroleum cream to our fingertips and facial high spots to stave off frostbite. Our pockets were filled with chocolate and energy bars for a ready boost of energy. We were rested and fit, but I wished we'd had longer to acclimatize to the extreme cold. While -40°F makes me feel all warm and fuzzy inside, even I found Cape Discovery's -55°F a bit off-putting.

We unloaded the plane in a hurry so the engines wouldn't seize up. We anticipated highly fractured sea ice for the first 200 miles. To tackle the near-impassable maze of car-sized ice blocks, we were using 5-foot-long Kevlar sleds custom-designed for rough ice. We would cross the leads by paddling our lashed-together sleds. I bent the waist harness that was attached to the sled around me. I heard the foam padding between the fabric crack and break. I snapped into my skis and began moving to warm up. I pulled an energy bar from my pocket to gnaw on, only to find it frozen solid. I put it deeper into my fleece in hopes it would soften a bit.

We made 2.3 miles and camped on the edge of the Ward Hunt Ice Shelf. This would be our last relatively safe campsite before entering the live ice of the ocean. I'd been here before. The next morning, it took us about three hours to melt snow for water, eat breakfast, prepare for the day, dress, load the sleds, and take down the tent. Our daily plan was to awaken a little after 6 in the morning and hit the trail shortly after 9 o'clock. When we got into pack ice, which caused a lot of detours and up-and-down treks, we switched to snowshoes. We planned to consume 8,000 calories a day, which was the amount we'd need to ward off the extreme temperatures and to pull our sleds, each weighing between 170 and 190 pounds.

We continued to make slow progress north and decided to set up camp at 2:15 pm, giving us a respectable five hours of travel time for the day. It was all we could manage in the cold. While we had about seven hours of daylight each day, the sun was only above the horizon for a couple of hours.

On March 5, the temperature rose to a balmy -46°F as we wiggled and climbed our way north through the mountains of ice rubble. We made a notable 3.7 miles. We suffered frost nip on toes and fingers, and the cold exhausted us. Constant movement was all that kept us from freezing. We even had to eat our snacks on the move. The only time we stood still was to take a drink. Anytime we were waiting for someone to catch up, we were doing jumping jacks, running in place or swinging our arms and legs to keep warm blood moving to our frozen fingers. Our only rest came when we were lying in our sleeping bags—and only after we had gotten warm by kicking our feet and rubbing our arms for half an hour.

On March 6, the ice got even rougher, and we had to relay the sleds through patches of pack ice. One person pulled a sled while the other two pushed, pulled and otherwise manhandled it over or around the blocks of ice. After getting one sled through, we walked back and did it again with the next sled. And then again. It took us close to an hour to travel 100 feet, and it was not necessarily in a northerly direction.

By day's end we were exhausted and cold as we set up the tent. As Stuart and Max unloaded their sleds, I was inside getting the stove lit and organizing our meal. Pressurizing the cold fuel tanks can only be done with gloves on because skin would freeze and stick to the steel. My fingers on both hands were already white with frostbite down to the second knuckle. I struggled, trying to start the stove and warm my painful fingers at the same time. When I turned on the valve to prime the stove, gas poured out of every joint of the pump assembly. Shocked, I shut down the valve. I knew it would be a long time before I got the stoves running. I caught the fuel from spreading with a clump of toilet paper. I ordered Max and Stuart to grab an energy bar and get into their sleeping bags.

Trying to save my fingers from permanent damage, I knelt with my hands clutched around my groin while trying to figure out the stove issue. I unscrewed the pumps from the bottle with throbbing fingers and dove into my sleeping bag. I was too cold to warm the pumps with my body, so I reached for the butane lighter in my jacket. I placed the back half of the lighter in my mouth to warm the butane enough so it would light. Buried deep inside my bag I ran the flame of the lighter over each pump. Whichever one wasn't getting the flame was tucked under my armpit. Two hours later, I managed to get the stoves lit with only a small leak under one of the pumps. Out here losing a tent to a fire meant losing our lives.

The GPS showed that we had traveled only 1.25 miles, but the important thing was that we made some progress in difficult conditions. We had no trouble sleeping that night. By morning, the temperature had dropped to -50°F, and I was sure that our tent was only a degree or two warmer. Frost was an inch thick on the inside walls. I had to use a similar method of warming the pumps. Only this time I ignited some fuel in a titanium cup and heated both the pumps and fuel bottle over the flame. Warming up the fuel ensured that the O rings wouldn't cool down before the stove got primed and lit. I wouldn't recommend this gas-warming method for the handbook on safe camping—unless, of course, it's way below zero and your life hangs in the balance. I started sleeping with the pumps each night and carried them in my pockets during the day.

I made a note in my journal to chew out the Mountain Safety Research R&D team for using cheap O rings in their stoves. In the past, we had no problems with the stoves. From then on, I slept with my stove pumps anytime I was on the trail. The stoves were not the only things affected by the cold. Several Fastex buckles snapped off our equipment, and the Silva and Suunto compasses froze. Only the Brunton compasses worked. It wasn't an emergency, as we navigated mostly by the sun and prevailing wind.

During the night, Stuart had a mildly painful sensation in several of his toes. In the morning, we checked them out and discovered frostbite on the ends of several toes and under a number of toenails. While not a major catastrophe, it was important that they not freeze again. It wasn't going to be easy. The temperature was -49° F. Although it was tempting to stay put, we had to keep moving. Behind us, Ellesmere Island was dark magenta, with the sun poking out through a valley west of Cape Discovery. We three were the only human hearts beating within hundreds of miles. Even polar bears are not often found off Ellesmere at this time of year because of extreme cold and lack of food.

Day five brought low visibility, a temperature of -34°F and wind. The latter two greatly increased the risk of frostbite. We decided to take a rest day. The ice conditions were good the next morning, and we were able to use skis for the first two hours. Then we started walking, zigzagging actually, around obstacles. The temperatures were beginning to warm. One morning, we woke to -24° F, and it was -20° F by the time we started walking. It was overcast and snowing lightly, so we used the compass to navigate, although the sun peeked through at times to confirm that we were headed in the right direction. On March 12, we put in almost seven hours on the trail. Our goal was to increase the amount of time we traveled each day.

Although we didn't feel any warmth from it, we were glad to see the sun rising higher each day. We knew that we eventually would feel its warmth. Navigation was easy. All we had to do was watch our shadows to tell where we were going. At noon, with the sun directly behind us, our shadows pointed due north. At 10 am, they pointed northwest (11 on a watch face), and at 2 pm, our shadows pointed northeast (1 on a watch face).

By the ninth day, we had traveled about 45 miles north. It had warmed to -29°F but a 15-mile-an-hour wind battered our faces, and cut through our anoraks and pants. Our noses and cheeks were puffy and yellow with first-degree frostbite. That was the least of my worries, compared to the uncomfortable pain coming from my privates. Having been frostbitten there during other expeditions, they were more susceptible to freezing. I remedied the problem by stuffing my prized neck gaiter, knitted of musk-ox yarn, down the front of my wind pants. It worked. After dinner that evening, I made the dreaded run to relieve myself. When I returned to the tent, I realized my coveted neck gaiter was gone. Since I couldn't find it in the tent, I went back outside to look.

"Did you find it?" Stuart asked.

"Yeah, I found it. It was held down nicely by a good-sized turd." They must have heard us laughing back in Resolute.

Even though it was very cold out, it only took two layers of long underwear to stay warm while we dragged our sleds over the ice blocks. The instant we stopped for any reason, we had to pull on our PrimaLoft parkas. We usually stopped just long enough to take a drink from the thermos and chew on some chocolate or pemmican. After a minute or so, mainly spent swinging our feet and arms, we were off again for another hour and a half. The downside of eating on the trail was that we used valuable energy to digest the cold food in our stomachs, which pulled life-giving blood away from our extremities. It took at least 30 minutes to get the feeling and warmth back into our fingers and toes.

Although it was too cold to eat much during the day, we started snacking the minute we got in the tent. Then we ate an enormous dinner. Both men and dogs crave fat in the Arctic. Cold produces a searing hunger that only fatty food can satisfy. It serves as a form of antifreeze. In his 1890 book, *The First Crossing of Greenland*, Norwegian explorer Fridtjof Nansen told of running short of fat and craving a pound or two of butter. Each night, we threw a stick of butter into whatever we were having—pasta, rice, dried potatoes, refried beans, soup. It was essential to eat a high-fat diet to fend off the cold, but it was hard on our digestive tracts.

We ran across our first set of bear tracks on our 12th day on the trail. I wondered why the bear was in this particular spot. The answer lay just over the next pressure ridge. Directly ahead of us was a series of leads about 1.5 to 2 miles wide and covered with thin ice. Where there is thin ice or open water there are seals. For us it meant a huge detour if the ice wasn't thick enough to cross. To determine if the ice would hold our weight, I gave it several pokes with my ski pole. If by the third poke the tip broke through, we skirted the edge until we found a place to cross. When the ice took five pokes we went across.

The thin but flexible sea ice bent under our weight. I thought that if we kept moving we wouldn't break through. However, if I was wrong about this and one of us fell into the water, it meant likely death from hypothermia. The ice would keep breaking around a person struggling to get out, and no one would be able to get close enough to help without ending up in the water, too. The only chance would be to throw a rope to the person in the water.

While the weight of our food and fuel had decreased substantially, the weight of our sleeping bags had gone up significantly. We slept in a bag rated to -30° F with an outer bag over it. The outer bags absorbed moisture, which turned to ice, adding several pounds to the weight of the bags. To keep down the amount of moisture, we slept in vapor barrier liners. This was similar to sleeping in a plastic garbage bag inside the sleeping bag. It wasn't pleasant, but it kept body moisture from infiltrating the sleeping bag.

On March 21, we took our first break in 14 days and waited for our resupply drop. By now we were adding more than two sticks of butter to our daily rations to counteract the extreme cold. The wind howled during the night but began to drop at dawn. By morning, it was perfectly clear and the temperature was a comfortable -21° F with a light wind. We discovered we had drifted three-quarters of a mile north during the day and a half we had been camped. The plane arrived a little after 11 am and the pilot landed half a mile northwest of us. We unloaded our supplies and spent the next couple of hours resorting our gear and getting ready to travel again. We set off at 3 o'clock that afternoon to put in half a day of travel. We had forgotten how heavy the sleds were when carrying 20 days of food and fuel. Even though it was hard slogging, we managed 4.5 miles in 4.5 hours on snowshoes. It was after 8 pm by the time we set up camp.

We woke March 26 to a temperature of -30° F, clear skies and no wind—a perfect day for travel. We stayed on snowshoes so we could manage the sleds over obstacles. A brief appearance of the southern sun at noon allowed us to be guided directly north by our silhouettes. I looked at my bent, hardworking shadow struggling over every hump of snow. It seemed to be looking for something it could not find. I felt sorry for it, as if it belonged to someone else, and I was overwhelmed with a grief I could not explain. I looked back into the sunlight, searching for warmth and companionship.

When we woke up the next morning, everything in the tent was covered in thick frost. Shifting in my sleeping bag caused an avalanche of ice crystals to cascade down my warm neck. That evening, we were thrilled to learn from the GPS that we had made 10 nautical miles, our best effort to date and our first double-digit day. Small victories were usually short-lived. Two days later, both of my pole baskets broke, and the tips of my Asnes skis started to delaminate from the constant cold and rough ice.

On April 2, we crossed N 86. It was also our first day of 24-hour sunlight. I shot off one of our bear-scare flares in celebration. Early in the afternoon, we hit a monster lead that was largely refrozen. It was the largest we had seen and was roughly 2 miles across. The ice was 2 to 3 inches thick, enough for us to cross, but when we got out to the middle, there was a 30-foot-wide channel that was barely frozen and would not support our weight. While Stuart got into the one dry suit we had, I lashed the sleds together to make a catamaran. Stuart slipped into the water and backstroked across it while breaking the ice. Then he pulled the sleds across with Max on top. I pulled the sleds back to my side and went across. The whole operation took 35 minutes. We crossed N 86 30, which marked the halfway point in terms of mileage. We had covered 215 miles. We had 206 to go.

CHAPTER 30

CHEATING DEATH—ONCE AGAIN

Monday, April 6, 2009, marked the 100th anniversary of Robert Peary's arrival at the North Pole, but I will remember it as the day Stuart, Max and I nearly died. I woke at the usual hour, moved aside all the drying socks, hats and gloves from my cooking area, and got the stoves started. It had blown and drifted snow most of the night. Forty-five minutes later, I realized that I had forgotten the breakfast ration in my sled. Once outside, I became immediately dizzy, stumbled and landed face first in the snow. I struggled to get on my feet, but couldn't. I crawled on my hands and knees toward the tent, afraid I would pass out completely in the -20°F air and freeze to death. It was carbon monoxide. With my hands nearly frozen, I tore at the tent door zipper and flopped just inside the tent with my feet still outside.

Completely dizzy, I told Stuart to zip open the back door to get fresh air, and then I vomited.

"I think we're getting asphyxiated," I muttered.

Both said they were okay, but when Stuart went outside to relieve himself he, too, staggered and fell. A few seconds later he came crawling back into the tent. "Not good," he said. I looked at the two tent vents and found the culprit. The vent screens were completely plugged by drifted snow. I took out my knife and cut the screens completely out. No need to worry about mosquitoes here. We lay there for an hour breathing in fresh air.

This close call was a stupid mistake. I knew that we would feel nauseous for several hours and the best remedy would be to get on the trail. Still a bit sick, I spilled the four-liter cook pot of water onto the tent floor. We immediately lifted our ground pads to protect our sleeping bags. Oh well, it would freeze in 15 minutes and we could throw the ice chunks out when we broke camp. Max went out to get more snow blocks to melt for water only to discover after an hour of melting that the snow was laced with salt. I was getting irritated. He knew better, and I knew he was just being lazy. I threw the salty slush out and snippily told him to find some fresh snow this time.

Late in the morning, though still suffering from headaches and nausea, we started skiing north. Toward the end of a nine-hour day we began feeling better. We saw the tracks of a mother polar bear and cub, and an Arctic fox obviously hoping to scavenge a morsel of food from them. We hit a lead 300 feet wide. We skied west, and after an hour, the lead narrowed. Under us, at N 88, a mountain range on the ocean floor was creating lots of current, moving the ice and opening leads. This was exacerbated by the pull and push of the full moon. We needed to take extra care in crossing the shifting ice. Some thin ice and ice blocks floated in the lead, and we hopped on them to cross. A chunk tilted and Stuart put a foot into the water.

"How's your foot?" I asked.

"Soaked but not cold."

"It should be okay as long as we keep skiing. If it starts to get cold, let's stop and change out your liners and socks."

By the end of the day, our energy reserves were gone and we fought to keep from freezing as we set up camp. We ended up with 11.2 nautical miles for the day, even though we had to detour 45 minutes west around a lead that was 150 feet wide. The downside was that we'd waited too long to attend to Stuart's foot. His wet foot had gotten cold during the last couple of hours of skiing. We hadn't worried about it because his other foot had felt the same. I told Stuart to swing his feet and wiggle his toes no matter how difficult it was. Once we had the tent up and the stove going, we pulled off his boots and socks. Two of his toes were wooden and purple down to the first joint. Purple was a sign of tissue damage. Blood vessels and cells had frozen and burst. Within an hour, his toes thawed and throbbed painfully. Painkillers helped a little, but Stuart had a long night.

By morning, bloody blisters enlarged his toes to twice their size. I bandaged the area to prevent the blisters from breaking and rubbing against the inside of his boot. I told Stuart they were much more susceptible to freezing now, and if they froze again, the damage would be 10 times worse. Robbed of rest and with a bad foot, he still went out and put in a 10-hour day.

We had 180 miles to go. Each day on the trail made me more aware that we were not a well-matched group for an expedition. Max didn't seem to know how to be a good teammate. In my opinion, he wasn't pulling his weight with chores. Not only was he expert at conserving his energy at our expense, I had also figured out that he was hoarding food.

One of the hardest things for me about leading an expedition is dealing with the personal conflicts that are bound to emerge. Stuart, who was more than pulling his own weight, was angry at Max and frustrated with me. He thought I should have confronted Max about how he was sloughing off his responsibilities. I knew I had to confront Max, but it was difficult for me. There's a reason most expeditions have an even number of members. A three-member team is probably the most inherently difficult. No matter how diplomatic you try to be, when there's a disagreement a leader is seen to favor one side or the other unless you stay out of it completely. And, of course, a team leader can't just stay out of it. Ours was a textbook case of why you shouldn't go with a team of three.

Still, I was determined to deal with this head-on. I may not have been skilled at finding the best way to deal with conflict on the trail, but I was not going to make the same mistake I'd made in the past, hoping problems and tensions would fix themselves. I finally showed my anger. "If Stuart doesn't make it to the pole, that means you don't make it either," I told Max. "This is a team effort, not a support team for Max." He gave me a litany of all that was unfair. "Life's not fair," was what he got back from me. Unfortunately, when I finally confronted Max, it didn't change anything. In fact, Stuart didn't talk to Max the last 30 days of the expedition. In a way, I preferred that to their earlier shouting matches.

On Easter Sunday, we treated ourselves to dehydrated lasagna for dinner. I also treated myself to a clean change of long underwear, the first in five weeks. When I pulled off the bottoms, I was shocked to see a collage of pus-filled scabs, blisters and swollen flesh on both my knees. Apparently I'd gotten this deep frostbite in the beginning of the expedition when I knelt on the frigid floor of the tent. I hadn't yet installed the foam floor and ground pads. In my constant focus on keeping us alive and moving in those first few weeks, I had completely blocked out the pain and damage to my knees. Another note to myself: have kneepads built into wind pants in the future. Most of the blisters on Stuart's toes had now popped, and I drained what blisters were left with a needle. His foot smelled rotten. To prevent infection, I began to cut away all the dead skin and tissue every other day for the remainder of the expedition with a small surgical scissors. Then I cleaned the area and rebandaged the foot.

We constantly worried about the southern drift. One night, we went 1.5 nautical miles backwards and about 4 miles east. For three days straight, a low-pressure system pushed a northwest wind and drifted us southeast, the worst possible direction. We were drifting right into the transpolar drift stream, which headed straight south at least 4 miles a day. We continued to travel northwest instead of directly north to counteract the easterly drift. The southerly drift was discouraging, but we were still moving north. The wind couldn't blow forever. We were now less than 100 nautical miles from the pole.

On April 20 we put in a full 12 hours and were rather shocked to see that we had advanced only 12.5 nautical miles. That meant we had most likely drifted back 4 or more miles during the 12-hour march. That night's drift told us a lot about our chances for making significant progress in our remaining time. The good news was that we were less than 39 miles from the pole—at least for the moment. Who knew where we'd be in the morning. It was hard not getting discouraged by the continued strong drift. Skiing 19 miles could mean making only 15 miles of progress north. At night, we lost miles just by stopping. We stayed still, but the ice did not.

Even though we were eating about 8,000 calories a day, we still lost weight. For dinner, we consumed a total of eight servings of Mountain House freeze-dried meals. We had a hard time keeping warm in our sleeping bags even though the temperature was climbing. Even our shadows looked hilariously skinny. With no fat reserves, only constant motion kept us warm. What motivated us to continue and to sleep for only five hours at a time, was our race against time. If we failed to make the pole by April 26, we risked missing the Russian evacuation flight back to Ice Station Borneo and, ultimately, home. By now, for every mile we skied, we lost about a third of a mile to the "treadmill" pushing us back.

On April 24, totally spent, I led for the last hour of the day. Thirty minutes later, I couldn't keep my head up or legs moving no matter how much I tried. I fell asleep standing up. Stuart came along side me and tapped my shoulder. "Perhaps we should camp?" he said. While we rested, we drifted back a mile and a half. We took our time getting ready to ski the final 9 miles to the pole.

We left at 2:15 am on April 25 in good weather to complete our last leg. The terrain was great, and we were sailing along until we hit a couple of small leads, which weren't much trouble to negotiate. At 2.75 nautical miles from the pole, we hit a lead that was 40 feet wide and had no end in sight. The ice was not even 2 inches thick and it thinned on the far side. We couldn't ski across. The ice would not support our weight.

Max put on the dry suit, grabbed a rope and slithered across on his belly. We used the rope to pull across the sleds with Stuart and me on top of them. The plan worked perfectly, and we were across in less than half an hour. The sleds rode about 6 inches out of the water so we had to be careful not to drop our toes in.

About 2 miles from the pole, I gave both Max and Stuart a GPS in order to have them guide us home. On the ice, heads down, looking into the screen for direction, Stuart veered to the right, Max to the left. I shuffled north between the two and couldn't help but laugh to myself. It was the perfect image for the whole trip. Here we were, almost to the pole, and my team members were heading in slightly different directions.

Half a mile from the pole, they were 300 yards apart, but the gap was closing. Intently looking at the GPS display showing N 89 59.59.9, they nearly bumped heads when they gave a simultaneous yell of, "The pole!"

It was 9:22 am on Saturday, April 25, 2009. After 53 days of travel on the ice, we were relieved and happy to reach the North Pole. We had skied more than 650 miles to cover the 478 straight-line miles because of detours and backwards drift. We relaxed in the tent for an hour before starting a long round of phone calls, including Max's call to the president of Lebanon. We switched our watches to Norwegian time and took more photos while we waited for the chopper.

We left the pole on a Russian chopper and had an hour flight to the Borneo ice station at N 88. From there we boarded a jet for a two-hour flight to Longyearbyen, Norway, at N 78. The first order of business was to take showers after 54 days without one. When we weighed ourselves, we found that I'd lost 30 pounds, Stuart 34, and Max 20.

While I was happy to have been at the North Pole again, and to have honored Peary and Henson's accomplishment, I was deeply disturbed by what we'd found. I'd never seen or heard of so many gigantic leads at this time of year. Mostly, we saw young, annual ice, with nearly no multiyear ice floes. These conditions were clearly a result of climate change.

A century earlier, standing at the pole after a heroic battle with frigid temperatures and thick pressured ice, Peary could never have imagined that the sea ice beneath his feet would melt completely away in just over a century, and that it would do so at the hands of humans. My only consolation was that our Web site was receiving nearly a quarter-million hits, an indication that our expedition was increasing people's knowledge about this irrefutable and irreversible damage to our planet. For the moment, I was satisfied that our commemorative Peary-Henson expedition was making a difference.

AFTERWORD

My days of exploring the Arctic may be numbered, but as long as I'm alive, I'll work for the state of its health. As one of the last explorers to traverse the ever-thinning ice of the Arctic Ocean with any degree of solid footing, I feel obligated to speak for this place of mystical light and dark, and for its people and its wildlife. On every expedition I've taken, I've seen incontrovertible proof of the region's rising temperatures and melting ice. You don't have to be a polar explorer to see this for yourself. With today's technology, anyone with access to the Internet or television can see images of the melting ice cap.

It's difficult for me to understand why so many people refuse to believe the evidence amassing all around us. Of greatest irony to me is that one of the most polarizing issues in the United States today is whether changes at the poles are, in fact, proof of the climate change crisis. Nearly every respected national and international scientific organization agrees that the earth's surface temperatures have increased, primarily due to human-induced greenhouse gas emissions. In fact, the science academies of all major industrialized nations endorse this position. Scientists all over the world have collected data independently and reported how climate change has led to rising sea levels, increased frequency and severity of storms, desertification and drought. But you don't even have to look at the research. All you have to do is look around. Everyone knows about the Indian Ocean tsunami and Hurricane Katrina. Less spectacular in terms of the world media, but just as devastating, are increased floods and wildfires all over the planet.

While the Arctic Inuit people are severely and directly impacted by climate change, so are the world's poor. The planet's rising temperatures increase insect breeding and resulting disease. An increased mosquito population alone spreads dengue fever, West Nile virus and yellow fever to human populations who've not experienced the diseases before, and, therefore, have no natural immunity to them.

Until very recently, scientists believed it was too late to reverse the damage already done. However, a study published in *Nature* on December 16, 2010, reported that lowering greenhouse gas emissions now will, in fact, curb the melting of the sea ice. This study projects that by the end of the 21st century some of the lost ice may actually be recaptured. That is good news for everyone: the Inuit, the polar bears, and, of course, the whole planet.

Time will run out only if average citizens—like me—don't stand against the extremists and the companies who benefit from the status quo. It we stand silent, we let them define the health of our planet. We need to act now and we need to act on three levels: individual, national and global.

For individuals it's a simple path. It's not an easy path because changing human behavior can be difficult, but it's not complicated. We can all buy local goods. When we do, we conserve the energy needed to preserve and transport goods from other places. We also are supporting local businesses. When we do errands in one drive rather than several—and when we drive fuel-efficient cars—we use less fuel. Better yet, we can walk, bike, carpool and take public transportation. We can turn down the heat, switch off unnecessary lights, fix broken possessions, recycle, use energy-efficient appliances and plant new trees. We impact the planet positively when we invest in renewable energy (such as wind, solar and hydro), and when we donate to and volunteer for environmental groups. There are so many ways we can be good global citizens.

We also have the power to act collectively, both as citizens and as legislators, to ensure that our nation acts in the best interest of our planet. We can't have it both ways. We can't complain about rising fuel costs and not do what we can to curb our own use. We can't complain that our legislators aren't doing enough if we don't speak up and tell them our concerns. Working for and voting for state and federal acts that eliminate subsidies—in amounts of hundreds of billions of dollars—to fossil fuel and nuclear industries would be a good start.

We might consider following Scandinavia's lead: tax fossil fuels to discourage their use, and fund health care and education with that revenue. We could also use such a tax to support alternative energy sources. Perhaps the most significant step for our country is agreeing to a legally binding treaty that cuts current carbon dioxide emissions by 80 percent by 2050. The United States has some catching up to do.

While each individual and collective national act makes a difference, our planet will only be healed if nations also work in unison. In terms of environmental impact, nowhere on earth is the need more evident than in the Arctic. One of the major dangers to the Arctic today is planned exploitation of its resources by Arctic countries. Companies and governments in all these countries—Canada, Denmark, Norway, Russia and the United States—stand ready to strip the Arctic of its natural resources and wildlife. Perhaps the greatest irony of all is that the mining of fossil fuels—the very element that has placed our planet in such peril—is at the top of the resource wish list!

Working for passage of a proposed Arctic Treaty would go far toward protecting this fragile environment. The core terms of the treaty call for use of the Arctic Ocean for peaceful purposes and scientific research. This treaty would ban oil, gas and mineral exploration as well as commercial fishing. It also calls for the preservation and conservation of living resources in the Arctic Ocean. Such a treaty would exempt, of course, the first 24 nautical miles from the coastline of each Arctic country—in accordance with the territorial and contiguous zones defined in the United Nations Law of the Sea.

We need only look to Antarctica to see how effective worldwide protective action can be.

I know there are many people like me, individuals who want to create a healthy planet. If we don't act now, we ourselves may not suffer greatly, but our children and their children will, and we will deserve their harsh judgment if we fail to do what is in our power.

Though I sometimes get discouraged and overwhelmed, I'm mostly hopeful that enough of us will stand up and do the right thing. I'm an optimist. An explorer has to be.

ACKNOWLEDGMENTS

I have worked on this manuscript for about 10 years. I have found it difficult to tell my story, mostly because I wanted my readers to see and breathe and feel this place that I find so vast and mystical. It took me years to accumulate the material, gather up old journals and begin to write.

I owe my greatest appreciation to my editor, Ann Ryan, and my hometown friend, Jim Boyd. Jim helped me organize and edit a rough 500-page journal. This was no small task and it took him the better part of a year. Without Jim's dedication, along with the efforts of Kelly Dupre, Buck Bensen, Judy Johnson, Annie Princen and Steve Hoffman, who gave helpful critiques of the manuscript, I couldn't have brought it to the next stage.

Writer and editor Ann Ryan was the gift I had been looking for all these years. It was an absolute pleasure working with her. She edited and polished the manuscript while staying true to my voice. She was able to put on paper exactly what I'd been attempting to do.

I also want to thank Kelly Dupre, who literally held the fort during all the days and months that I was on my expeditions. The long nights spent wondering whether I was alive or dead and the painful good-byes never got any easier. Her talents, as an artist, educator and author were essential to the successful outcome of both this book and all my expeditions, for which she customized our clothing, designed graphics and did anything else I needed, including spending hours packing food.

MY FAMILY

I want to thank my family for the many ways they've supported me over these past decades. To this day, my mother, Kate Cartier, tries to fatten me up before I leave on an expedition. My dad, Jim Dupre, introduced me to winter, and my stepmother, Bette, offers me warmth and hospitality. And I'd like to thank my sister, Janie DeLuce, and her husband, John, who are often the ones who get me to and from the Minneapolis airport—many times early in the morning and late at night. Thank you to each of you.

1989 BERING BRIDGE EXPEDITION

I want to thank Paul and Sue Schurke for becoming partners in an Inuit dog team and introducing me to Arctic expeditions. Even before we met, the Schurkes inspired me through an epic dog-sled expedition to the North Pole in 1986 with Will Steger. This solidified my Arctic fever and launched my career. Paul showed me how to do 50 things at once, or, better yet, how to delegate—both key tools for expedition planning.

1991–1992 NORTHWEST PASSAGE

I want to acknowledge all the hard work of the early days of the expedition when darkness, cold and fatigue struck our then-young team. My best wishes to Jon Nierenberg, whom I look forward to meeting again someday to swap stories. My best to Tom Viren, now Dr. Viren, for his wisdom and kind heart. I want to thank Malcolm Vance, with whom I fondly shared 3,000 miles of Arctic experience.

We forged a bond of friendship one only gets during long and diffi-cult travel. And thanks also to my longtime friend and photographer Larry Roepke for lots of good laughs and fine cigars.

1997–2001 GREENLAND

From the conception of this expedition to its 2001 completion, a multitude of gracious individuals came to our aid in making this dream come true. I would like to thank John Hoelscher for giving five and a half years of his life to this project, which never would have been possible without him. We endured appalling conditions, about which John never complained. Our trials together created an interwoven bond of friendship that cannot easily be broken. I would especially like to thank John for sharing his Greenland reflections and insights, which helped me in the writing of this book.

Thank you also to our friends at National Geographic: Rebecca Martin (director of National Geographic Expeditions Council), Peter Miller (Expeditions Editor), Mark Christmas (National Geographic Online); and Rebecca Young (The Polartec Challenge Grant). Thank you also to Rod Johnson, owner of Midwest Mountaineering, which has supported our expeditions with gear for years.

I will always be grateful to all the volunteers and friends in my Minnesota hometown of Grand Marais. They spent hours and hours working in the office and packing thousands of pounds of people and dog food that were shipped to depot locations around Greenland.

Thank you also to the individuals who gave John and me sup-port, hospitality and knowledge, thus making the Greenland journey even more memorable and enjoyable. **In the United States:** Dr. John Wood, Buck Benson, Mark and Wendy Hanson, Gary and Maryann Atwood, Linda Zink, Betsy Bowen, John Gorsky and Clark Baldwin.

In Denmark/Greenland: Torben Diklev, Tine Lisby Jensen, Hanne Sørensen, Hans E. Pedersen, Oodaq Duneq, Hans Jensen, Jens Carl Jensen, Bent Olsen, Allan Chemnitz, Uilog and Ojstein Slettermark, Poul Hendriksen, Alega Hammon, Leong Wai Meng, Ove Rosing Olsen, Jan Thrysøe, Captain Fritz Ploug Nielsen, Gert Jakobsen, Denny Rune, Marie Qujaukitsoq, Tequmeq Peary, Mamarut Kristensen and Jens Danielson. **In Australia:** Wynne Hoelscher, Danny O'Reilly and Howard Welan of Australian Geographic.

2005–2006 ONE WORLD EXPEDITION

I express heartfelt appreciation to Ann Possis, our 2005 expedition manager, who added a great deal of professionalism and fun to the whole process of raising support and tackling logistics. She was also invaluable for keeping us from getting lost in big cities. I want to thank Eric Larsen's parents, Andy and Judy, for hosting fundraising events in Wisconsin, and my good friend Buck Benson for giving both financial and electronics support as well as keeping me motivated to ski rather then drink coffee. A special thanks to John Hoelscher for handling safety and logistics, to John Wood for his medical expertise in developing our first-aid kit and acting as the expedition's on-call physician, and to Jan Lemke for helping me organize and begin moving the fledgling idea forward in 2004.

Thank you to my dear friend Mark Hansen for helping customize our equipment, and for listening to my hair-brained ideas—and my venting. Thanks to Sarah Allen for her volunteer work on graphic layout and web design. I am grateful to John Huston, our calm and collected 2006 expedition manager who navigated the tricky waters of handling our sponsors, the media and ever-changing overseas logistics. I am grateful for web support from Tim and Elisabeth Harincar, and for the hours of volunteer time given by my good friends John Gorski and Matthew Brown, the going-away party music of Jacob and Josh Schmitt with 'Vintage Mink' band. And thanks also to friends and supporters Tom and Ann Rider, owners of Lutsen Mountain & Papa Charlie's, and to Anna Latz of Heavy Duty Sewing for sewing all of our cargo bags and covers for our expedition canoes.

Thanks to Clyde Hansen for developing the marketing and working relationship between Greenpeace and us, and to our Greenpeace friends, Kert Davies, John Passcantando, Ellen McPeake, Nathan Santry and Mike Harold. I will always be grateful to Rolex and the Rolex Awards for Enterprise (and Barbara Geary and Rebecca Irvin); the National Snow and Ice Data Center (NSIDC) (and Ted Scambos and Walt Meier); and the University of Washington and its Department of Atmospheric Sciences (and Thomas C. Grenfell and Ignatius G. Rigor); and Gloria R. Leon, professor emeritus of psychology at the University of Minnesota.

2009 PEARY-HENSON CENTENNIAL EXPEDITION

I express a special thank you to my friend and team member Stuart Smith, whose journal entries helped form this story. And I want to express my gratitude to my Polar Explorers and Northwest Passage Outing Club friends and arctic cohorts, Rick Sweitzer, Annie Aggens, Kieth Heger, Dirk Jensen and Nancy Vedder in Chicago. Their professionalism in the adventure outfitting business is unmatched. My best to Roland Wall and all my friends at the Academy of Natural Sciences in Philadelphia for their wonderful hospitality.

ABOUT THE TYPE

This book was set in Calluna and Calluna Sans, typefaces created by Jos Buivenga in 2008. Buivenga, a self-taught type designer from the Netherlands, also designed Anivers, Delicious and Museo. Calluna was chosen for its graceful, fluid style, which makes for an easy read and an elegant display.

ABOUT THE DESIGNER

This book was designed by Adria Chilcote, a graphic designer born in the United States and based in Berlin. She was chosen to design this book because of her mimimalist style and fluency with typography. Chilcote does design work for clients on three continents.

ABOUT THE PUBLISHER

This book was published by Keen Editions, an independent publisher dedicated to helping authors publish carefully edited and finely designed books. Ann K. Ryan is the founder and executive editor of this innovative press, which allows writers and illustrators to retain rights and profits in a way traditional publishing models do not.

ABOUT THE PAPER

This book was printed by Bang Printing using paper certified by the Sustainable Forestry Initiative (SFI), which is the world's largest forest certification standard. A commitment to sustainable forest management is a means of protecting water, soil and wildlife .